Teaching about Alcohol

TEACHING ABOUT ALCOHOL

Concepts, Methods, and Classroom Activities

- **PETER FINN**
  Senior Research Analyst
  Economics and Environmental Analysis Area
  Abt Associates Inc.

- **PATRICIA A. O'GORMAN**
  Director
  Division of Prevention
  National Institute on Alcohol Abuse
  *   and Alcoholism*

ALLYN AND BACON, INC.
Boston · London · Sydney · Toronto

```
Library of Congress Cataloging in Publication Data


Finn, Peter      1940-
   Teaching about alcohol.

   Bibliography:  p.
   Includes Index.
   1. Alcoholism--Study and teaching--United States.
   2. Youth--United States--Alcohol use. I. O'Gorman,
Patricia A., joint author.
II. Title.
HV5128.U5F56      613.8'1'071073      80-25929
ISBN 0-205-07195-3
```

Series Editor: Hiram G. Howard

Printed in the United States of America

10 9 8 7 6 5 4 3   86 85 84

To Myrna, to my Father, and in memory of my Mother
P.F.

To my parents, to Rob, and in memory of grandpa Stephen
P.O'G.

Contents

CONTENTS

Foreword

Teaching About Alcohol: Concepts, Methods, and Classroom Activities brings alcohol education into the 1980s. The text presents information and concepts that have been evolving historically, but have lacked direction and cohesiveness.

The need for this text is identified in a brief historical view of alcohol education in twentieth-century America. In the early 1900s alcohol education was temperance education with abstinence as its major goal. The National Prohibition period from 1920-1933 focused on the deleterious effects of consuming alcohol; abstinence in the present and future was also the goal. Following Repeal in 1933, alcohol education reflected the ambivalence of society. Little textbook space focused on alcohol and the goal of alcohol education was vague. Throughout the 1940s alcohol education was interpreted as "alcoholism" education, emphasizing the "evils of alcohol."

The potential importance of alcohol education as a vital technique for the prevention of alcohol problems was acknowledged in the 1950s. Though the stated emphasis was on factual and scientific knowledge, the textbooks of the period indicate an evident stress on the "evils" approach using select facts and information. The 1960s affirmed alcohol education's role as a responsibility of the schools and stressed that the topic required accurate facts and honest information. Studies of youthful drinking in the sixties documented the finding of earlier research: young people consume alcohol. It was also recognized that there was no single national pattern of drinking nor was there a single national pattern of alcohol education. The teacher, considered the single most important element in alcohol education, was not provided accurate information or techniques on how to handle the subject in the classroom. The needs of students in this area and the reality of the youthful world were again stated by researchers and again not translated into a form for educators.

Having identified major obstacles to alcohol education, the 1970s continued the process to enable alcohol education to become a reality. Alcohol education materials began to address the needs of the field. The quantity and quality of alcohol education materials increased throughout time; though the major portion of the published materials were still prepared for the general audience, the materials for educators and students (college, senior-high, junior high, and elementary) expanded, indicating an increasing awareness and importance of alcohol education. The percentage of titles published as curriculum guides increased in the seventies and the overall quality of these guides rose steadily. The publications for students also indicated a more relevant trend; the topics (e.g. teenage drinking, etc.) were more representative of students' needs than in the earlier time periods.

The 1980s are facing a clearly defined challenge in the area of alcohol education: it must become a reality. We can no longer verbalize the need for accurate and honest information without providing it, and the needs and interests of students must be integrated into the curriculum. Society's ambivalence and misinformation need to be identified and discussed with students so that they perceive the substance alcohol and their attitudes surrounding its use with clear and rational thinking. It is also necessary to motivate individuals to clarify their values regarding alcohol and make responsible decisions related to its use and nonuse.

The most significant element required to meet the challenge of the 1980s is the educator. The educator must have clarified his or her own attitudes about alcohol use and alcohol problems, have basic information on alcohol and alcoholism, understand societal ambivalence and misinformation, and be comfortable with the open atmosphere necessary to stimulate student thought and discussion of the subject. Educators need content and technqiues to be able to fulfill this role. *Teaching About Alcohol: Concepts, Methods, and Classroom Activities* meets these needs.

The text is accurate, organized, and understandable and can be used by a beginning alcohol educator, an experienced alcohol educator, a teacher training or in-service program, a professional in the alcohol field, a community educator, or a guidance counselor. It provides perspective, rationale, and balance in each of its chapters.

As with an excellent text in any field, this text begins with goals and objectives. This is more important in the alcohol field than most others due to the goal swings and vague objectives that have been present in the past. Alcohol education is defined as "the process of helping youngsters (1) become familiar with a variety of facts, attitudes, values, and behaviors regarding alcohol use, nonuse, and abuse, (2) evaluate this information and these feelings, and then (3) act on their evaluations." This definition provides perspective for the educators and supports reality. Educators are encouraged to promote health, to enhance human potential, to enrich lives, as well as to provide information. In this approach the mastery of information is not the end, rather it is the ability to use that information in making decisions that is the goal.

Alcohol education as a technique for primary prevention is introduced in chapter 2 with an historical account of alcohol use in American society. This background is necessary due to the societal ambivalence and misinformation regarding alcohol that is rooted in our history. It is also necessary because of the earlier stress on alcohol problems which assumed that the youthful population was able to intervene or treat adult alcohol problems. The classroom is the appropriate place for primary prevention for all children: nondrinkers, drinkers, and children of alcoholics. Though it is noted that there has been little evidence to substantiate the effectiveness of this prevention approach, it is also clear that little emphasis to date has been placed on alcohol education in the classroom. *Teaching About Alcohol: Concepts, Methods, and Classroom Activities* presents a carefully structured background that will facilitate implementation. As educators use this text, the potential for evaluating the effectiveness of this approach will be created.

Chapter 3 provides content information on alcohol use, nonuse, and abuse. This section is concise, clearly written, and presents the background needed by any individual who wishes to educate about alcohol. The chapter could stand alone as an information publication, yet its inclusion further demonstrates the authors' understanding of and concern for educators. Knowing that many teacher training institutions do not provide content information on alcohol, its use and effects, this chapter is significant in that salient facts are delineated within a philosophical and attitudinal framework.

Chapter 4, "Alcohol and Youth," provides additional information necessary for educators by dealing with the reality of youthful drinking in a nonjudgmental manner. If educators are going to be comfortable and confident in the area of alcohol education, it is essential that adolescent drinking be viewed as part of society's drinking patterns and as a reflection of those patterns. In this perspective, youthful drinking becomes part of the whole and can be thought of in its positive as well as its negative aspects. When youthful drinking is isolated or considered in itself as a whole, it stimulates a more negative response. Appropriately the text then provides instructional strategies to enable educators to present information about alcohol. The strategies (e.g. small group discussion, interviews, peer teaching, etc.) are clearly explained with both pro and con aspects, how to use them, and the appropriate techniques for follow up.

One unfamiliar with the history of and attitudes toward alcohol education might misinterpret the meaning of chapter 6, "Alcohol Education at the Elementary Level," and assume that since separate chapters are not devoted to the junior high and high school level these are not as meaningful. This is not the case. Prior to the 1970s, most alcohol education programs that occurred took place at the high school level with rare appearance at the junior high level. Research findings indicate that approximately 70 percent of our adolescent population uses beverage alcohol and that the majority of these young people have their first drink at home usually between the ages of 10 and 13. Therefore, introduction to alcohol often occurs during the elementary school years.

Yet most adults are not aware of this; even the parent population that offers the first drink is frequently not conscious of this as an introduction to alcohol. This is due to two major reasons: (1) many adults do not realize that any beverage that contains alcohol is considered an alcoholic beverage and that there is approximately the same amount of alcohol in a 12 oz. can of beer, a 5 oz. glass of wine and 1-1/2 oz. of distilled spirits, and (2) most adults negatively interpret the word drinking to mean "heavy," "problem," "alcoholic," etc. rather than the act of consuming beverage alcohol; therefore, they don't see offering a small glass of

an alcoholic beverage to their children as introducing drinking. The consequence of these two reasons is that little information and discussion surround the use of alcohol by the parents and the child, and little is communicated directly about why people drink, the effects of alcohol, etc. However, indirect learning occurs as the child witnesses adult drinking, its motivations and effects. The inherent message in the lack of discussion is that this is not a subject to discuss. Elementary school children have many questions regarding alcohol use. When the topic is introduced by a classroom teacher, it becomes a legitimate subject to discuss and question.

It is extremely important that alcohol education begin at the elementary school level and continue through junior high and senior high. In this way the questions, needs, and concerns regarding alcohol of the various age levels can be met in an objective manner. "How to Teach Objectively About Alcohol" is discussed in chapter 7. Objectivity is essential in alcohol education as well as other controversial areas, because the effectiveness of the approach is directly related to the honesty and attitudes of the educator and the ability to deal with the reality of the adolescent experience. Educators are encouraged to analyze their feelings and attitudes about alcohol and then decide which approach (i.e., candor or nonopinion) is appropriate for each individual. Guidelines are then offered to enable educators to achieve objectivity and select strategies to use with students. Since educators need to have a level of comfort with the parental and community response to alcohol in the schools, this is discussed in chapter 8. Essential elements to consider in communicating with parents are presented as are approaches to obtain parental opinions.

The need for teachers to be trained to be effective alcohol educators has been documented historically and is also noted throughout the text. The importance, goals and issues, attitudes, methods, and an illustrative training curriculum are detailed in chapter 9. "Developing and Evaluating an Alcohol Curriculum Unit with Sample Lesson Plans" is the content of chapter 10. Curriculum is defined, problems of time and course interaction are addressed, and the development and evaluation of an alcohol education curriculum are presented. Sample curriculum units for grades 4-6, 7-9, 10-12, and college are outlined by concept, focus, method, and time.

The second half of the text has three excellent sections that should enable educators to feel comfortable with the topic and able to use available materials and techniques to increase their effectiveness. The first of these sections, "Instructional Activities," is a classic and may prove to be the most widely used part of an alcohol education text to date. It provides thirty-three instructional activities that are identified and indexed by teaching topic and grade level and described in detail; follow-up questions and suggestions are also presented. The activities translate the philosophy, content, and balance of the text into techniques to use with students. This chapter helps to fill a major gap in alcohol education: that is, how to simultaneously provide information, clarify values, and teach objectively.

In the second section of the book, "Resources," alcohol education materials are listed and described according to content, type, grade level, and source. Audiovisuals are presented in the same manner facilitating ease of use; organizations and agencies are provided under a major topic heading (e.g., for the problem drinker or alcoholic, etc.) and local services and journals in the field are listed.

And the final section, a glossary of major terms, provides definition for basic items as well as for words that are often confused or misused (e.g., addiction, alcoholic, drunk, etc.).

Teaching About Alcohol: Concepts, Methods, and Classroom Activities is an excellent text that will help alcohol education "come of age." It presents a philosophical perspective, a balanced rationale, and excellent content; the text is accurate, organized, and understandable. The ease of use, awareness of the reader's perspective, and the abundance of techniques qualify its use for a variety of educators (school, community, industry) now and in the years to come. With the appearance of texts such as this, alcohol education may indeed become a reality and may also be able to prove that it is a technique for eliminating ambivalence, producing an informed public, and preventing alcohol problems.

Gail Gleason Milgram, Ed.D.
Director of Education
Center of Alcohol Studies
Rutgers University

Preface

This book is intended as a practical, comprehensive book on alcohol education for instructors at the elementary, secondary, and postsecondary levels. It is designed to meet *your* needs in teaching in this field and, through you, those of your students.

Alcohol is a far from neutral substance. It is alternately extolled as a promoter of conviviality and censured as being responsible for a $43 billion annual drain on our economy. A casual mention of it in a classroom may spark a flurry of questions, yet an allusion to it over lunch may elicit only knowing nods.

Since drinking is an emotionally charged topic, teachers must not only feel at home with the facts and issues but also feel comfortable with their feelings before discussing alcohol with others.

This book has been several years in the making and represents not only the viewpoints of the authors but also the perspectives and opinions of many others in the vast field of alcohol studies. As such, the book will be an invaluable instructional guide as you begin (or continue) to teach about alcohol, as well as a helpful resource for securing the basic factual information about alcohol that you will need in order to teach effectively in this area.

However, we need to stress right from the start that information — facts about alcohol — is not the key to alcohol education. To be sure, studies have shown that most youngsters (and adults, as well) are unfamiliar with much of the basic information about alcohol and its use and harbor many misconceptions. And certainly you will want to familiarize yourself with the information we have provided on these topics in chapters 3 and 4.

However, your students' ability to drink or abstain responsibly is not likely to hinge on any information you provide them, because feelings, attitudes, and values are more crucial to their current and future drinking behavior than are cold, abstract facts. Even with adults, we have all seen how ineffective knowledge of "the facts" about safety belts has failed to motivate most people to buckle up when they drive.

Your most important function as a teacher of alcohol education may not be as a provider of information but rather as a *role model* of responsible and healthy attitudes toward drinking and not drinking. As a teacher or guidance counselor you are one of the most prominent role models that your students have. In fact, since some youngsters may spend more time with you than with their parents, you and other teachers may well be the most constant adult role models that your students have. As a result, your attitudes toward alcohol use, abuse, and nonuse and your behavior in teaching about them will probably be better recalled than what the facts themselves were.

A second critical function you will have as a teacher of alcohol education is that of a *facilitator* of student learning. Rather than you supplying youngsters with the answers to the many questions about alcohol and drinking, you will serve their interests best in the long run if you help enable them to develop decision-making skills that they can then apply on their own to dilemmas involving alcohol use and nonuse.

To help you be an effective role model and engage your students constructively in decision-making activities that involve their feelings, values, and attitudes, we have addressed the following topics in this book:

- selecting *goals and objectives* for your alcohol education unit (chapter 1)
- using the classroom as one approach to the *primary prevention* of alcohol problems (chapter 2)
- learning *background information* on the manufacture, history, use, and behavioral and physical effects of alcohol (chapter 3)
- understanding *youthful drinking* (chapter 4)
- implementing effective *instructional strategies* for teaching about alcohol (chapter 5)
- teaching about alcohol at the *elementary school level* (chapter 6)
- teaching *objectively* about drinking (chapter 7)
- involving *parents and the community* in support of your alcohol education efforts (chapter 8)

- participating in *teacher training* for alcohol education (chapter 9)
- developing and evaluating an alcohol education *curriculum unit* (chapter 10).

The second half of the book consists of a wide range of instructional activities, each with complete instructions for use, from which you can choose to implement those which are appropriate to your students' concerns and needs, your own teaching methods and approaches, and your time limitations.

A list of agencies and organizations you can contact for additional information, a list of pamphlets and books for students, and a glossary of alcohol-related terms have also been included.

The broad range of information and issues we have included in this book makes it possible for you to use the volume in a variety of ways, depending on your prior experience teaching about drinking and your purposes in getting involved with alcohol education.

- As a *beginning alcohol educator*, you can read the entire book before teaching about alcohol.
- As an *experienced or partially experienced alcohol educator*, you can read those chapters that you feel address gaps in your knowledge and skills or that provide a useful review of what you already know and can do.
- As a *guidance counselor*, you can read those chapters that will help you in your counseling efforts with youngsters who have concerns related to their own drinking or that of members of their families (see especially chapters 1–4 and 6–8).
- As a *trainer or educator of teachers or counselors*, you can assign specific chapters to your teacher and counselor trainees to supplement your other training materials or use the book itself as the core of your training program in alcohol education.

Whatever your background, goals, and skills, you will find a variety of detailed learning activities in the second half of the book that you can feel comfortable teaching, that will enable you to act as a positive role model to your students, and that will help them to develop and reinforce decision-making skills which will lead to healthy drinking and abstaining habits.

We are grateful for the thoughtful comments of several reviewers of this book when it was in manuscript stage, including Dr. Howard T. Blane, Dr. Gail G. Milgram, Dr. Robert D. Russell, and Dr. Roger Seehafer. While their criticisms helped improve the book in many ways, they are in no way responsible for errors of fact or biases in approach or interpretation which may remain. We also wish to thank Linda Clement for the illustrations in chapter 3. Joanne Klotz expertly typed the several manuscript drafts. We want to express our gratitude to Hiram Howard, our editor at Allyn and Bacon, for his nurturance and enthusiasm during the long preparation of the book. Peter Finn gratefully acknowledges the supportive atmosphere provided by Abt Associates Inc. and its Economic and Environmental Analysis Area during the past ten years which substantially facilitated his work as coauthor of this book. Patricia O'Gorman wishes to thank the National Council on Alcoholism and the constituency groups around the country for their support and inspiration, and Marty Mann for being the great "herself."

Teaching about Alcohol

1

The Goals and Objectives of Alcohol Education

Alcohol education is one strategy for preventing alcohol abuse and alcoholism that many believe has the potential to be very effective. However, not everyone agrees on what "alcohol education" actually is. For example, to some it's providing students with information about alcohol use and abuse. To others it means advising youngsters not to drink until they are legally allowed to do so and then drinking only in moderation. Many people feel alcohol education consists primarily of exploring the causes and consequences of alcoholism.

We have defined alcohol education as the *process* of helping youngsters to (1) become familiar with a variety of facts, attitudes, values, and behaviors regarding alcohol use, nonuse, and abuse, (2) evaluate this information and these feelings, and then (3) act on their evaluations.

The fundamental purpose of alcohol education shares the aim of all education—to develop productive and happy human beings. Alcohol education strives to give people the skills to function untroubled as teenage and adult drinkers or abstainers and to act positively in helping relatives and friends who have alcohol-related problems to do the same.

To achieve this purpose, alcohol education programs must seek to do more than impart factual information about alcohol and alcoholism. We must refrain from stuffing students full of facts they will never use. In such a process we are training the memory but not the mind. We must eschew the temptation to teach youngsters to *fill* their heads rather than to *use* their heads. We must help students become aware of and explore their reasons for their opinions, feelings, and actions and assist them from the earliest grades to practice decision-making techniques so that they will be equipped to handle many of the difficult choices they will have to make, among which will surely be their use or nonuse of alcohol and will likely be their response to other people who use or abuse it. In this way, not only are we promoting their future

1

health behavior but also their constructive responses to others' use and nonuse of alcohol.

GOALS OF ALCOHOL EDUCATION

In order to accomplish this overriding aim of promoting human productivity and happiness, alcohol education must help youngsters to drink or abstain in a manner that enhances or at least does not harm their own or other people's physical and emotional health, family life, and employment. There are several goals alcohol education must seek to achieve that will enable students to use or abstain from alcohol in this healthy manner. These goals are that students:

1. Understand the role of feelings, attitudes, values, family histories, and the social environment as factors that influence people's decisions to use, abuse, and abstain from alcohol and be able to examine objectively their own feelings about drinking and not drinking.
2. Seek and make use of unbiased information concerning alcohol, its use, abuse, and nonuse, and its positive and negative effects on individuals and society.
3. Understand that there are conflicts in American society regarding the use and nonuse of alcoholic beverages because of different ethnic, social, religious, cultural, and educational backgrounds of people in different communities and households.
4. Be aware of the pervasive and changing role of peer pressure in different environments and its impact on decision making about drinking and not drinking and develop the ability to distinguish between appropriate and inappropriate peer pressure.
5. Appreciate the widespread benefits that most Americans and many cultures derive from the moderate use of alcohol.
6. Make harmful drinking practices socially unattractive phenomena and encourage healthy drinking practices, such as serving food with alcohol, helping guests pace their drinks, refusing to buy alcohol for or serve alcohol to minors outside the immediate family, and promoting the use of soft drinks among those who do not wish to drink or should not be drinking.

7. Understand the extent to which alcohol abuse has produced monumental problems in health and safety, economic behavior, personal relationships, and the criminal justice system.
8. Understand the nature and extent of alcoholism as a relatively widespread, crippling, but treatable disorder and avoid stigmatizing the alcoholic and his or her family.
9. Know about the agencies and organizations in their communities that provide assistance to those with alcohol problems.
10. Develop a sense of responsibility for their own welfare and that of others in regard to the use and nonuse of alcohol, including seeking help if they have a drinking problem and identifying and securing help for other people with drinking problems.

These goals of alcohol education are designed to promote the aim of helping youngsters to become productive, happy human beings. In order to achieve these goals, however, you need to focus your attention on several *immediate, short-term objectives*, the achievement of which is the prerequisite for accomplishing these ultimate goals. Unlike goals, objectives help you to focus on the discrete, "bite size," manageable targets your instruction should be designed to achieve and thereby provide practical guidelines for how to engage in the nitty-gritty of alcohol education—developing curriculum, selecting teaching strategies, identifying content, preparing lesson plans, and actually teaching. A detailed discussion of how to select objectives and evaluate your success in achieving them may be found in chapter 10.

SOME BASIC PRINCIPLES OF ALCOHOL EDUCATION

Below are the basic principles of alcohol education that, if properly implemented, will enable you to achieve the goals of alcohol education which we have suggested above. Each of these principles is discussed in detail in one or more of the remaining chapters of this book. You may wish to turn directly to the chapters that expand on those principles that concern you the most.

1. Examine Your Own Attitudes toward Alcohol. Your attitudes are critical. They show in everything you do and are quickly picked up by those around you. In order to teach about alcohol it is essential to understand how you, the educator, feel about drinking and about persons with alcoholism and people who abstain. Once you are comfortable with your own feelings, it is easier to deal objectively with the feelings of your students. (See chapters 7 and 9.)

2. Respect the Integrity of the Home. In public education, we are teaching youngsters from all families in the community. Since there is no consensus in our society regarding appropriate drinking and nondrinking behaviors, these community members are likely to have different views about what consitutes acceptable use of alcohol and different drinking practices. These parents' different beliefs and behaviors must be respected, regardless of whether you agree with them or not. This means not criticizing specific drinking patterns, including abstention and frequent intoxication. However, respecting different drinking attitudes and practices in your community does not mean ignoring them; rather, it means ensuring that a variety of attitudes and behaviors related to alcohol are discussed in the classroom without your expressing opinions regarding their "rightness" or "wrongness." If your students make judgements regarding drinking attitudes or practices, make sure that you balance their comments with objective information and solicit different viewpoints from other members of the class. (See chapters 7 and 8.)

3. Begin with the Concerns of the Student. The most effective teaching is that which is geared to the immediate needs and concerns of students. It must begin where the group or individual is and move on from there. The relation of new ideas to those already gained is an essential bridge in the process of teaching. In the teaching of alcohol studies, you should try to get to know your students' level of achievement, their major interests, and their experiences with alcohol. Only then can you capitalize fully on their aptitudes and concerns to maintain or create a keen desire to learn more about alcohol. (See chapter 10.)

4. Focus on Attitudes and Feelings. Most people's decisions about drinking are made not only on the basis of rational considerations but also as a result of nonrational motives. Some of the major nonrational considerations with respect to decisions to drink or abstain and how much and when to drink involve peer pressure, role modeling, self-concept, and risk-taking. You will be able to best help your students make healthy decisions about drinking and not drinking if you use instructional approaches that assist them in becoming aware of and understanding these nonrational motives. Create an open class atmosphere in which pupils feel free to express their thoughts and concerns about drinking and abstaining to you and to each other. (See chapters 5 and 7.)

5. Teach about Alcohol Objectively. To meet the community's perfectly legitimate concern that schools not promote drinking behaviors or attitudes that are not consonant with those of parents, you should avoid moralizing about drinking and abstaining, focusing on "the evils" of drinking, and overstressing the dangers of drinking—approaches that were popular in alcohol education from its inception in the nineteenth century as a result of the Temperance movement until very recently. Discuss and have students investigate what a majority of Americans feel are the positive aspects of responsible alcohol use, such as taste, relaxation, appetite stimulation, and conviviality. Include discussions of responsible abstinence with discussions about responsible drinking. Encourage students to investigate and discuss reasons for abstaining and attitudes of abstainers toward drinking. Welcome all student opinions nonjudgmentally. Avoid giving personal advice. Develop the ability to understand your own attitudes and feelings about alcohol and to determine when to keep them to yourself and when to express them honestly. Try to understand and develop the ability to explain several alternative positions with regard to drinking and abstaining without advocating a particular point of view. Above all, concentrate on promoting the *process* of decision making rather than recommending the adoption of specific attitudes or behaviors. (See chapter 7.)

6. Avoid the Psychology of Fear. One purpose of alcohol education is to prepare young people gradually for the decisions they will make regarding alcohol use and nonuse. This is accomplished best by presenting information in an unemotional atmosphere. It is usually not accomplished by attempting to frighten. If you should sense that a student is becoming upset in your class, it is important to try to immediately reduce his or her fear. For example, if speaking about parents with alcoholism appears to be creating tension, mentioning where help can be sought for those with alcoholism in their families may lessen his or her fear. Being informed about your community resources is therefore important when you teach about alcohol. (See chapter 7.)

7. Teach Alcohol Education, Not Alcoholism Education. Most youngsters are concerned about here-and-now problems and issues related to drinking, such as peer pressure, risk-taking, the effects of alcohol on their bodies and minds, alcohol and sex, and drunk driving—not just or even primarily alcoholism, which most of them regard as a remote possibility for themselves and an attempt to frighten them away from any use of alcohol. Alcohol education includes explorations into the causes, nature, prevention, and

treatment of alcoholism, but its range is much broader: It includes the study of the enjoyment most people find in drinking, the role of alcohol use in social, economic, and political life, the effects of moderate as well as excessive alcohol use on the mind and body, alcohol-traffic safety, why people drink and abstain, peer pressures, and the role of the mass media. (See chapters 3 and 4.)

8. Don't Try to Cover Too Much. The study of alcohol involves a vast number of issues—from drunk driving to the pleasures of drinking and the nature of alcoholism. You have an important role to play in making decisions about the teaching methods and content of your alcohol course or unit. You will be able to select topics to teach that will be of most benefit to your students if you encourage them to play a major role in planning the material to be covered and how it will be treated. (See chapter 10.)

ADDITIONAL READING

Blane, Howard T. "Education and the Prevention of Alcoholism." In *The Biology of Alcoholism*, vol. 4, edited by Benjamin Kissin and Henri Begleiter. New York: Plenum Press, 1976.

———. "Issues in Preventing Alcohol Problems." *Preventive Medicine* 5 (1976):176-186.

———. "Recent Trends in Alcohol Education," *Health Education* 7 (1976):36-38.

Finn, Peter. *Alcohol and Alcohol Safety*, vol. 1. Washington, D.C.: U.S. Government Printing Office, 1972.

Milgram, Gail G. "A Historical Review of Alcohol Education Research and Comments." *Journal of Alcohol and Drug Education* 2 (1976):1-16.

National Council on Alcoholism. *What Is Alcohol Education?* New York, 1975.

O'Gorman, Patricia A., ed. *Adolescent Education: Proceedings of the Region III Conference.* New York: National Council on Alcoholism, 1975.

———, and Stringfield, Sharon, eds. *Alcohol Education: What It Is and How To Do It.* New York: National Council on Alcoholism, 1979.

Room, Robin. "Governing Images and the Prevention of Alcohol Problems." *Preventive Medicine* 3 (1974): 11-23.

Russell, Robert D. *What Shall We Teach the Young about Drinking?* New Brunswick, N.J.: Rutgers Center of Alcohol Studies, 1970.

Unterberger, Hilma, and DiCicco, Lena. "Alcohol Education Re-evaluated." *Bulletin of the National Association of Secondary School Principals* 52 (1968):15-29.

Williams, Allan F.; DiCicco, Lena M.; and Unterberger, Hilma. "Philosophy and Evaluation of an Alcohol Education Program." *Quarterly Journal of Studies on Alcohol* 29 (1968):685-702.

2

Primary Prevention
in Alcohol Education

Primary prevention in alcohol education is often confused with both early intervention (also called secondary prevention, diagnosis, and early case finding), and also with treatment (also known as tertiary prevention). Early intervention is known as *secondary* prevention because it attempts to prevent the worsening of an incipient problem after it has begun. Treatment is known as tertiary prevention because it deals with the prevention of relapses in people who have already experienced the full-fledged problem. *Tertiary* prevention is also often used synonymously with the treatment of people who are currently alcoholics or problem drinkers—in which case it is a misnomer to use the term "prevention" at all, since the problem is already well developed.

Primary prevention is a more recent addition to this schema of dealing with drinking problems in people. On the simplest level, primary prevention means to keep a problem from developing before it has even started. This simple statement belies a complex series of events, because preventing the development of a problem may involve a number of strategies, from promoting basic health care behavior in the classroom to changing laws.

The strategies used to achieve primary prevention are varied and need to be chosen according to the nature of the problem to be prevented and the type of person or group to be helped. The most commonly used strategies to achieve the primary prevention of alcohol problems are the following:

- passage of laws to regulate the manufacture, sale and use of alcohol—for example, making 21 the legal age of purchase of alcohol
- promotion of group sanctions or norms—for example, insisting on or expecting friends to serve food and nonalcoholic beverages at parties
- education of the public at large—for example, making people aware that even one time

excessive alcohol use, when combined with such activities as driving or boating, can produce fatal results

- education through the schools—for example, teaching that a 12-ounce can of beer contains about as much alcohol as a 1½ shot glass of whiskey or a 5-ounce glass of wine.

HISTORY OF PRIMARY PREVENTION EFFORTS

Much of our thinking today concerning primary prevention is due to our country's long and controversial history of attempts to forestall alcohol problems. Early efforts to prevent alcohol problems in the United States date back to the beginning of the 1700s when certain religious groups attempted to have their members refrain from any use of "spiritous liquors" but did not discourage—and even encouraged—beer. (This largely arbitrary distinction between "dangerous spirits" and "harmless" wine and beer is still part of our thinking—witness the U. S. Senate bill that in 1979 would have labeled hard liquor as "dangerous to your health" but not wine or beer.)

The Temperance movement of the 1800s expanded on the goals of abstention to include all alcohol use and attempted to impose this standard as a new national norm. The Temperance movement started with informal grass roots meetings of private citizens and expanded into formally constituted community organizations that attempted first to close down retail alcohol outlets and eventually to institute legislation against all alcohol use, manufacture, and sale.

Along with attempts to promote group sanctions against any alcohol use, the Temperance movement in the latter part of the nineteenth century fostered the introduction of alcohol education in the public schools, where its primary thrust became one of warning youngsters against the "evils" of any alcohol use and vigorously exhorting them to abstain. It was during these years prior to World War I that every state passed legislation requiring that this approach to teaching about drinking be instituted in the public schools.

Eventually, with help from other groups in society concerned both with the effects of alcohol abuse on the war effort and also with the type of people who were most visible in their use and misuse of alcohol ("foreign immigrants"), the Temperance movement succeeded in securing the passage of the Eighteenth Amendment, which outlawed the manufacture, sale, and transportation of alcoholic beverages between 1920 and 1933. (A majority of states had already passed similar legislation.) With the advent of Prohibition, alcohol education in the schools was often discontinued under the assumption that it was now superfluous given the "dry" status of the country.

With the end of Prohibition came new efforts to prevent alcohol problems through a welter of state and local laws that attempted to control and regulate what Prohibition had failed to eliminate. Hours and days of sale were regulated, as was the legal age of purchase of alcohol. Laws governed such areas as whether or not a retail outlet had to be open to public view, how close to a church or school it could operate, and whether it needed to have curtains in the windows to "protect" the passing public from the activities inside.

At the same time, interest in alcohol education revived slightly as a primary prevention strategy with which to complement the regulatory approach through legislation. However, throughout the 1940s, 1950s, and 1960s, alcohol education, when it was taught at all, remained largely in the Temperance movement mode of focusing on the evils of drinking. However, the approach this time was not so much through the explicit advocacy of abstention as through the presentation of highly selected "objective facts" that purported to demonstrate scientifically the dangers of any alcohol use by youngsters and of a great deal of adult drinking behavior.

During the 1970s, however, alcohol education received both greatly increased attention and a different thrust as a result of two phenomena. First, throughout the 1960s, in response to a dramatic increase in nonalcohol drug abuse among middle-class teenagers, schools mounted a major educational campaign to educate students to the dangers of LSD, heroin, and marijuana. One of the long-term results of this campaign was a renewed appreciation of the fact that alcohol abuse was an even greater problem among the young than the use of these other drugs. Partly as a result of this realization, schools began to focus increasing attention on teaching about alcohol. However, this time they were urged by alcohol experts and many educators who drew upon the latest drug education approaches to avoid attempting to promote specific drinking behaviors by students through an objective presentation of just the risks of alcohol abuse and instead help youngsters to develop competent decision-making skills, that, it was assumed, would enable them to learn to abstain or drink without problem. Coupled with this approach to alcohol education was a more honest recognition than before that teenagers *did* drink and that to expect them to abstain until they reached the legal purchase age was unrealistic.

Yet, while these new alcohol education approaches have been promoted in educational circles and renewed attempts have been made to include teaching about drinking in every school system, the actual implementation of alcohol education in most schools throughout the country has not changed much since the 1940s: alcohol education is not taught in a significant number of schools in any meaningful way (one-day assemblies or a single class period devoted to alcohol is not alcohol education), nor have most instructors who have taught about alcohol done much more than introduce "the facts" to their students—although often with a good deal more objectivity than did previous generations of teachers.

Along with this modest revival of interest in alcohol education spawned by the problems stemming from the drug culture and coinciding with the new thrust toward the promotion of decision-making skills, came a second stimulus—a primary prevention approach fostered by the government to change social norms about drinking. The newly formed National Institute on Alcohol Abuse and Alcoholism (NIAAA) mounted a nationwide public education campaign in the early 1970s to promote what it called "responsible" drinking. The NIAAA funded several groups to develop responsible drinking campaigns, the most notable being the U.S. Jaycees. However, in the mid-1970s NIAAA repudiated the notion of responsibility in relation to drinking because a consensus could not be achieved on what this meant. Instead, the focus shifted to one of "making responsible *decisions* about alcohol." This theme, which coincided with the educators' new emphasis on promoting decision-making skills in the classroom, was further promoted across the country by such groups as the Boys Clubs of America

and the National Parent Teacher Association. As we stand today, the concept of promoting alcohol-specific, decision-making skills represents the major prevention focus for the classroom.

THE ROLE OF EDUCATION IN THE SCHOOLS AS PRIMARY PREVENTION

Given this background on the history of primary prevention attempts in America to reduce the incidence of drinking problems, we can now focus on the primary prevention strategy of most concern in this volume: classroom education. Two warnings are in order before we begin. First, the only appropriate form of prevention effort for the classroom teacher is *primary* prevention. You are simply not qualified to provide secondary or tertiary prevention—early intervention and diagnosis or treatment. Only a trained counselor or other experienced caregiver can do this. However, this does not mean that if you suspect a student of yours has a drinking problem that you should not inform the guidance department of your concern. And certainly if a youngster tells you he or she has a drinking problem or is troubled by somebody else's drinking, you should refer the pupil to the guidance department. What the exclusion of secondary and tertiary prevention from your agenda means is that you should not actively look for drinking problems among your students nor, if any drinking problems inadvertently come to your attention, should you try to help these students yourself. Alcohol education can be a controversial area that does not need to be further confused or endangered by misplaced attempts of teachers to solve their students' personal drinking problems.

A second caveat with regard to classroom education as primary prevention is that what you do with your students should be seen as one component of a total primary prevention strategy designed to help youngsters avoid alcohol abuse. Classroom education alone cannot be effective with most youngsters if what you teach in school is not reinforced and expanded upon by the primary prevention efforts of lawmakers, government agencies, civic groups, and, perhaps most crucially, parents. As such, classroom education should, where possible, coordinate its goals and approaches with those of the community and the nation—to the extent that a consensus on drinking exists at these levels. In chapter 8, we discuss in detail how you can shape your teaching about drinking in ways that are consistent with the values and attitudes of the parents in your town.

Alcohol education needs to be careful about what goals and objectives it seeks to achieve not only to ensure that they are consistent with the concept of primary prevention but also to make certain that what you attempt to accomplish in the classroom is something that you can realistically expect to achieve given the amount of time you are able to devote to alcohol education, the learning abilities of your students, and the support you can expect to receive from your school administration and the community. We have described the goals and listed the objectives that we believe your efforts should focus on accomplishing in chapter 1. Once again, we stress that no one can expect you to accomplish all or even one of them by yourself. Reinforcement from other sectors of society alone will make this possible for the vast majority of your students.

How can your instructional efforts help students to avoid problems related to alcohol use? First, you can help your students to initiate or further the process of identifying, examining, and evaluating their feelings about drinking and abstaining so that they are better able to develop constructive attitudes toward alcohol use, abuse, and nonuse and to learn to engage in behaviors that are consistent with these positive attitudes. Second, you can help pupils become familiar with contrasting attitudes toward drinking and abstaining and with a variety of patterns of alcohol use and abuse. As a result, rather than uncritically accepting their current values and thoughts about this area of human behavior, they will be able to open themselves to selecting new activities and developing different feelings that may be more likely to help them avoid drinking problems than were their previous ones.

Third, you can help youngsters develop effective decision-making skills by engaging them repeatedly in the process of recognizing problems, identifying alternative methods of resolving them, gathering information relevant to choosing a solution, selecting a method for resolving them, testing out their decisions in actual practice, and evaluating how effective their decisions were based on actual experience. Chapter

11 provides numerous exercises that will help your students develop these decision-making skills. Finally, you can assist your pupils secure accurate information about alcohol use and its associated pleasures and risks to facilitate their developing healthy attitudes and engaging in wise decision making.

TARGETING PRIMARY PREVENTION AT HIGH RISK GROUPS

Your efforts to help youngsters avoid drinking problems will be most effective if you are familiar with those kinds of individuals—youngsters and adults—who are most likely to develop a drinking problem. While it would certainly be desirable for you to learn whether there are students in your classes who are especially at risk of developing a drinking problem so that you could tailor your primary prevention efforts to the particular needs of these pupils, it will be difficult for you to be able to secure this information—even if it were ethically appropriate for you to do so.

Furthermore, even if you knew which youngsters in your class fell into high risk groups, given the heterogeneity of youngsters in most schools, it might be of little value to find out that you have three students who are at risk because they have an alcoholic parent, and four students because they are taking medication, while the rest of the class falls into no particular high risk category. Nonetheless, being aware of the types of demographic, familial, and other characteristics that make it more likely for one group of people to develop a drinking problem than another group is useful background information to have so that your teaching efforts are at least sensitive to the special needs the students in your class may have if they are members of these high risk groups. But most importantly, knowing which groups in society are at risk of developing an alcohol problem will enable you to help your students become similarly informed and thereby assist them in identifying their potential for developing an alcohol-related problem. As a result of this knowledge, they may be better able to evaluate whether, when, where, and how much they can safely drink—and when a friend or family member needs to be cautioned about his or her drinking behavior.

At-risk groups fall into basically two general categories. The first consists of those who, due to a current and transient state, are at risk for the development of a severe problem if they drink, such as the following:

a. Those taking medication for which alcohol use is contraindicated (such as, tranquilizers, aspirin, cold remedies)
b. Those performing complex motor tasks, especially youth and the geriatric population, and others whose general motor level may be as yet undeveloped or deteriorating (for example, driving cars, operating machinery, walking up or down stairs)
c. Pregnant women and couples contemplating having children
d. Those under high stress

The second category of at-risk groups consists of those individuals who are considered unusually susceptible to developing an alcohol problem over an extended period of time, such as:

a. Children of alcoholics
b. Children of rigid abstainers
c. Children of those living within sociocultural environments which have a high rate of problem drinking

As can be seen by viewing this list of those who may be periodically or continuously at risk for developing an alcohol use-related problem, many people who consume alcohol at some time or other can be regarded as at risk for the development of a problem. From an educational point of view this means assisting students in becoming aware of and developing appropriate attitudes and behaviors concerning the specific risks that are faced when alcohol use is introduced into certain situations or consumed by certain people—for example, abstaining or drinking with great care if one is pregnant, taking certain medications, or the child of an alcoholic.

A brief discussion of one particular at-risk group—pregnant women—can serve as an example of the kind of information with which students should become familiar as part of a primary prevention effort in the classroom. The full Fetal Alcohol Syndrome (FAS) is characterized by such symptoms as low birth weight, failure to thrive, facial irregularities such as narrow eye slits, learning deficits, mental re-tardation, limb abnormalities, and cardiovascular problems.[1] Any one of these features may appear separately and not in combination with the others. When this occurs, it is called an alcohol-related birth defect. This is felt to be much more pervasive than FAS.[2]

A controversy has revolved around just how much a woman can drink safely if she is pregnant. For example, the National Council on Alcoholism had a press conference at which it stated that pregnant women should not drink at all, while a statement from the National Institute on Alcoholism and Alcohol Abuse 24 hours later asserted that drinking up to two drinks or one and one-half ounces of alcohol per day was safe.

The most recent research suggests that drinking above a certain blood alcohol content (BAC) may risk FAS or an alcohol-related birth defect.[3] Since the relationship of amount drunk to BAC is based not only on the amount consumed but also on how much a drinker weighs and whether he or she has just eaten (see discussion of BAC in chapter 3), and since some women's ability to tolerate alcohol changes when they are pregnant (just as their ability to tolerate fats and sugars changes), no quick rule-of-thumb can be provided.[4]

Another research question that has yet to be established is the role of excessive alcohol use in males. We know that alcohol abuse is correlated with infertility in men. What we do not know is the effect of shorter term alcohol abuse on male's ability to produce a healthy child—that is, whether a child conceived during a period of

[1] Sterling Clarren and David Smith, "The Fetal Alcohol Syndrome: A Review of the World Literature," New England Journal of Medicine, 298 (1978):1063–1067; U.S. Department of Health, Education, and Welfare, "The Fetal Alcohol Syndrome and Other Effects on Offspring," in Alcohol and Health, Third Special Report to the U.S. Congress. Technical Support Document (Washington, D.C.: U.S. Government Printing Office, 1978), pp. 167-193.

[2] Henry L. Rosett, "The Effects of Maternal Drinking on Child Development: An Introductory Review," Annals of the New York Academy of Science 273 (1976):115-117.

[3] Gerald Chernoff, "The Fetal Alcohol Syndrome in Mice: An Animal Model," Teratology 13 (1977):223-230.

[4] Recent research suggests that the less a pregnant woman drinks the better, with abstention the safest course of action.

heavy drinking is likely to also show the signs of FAS or have an alcohol-related birth defect.

CONCLUSION

This brief presentation about the Fetal Alcohol Syndrome is a good illustration of the entire concept of primary prevention as it applies to alcohol education. It exemplifies the role you can play in providing students with information and in helping them to develop attitudes and make decisions that will help enable them to avoid a drinking-related problem before it ever occurs. This is the central goal of all alcohol education: to assist youngsters to abstain from or use alcohol in a manner that will enhance their well-being and enjoyment of life and prevent them from harming themselves or others. It is sometimes said that "an ounce of prevention is worth a pound of cure." Certainly this is true

in the area of alcohol-related problems. However, this does not mean that it is *easier* to prevent a drinking problem than it is to cure one. Primary prevention, as we have suggested, requires sensitivity and hard work to be effective, whether it is conducted through legislative efforts, public education, in the home, or in the classroom. Indeed, there are few carefully designed and executed programs around the country that demonstrate the success of this primary prevention approach. Part of this lack of evidence stems from the difficulty of measuring something that we are trying to prevent from happening: it is not easy to measure a nonevent—the absence of alcohol problems. However, we are confident that if you conscientiously implement the principles of alcohol education as recommended in this chapter and in the rest of this volume, you will be able to contribute to the prevention of alcohol problems among a significant number of your students.

ADDITIONAL READING

General

Bailey, J. P., Jr., and Wakeley, J. T. *Analysis of Education Programs for Primary Alcoholism Prevention.* Research Triangle Park, N.C.: Research Triangle Institute, 1973.

Blane, Howard T. "Education and the Prevention of Alcoholism." In *The Biology of Alcoholism*, vol. 4, edited by Benjamin Kissin and Henri Begleiter. New York: Plenum Press, 1976.

———. "Issues in Preventing Alcohol Problems." *Preventive Medicine* 5 (1976):176-186.

Bruun, Kettil, et al. *Alcohol Control Policies in Public Health Perspective.* Helsinki, Finland: The Finnish Foundation for Alcohol Studies, 1975.

de Lint, Jan. "The Prevention of Alcoholism." *Preventive Medicine* 3 (1974):24-35.

Ferrier, W. Kenneth. "Alcohol Education in the Public School Curriculum." In *Alcohol Education for Classroom and Community*, edited by Raymond G. McCarthy. New York: McGraw Hill Book Company, 1964.

Finn, Peter. "Attitudes Toward Drinking Conveyed in Studio Greeting Cards." *American Journal of Public Health* 70 (1980):826-829.

Freeman, Howard E., and Scott, John F. "A Critical Review of Alcohol Education for Adolescents."

Community Mental Health Journal 2 (1966): 222-230.

Globetti, Gerald. "Alcohol Education in the School." *Journal of Drug Education* 1 (1971):241-248.

———. "A Conceptual Analysis of the Effectiveness of Alcohol Education Programs." In *Research on Methods and Programs of Drug Education*, edited by Michael Goodstadt. Toronto: Addiction Research Foundation, 1974.

Lender, Mark Edward. "The Role of History in Early Alcohol Education: The Impact of the Temperance Movement." *Journal of Alcohol and Drug Education* 23 (1977):56-62.

Milgram, Gail G. "A Historical Review of Alcohol Education Research and Comments," *Journal of Alcohol and Drug Education* 21 (1976):1-16.

Morgan, Patricia Anne. "Examining United States Alcohol Policy: Alcohol Control and the Interests of the State." Working Paper No. E-56. Berkeley, Calif.: Social Research Group, 1978.

Mosher, James F. "Alcoholic Beverage Controls in the Prevention of Alcohol Problems: A Concept Paper on Demonstration Programs." Berkeley, Calif.: Social Research Group, 1978.

Parker, Douglas A., and Harman, Marsha S. "The Distribution of Consumption Model of Prevention: A Critical Assessment." Paper prepared for the NIAAA symposium on normative approaches to prevention at Coronado, California, April 1977. Washington, D.C.: National Institute on Alcohol Abuse and Alcoholism, 1977.

Popham, Robert E.; Schmidt, Wolfgang; and de Lint, Jan. "The Prevention of Alcoholism: Epidemiological Studies of the Effects of Government Control Measures" *British Journal of Addiction* 70 (1975):125-144.

Russell, Robert D. "Education about Alcohol . . . For REAL American Youth." *Journal of Alcohol Education* 14 (1969), 16-20.

Smart, Reginald G. *The New Drinkers: Teenage Use and Abuse of Alcohol.* Chapter IX, "What Can Schools Do to Teach Safe Drinking Habits?" and Chapter X, "What Can Governments Do about Preventing Drinking Problems?" Toronto: Addiction Research Foundation, 1976.

Unterberger, Hilma, and DiCicco, Lena. "Alcohol Education Re-evaluated." *Bulletin of the National Association of Secondary School Principals* 52 (1968):15-29.

Wilkinson, Rupert. *The Prevention of Drinking Problems: Alcohol Control and Cultural Influences.* New York: Oxford University Press, 1970.

Williams, Allan F.; DiCicco, Lena M.; and Unterberger, Hilma. "Philosophy and Evaluation of an Alcohol Education Program." *Quarterly Journal of Studies on Alcohol* 29 (1968):785-702.

Children of Alcoholics

Bowen, Murray. *A Family Systems Approach to Alcoholism.* New York: National Council on Alcoholism, n.d.

Cork, R. Margaret. *The Forgotten Children.* Toronto: Paperjacks, 1969.

El-Guebaly, N., and Offord, D. "The Offspring of Alcoholics: A Critical Review." *American Journal of Psychiatry* 134 (1977):357-365.

Fox, Ruth. "The Effect of Alcoholism on Children." *Proceedings of the Fifth International Congress on Psychotherapy Program in Child Psychology.* New York: National Council on Alcoholism, 1963.

Goodwin, Donald; Schulsinger, F.; Hermansen, L.; Guze, S.; and Winokur, G. "Alcohol Problems in Adoptees Raised Apart from Alcoholic Biological Parents." *Archives of General Psychiatry* 28 (1973):238-243.

Hornick, Edith. *You and Your Alcoholic Parent.* New York: Association Press, 1974.

Mayer, J., and Black, R. "The Relationship between Alcoholism and Child Abuse and Neglect." In *Currents in Alcoholism,* vol. 2, edited by Frank Seixas. New York: Grune and Stratton, 1977, pp. 429-444.

O'Gorman, Patricia A. "Alcoholism: The Family Disease." *Urban Health, The Journal of Health Care in the Cities* 27 (1974):38.

Seixas, Judith S. *Living with a Parent Who Drinks Too Much.* New York: Greenwillow Books, 1979.

3

Background Information on Alcohol Use, Nonuse, and Abuse

Alcohol was introduced into the colonies with the early settlers—in fact the Mayflower landed where it did at Plymouth in part, as one of the party wrote, because "we could not take much time for further search and consideration, our victuals being much spent, especially beer." Soon regional specialties developed that were based on the distillation of local fruits, the most popular being applejack.

In a sense, alcohol consumption grew as the United States did. The tavern was a center of social activity as well as political intrigue. As the colonies entered the world of international trade, rum eventually constituted one-third of the famous triangular trade route. Slaves from Africa were transported to the West Indies where they worked on sugar plantations and assisted in the making of molasses. Molasses was in turn traded to New England where it was manufactured into rum which, in turn, was used to purchase more slaves in Africa.

One of the adverse consequences of the introduction of "spirits" to the colonies was the effect that this new substance had on the American natives—the American Indian. In part because they did not have a cultural tradition to guide the use of these new "spirits," many American Indians soon developed social problems directly related to their alcohol use. In addition, many early American traders encouraged alcohol abuse among the Indians, both by their own example of frequent inebriety and by their attempts to make Indians dependent on a cheap commodity in exchange for which the traders could secure valuable furs. In fact some tribes in Eastern Canada became extinct soon after the introduction of alcohol because they were easily attacked and decimated by hostile but sober tribes.

On the whole, however, alcohol consumption was thought to be remarkably healthy and was consumed in great quantities by the early pioneers—usually starting before breakfast. The tradition of the heavy drinker coupled with massive binges culminated in the early nineteenth century with an annual, average per capita consumption level (the amount consumed by every adult 15 and over) of 7.1 gallons.[1] Our current annual per capita consumption is just under 2.7 gallons.

The Temperance movement in America had its roots in the Washingtonian movement (in which people were asked to sign the pledge), in the early religious organizations within the states that prohibited the use of alcohol, and in the reaction to the new wave of "hard-drinking" immigrants in the 1830s. These factors, coupled with the beginnings of the Industrial Revolution, which emphasized productivity and performance, led to a drop in the per capita consumption.

With reorganization of the Women's Christian Temperance Union in the 1880s and the formation of the Anti-Saloon League in the 1890s, the Temperance movement gathered new strength, culminating in the complete prohibition of the sale of alcohol beverages in 1920 in the Eighteenth Amendment to the Constitution. While Prohibition led to a reduction in alcoholism and in annual per capita consumption, it also created a dramatic increase in social problems. Prohibition was repealed by the Twenty-first Amendment in 1933. It is interesting to note that it has taken the United States until the 1970s to reach pre-Prohibition per capita consumption levels. Prohibition therefore did lead to a temporary but marked change in drinking behavior following repeal.

After repeal, the per capita consumption level gradually rose until the end of the 1950s and then soared.[2] However, the rapid increase in drinking in the 1960s may have been more apparent than real, for the end of the sixties also marked a huge decline in the amount of moonshining (illegally operated stills) in the country. The drop in moonshining resulted from the shrinking population in rural America, where moonshining had been most prevalent, a gradual increase in American prosperity, so that drinkers could afford the higher prices of legally manufactured alcoholic beverages, and the rapid rise in the cost of sugar, which priced many moonshiners out of the market.

Another change in American drinking practices has been a trend toward light-tasting

substances. This literally translates into a decline in bourbon sales and an increase in vodka sales (until a short time ago, a relatively unknown "spirit") as our most popular distilled beverage. With this has also come a shift to white wine from the once more popular red.

Interestingly enough, another change is also afoot, and this is the gradual lowering of the alcohol content in distilled spirits, and even some indication of a similar trend in beer and wine. This reduction in the alcohol level was initially a strategy to lower the relative price of alcohol, since alcoholic beverages are taxed according to the percentage of alcohol they contain. A side effect of this change may be that those who drink the same number of alcoholic beverages will be consuming less alcohol than before. However, a greater percentage of people now drink than did prior to the 1960s—especially women.

Significantly, 15 percent of those people who drink consume about 60 percent of the alcohol sold, and 20 percent of all beer drinkers consume 80 percent of all beer sold.

Today, approximately two-thirds of all adult Americans drink, which has given us the impression that we are a drinking society. However, for all the attention that our consumption of alcoholic beverages attracts, we rank fifteenth in per capita consumption out of twenty-six countries for which comparable figures are available. In addition, if we add the 15 percent of "drinkers" who in fact drink less than once a month, only slightly more than half the population can be considered to be regular drinkers.[3]

There are many ways that drinking practices in the United States have been measured. One of the most popular is based on the work of Dr. Don Cahalan and his associates at the University of California at Berkeley. He classified people according to the following parameters: "*Abstainers*—drink less than once a year or not at all; *Infrequent drinkers*—drink at least once a year, but less than once a month; *Light drinkers*—drink at least once a month, but typically only one or two drinks on a single occasion; *Moderate drinkers*—drink at least once a month, typically several times, but usually with no more than three or four drinks per occasion; *Heavy drinkers*—drink nearly every day with five or more per occasion at least once in a while, or about once weekly with usually

[1] U.S. Department of Health, Education, and Welfare, *Alcohol and Health*. Third Special Report to the U.S. Congress. (Washington, D.C.: U.S. Government Printing Office, June 1978.)

[2] Ibid.

[3] Ibid.

five or more per occasion."[4] Figure 3.1 illustrates the percentage of adult Americans which falls into each of these categories. Other, more recent studies have generally confirmed these findings.

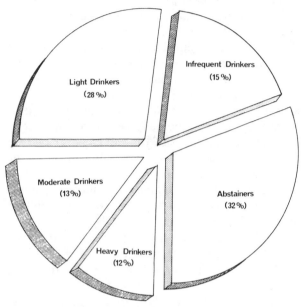

FIGURE 3.1. Percentage of Drinkers by Drinking Frequency. Reprinted by permission from *Journal of Studies on Alcohol*, Inc. From: Cahalan, D., Cisin, I. H., and Crossley, H. M. *American Drinking Practices*. (Monographs of the Rutgers Center of Alcohol Studies, No. 6.) 1969. Copyright by *Journal of Studies on Alcohol*, Inc., New Brunswick, NJ 08903.

Many studies have sought to determine how many Americans drink beverage alcohol and how many abstain, why they drink or abstain, how much and how often they drink, and under what circumstances they drink. Since most such studies rely on what people say rather than on observed behavior, the findings may be erroneous. However, numerous research studies suggest that the following generalizations about drinking in America appear to be accurate.*[5]

*As you read these statements, keep in mind that they distinguish carefully between *drinkers* (who may or may not drink extensively) and *problem drinkers*.

[4] Don Cahalan, Ira H. Cisin, and Helen M. Crossley, *American Drinking Practices* (New Brunswick, N.J.: Rutgers Center of Alcohol Studies, 1969), p. 19.

[5] U.S. Department of Health, Education, and Welfare, *Alcohol and Health*; Cahalan, Cisin, and Crossley, *American Drinking Practices*; Don Cahalan and Robin Room, *Problem Drinking among American Men* (New Brunswick, New Jersey: Rutgers Center of Alcohol Studies, 1974).

- Two-thirds of all Americans drink at least once a year; one-third do not. However, as we noted earlier, if those persons who are infrequent drinkers (less than once a month) are included with those who never drink, *nearly half of the American adult population cannot be classified as regular drinkers.*

- The percentage of drinkers in the adult population has risen in recent years, after declining in the post-World War II period. However, there appears to have been little change in the percentage of drinkers among men since 1958 but a steady increase among women.

- An estimated ten million Americans are problem drinkers or alcoholics.

- There is more drinking and problem drinking in urban and suburban areas than in rural communities and small towns. There are proportionately more drinkers in New England and the Middle Atlantic and Pacific Coast States than elsewhere, although these regional contrasts may be diminishing. The lowest proportions of drinkers occur in the East South Central States, followed by other southern areas and the Mountain States.

- People from higher socioeconomic groups are more likely to be drinkers than the middle and lower classes, but they are slightly less likely to be problem drinkers. The highest proportion of abstainers is found among the lower socioeconomic levels. The highest proportions of problem drinkers are found among the middle and lower socioeconomic groups.

- Drinking behavior shows a relationship to religious affiliation. Baptists, Methodists, and Mormons, for example, are more likely to be abstainers than are members of other religious denominations. Episcopalians, Catholics, and Jews are more likely to be drinkers than are members of other religious groups.

- The highest proportion of drinkers is found among Americans of Italian, Russian, and Polish ancestry. The Scotch-Irish have the highest proportion of abstainers. The number of heavy drinkers is proportionately highest among Latin-American and Caribbean ethnic groups and Irish-Americans.

- There are no significant differences in drinking behavior between whites and blacks except that proportionately more black women than white women are abstainers and problem drinkers.

- The proportion of adult women who drink has been increasing steadily since World War II. About half of adult women in America now drink once a month or more. However, until recently, available data indicated that men are nearly twice as likely to be moderate drinkers and three times as likely to be heavy drinkers in comparison with women. This gap in male and female drinking behavior appears to be narrowing.

- With advancing age people tend to drink less. More elderly people abstain, and heavy drinking among elderly drinkers declines. However, alcoholism among this group is increasing. The reasons for this are unclear but may include increased isolation and loneliness.

Americans who use alcohol in moderation drink for a variety of reasons. Many drinkers delight in the taste of wine. For some families, wine with their meal is a habit, like eating bread or dessert—and just as enjoyable. Countless drinkers also enjoy what to them is the unusual ability of a cold beer to quench a strong thirst on a hot day. However, most drinkers never really drink because they like the taste of alcohol. After all, a Bloody Mary can be enjoyed as well without the vodka in it (some people drink Bloody Mary mix all by itself). And it's no accident that the most popular hard liquor in America—vodka—has no flavor at all. Most moderate drinkers like the *effects* alcohol has on them after they have swallowed it. They like the way alcohol helps them to relax, forget minor worries, relate to people, and have more fun.

Many people also drink as part of special occasions in order to enliven things or bring out the special importance of the event. Numerous people drink beer at ball games, champagne at weddings, mulled apple cider at Thanksgiving, and hot buttered rum after skiing. These people do not drink in order to enjoy themselves—they are *already* having a good time. Rather, they drink to heighten their pleasure and have an even *better* time. In addition, for many people drinking with friends and family helps them to feel close to each other and share their happiness. Part of this sharing relates to doing something together—like offering a champagne toast, filling everyone's wine glass, or treating friends to a beer. Drinking provides these people with another chance to relate to each other in ways that express and promote friendship.

Finally, people who find it a little difficult to strike up a conversation with strangers at a party or social gathering often find that a drink or two helps them talk about themselves and listen to others.

People who abstain from alcohol also do so for a number of reasons. Often, they simply don't need to use alcohol to help them feel good: they're happy enough the way they are. They may have other ways to relax or share good times, such as through hobbies, talking, eating, playing sports or cards, bicycling, or watching television. Often, from family tradition, the thought of drinking to relax, feel happier, or share good times simply does not occur to them as an important or meaningful activity.

Many people do not like the idea of using any drug, including alcohol, except for medical purposes. Others don't enjoy the partial loss of control they experience after one or more drinks. While there is no evidence that moderate use of alcohol causes any permanent damage (with the possible exception of pregnant women), many people see no point in putting up with even the temporary damage to their stomach, liver, and brain that even one drink always causes. Sometimes illnesses, such as diabetes and ulcers, make it dangerous for a person to drink. Many people also abstain because of a religious conviction that drinking is sinful or at least not useful.

Some people want to drink but won't because they can't stand the taste of alcohol, are concerned about the extra calories it provides, or want to spend their money on what to them are more important things. There are also many alcoholics who have recognized their drinking problem and do not drink because they know what harm drinking causes them.

Adolescents have some of these same reasons for drinking and not drinking, as well as some reasons that may be unique to their age group. In chapter 4 we explore teenage drinking in detail.

MANUFACTURE OF ALCOHOL

The alcohol that we drink, ethyl, is just one of the several types of alcohol that exist, including methyl (wood alcohol), butyl, and isopropyl (rubbing alcohol). Ethyl, or beverage, alcohol is clear, colorless, and highly flammable, and has a slightly sweet smell.

Alcoholic beverages are divided into three categories: wines, beers, and distilled spirits. Beer and wine are produced by fermentation, distilled spirits by distillation.

In the process of fermentation, yeast, which is found naturally in the air and on fruit skins, acts on the sugar in fruit juices, converting the sugar to carbon dioxide and (ethyl) alcohol. Fermentation continues for 4–10 days until the yeast has converted all the available sugar into alcohol and carbon dioxide, usually yielding a concentration of 12–14 percent alcohol and 86–88 percent water (plus minor amounts of other substances).

Wine is produced when yeast converts the natural sugar of a fruit juice into alcohol and carbon dioxide. Most wines are made from the juice of grapes, but they can be produced using nearly any fruit. Red wine is produced by crushing and fermenting the entire grape, including the skin, while for white wine only the juice is fermented.

While the alcoholic content of wines cannot exceed 12–14 percent through the fermentation process, stronger ("fortified") wines, such as muscatel, vermouth, and sherry, have alcoholic contents of up to twenty percent resulting from the addition of distilled spirits.

Beer is produced when yeast and cereals (wheat, barley, rye) interact in a process that involves fermentation but is called brewing. Hops (part of mulberry vines) are added during this process and give beer its characteristic taste. Beer normally contains 3–6 percent alcohol.

Distilled spirits such as whisky, gin, vodka, and brandy consist essentially of the alcohol contained in wines and beers without the extra water these latter beverages contain and with different flavorings. Distilled spirits are manufactured in a process called distillation. Because alcohol has a lower boiling point than the other ingredients in wines and beers, when the latter are heated to a limited degree, the alcohol becomes vapor, which, through a cooling process, can then be reliquefied. The resulting high concentration of alcohol is then aged in charred barrels, a process that creates the distinct flavors of distilled spirits. This process probably dates back to 2000 B.C., but was rarely used until the Middle Ages.

Different types of distilled spirits are based on the major type of cereal used during fermentation. The breakdown is as follows:

Bourbon	51 percent or more corn
Rye	51 percent or more rye and corn or meal
Scotch	Malt only

Gin and vodka are both made from neutral spirits and water. Gin has juniper berries, orange peel and other ingredients added for flavor. Vodka has no added substances. Rum is made by fermenting molasses.

Normally, distilled spirits are watered down to get 40–50 percent alcohol by volume,* but the alcoholic content is called "proof," a term that is always double the actual percentage of alcohol. (For example, 80 proof on the label means 40 percent alcohol.) The term proof derives from the old English test of whiskey in which the English would moisten gunpowder in whiskey and then attempt to ignite it. If the powder exploded, it was too strong; the proper strength of distilled beverages would burn slowly with the powder in a blue flame. Straight alcohol and water in equal proportion will cause such a flame, so this strength was considered perfect and was referred to as 100 proof—that is, 50 percent alcohol, 50 percent water.

EARLY ALCOHOL USE

The use of alcohol can be traced to the beginnings of civilization, when many of the early uses of alcohol had to do with religious rituals. Most ancient civilizations had a god or goddess related to alcohol.

The process of distillation was not widely used until the Middle Ages. Wine was the popular drink. The Bible contains many references to wine where its virtues are extolled. Gradually, the use of wine began to spread westward and soon became popular in Greece where social gatherings were known as "drinking together." Wine's use began to become excessive and raised concern among the great philosophers. In fact, Greece is one of the first examples we have of a society that actually had two separate styles of alcohol use in which alcohol was one of the focuses. Many parts of Greece were the scene of the early Bacchanalian feasts of wine, sex, and violence, whereas smaller

*It is possible in many states to purchase grain alcohol which is 95 percent alcohol or 190 proof.

cities such as Sparta attempted to dilute and monitor the amount of alcohol consumed.

Early Rome was the scene of restraint in drinking practices. Men who consumed an excessive amount were thought to be foolish while women who drank at all were killed. Drinking behavior in the later Roman Empire began more to resemble that of the Greeks, and this caused concern among the early Christians who preached sobriety. The Romans introduced wine to the Gauls whom they conquered, and this was the beginning of the famous vineyards of France and Germany.

The Middle Ages with its reawaking of interest in science spurred the popularity of distillation, and soon many countries were producing their own spirits. By the 1600s there were even some distillation companies forming as these spirits began to be traded "internationally," while eighteenth century London found itself coping with a serious problem of gin abuse, immortalized in Hogarth's series of drawings on "Gin Alley."

While alcohol has been used in different ways throughout the course of history, its effects on the mind and body have always been the same—for alcohol is alcohol, no matter when or where it is used.

PHYSICAL AND BEHAVIORAL EFFECTS OF ALCOHOL

Alcohol passes through a person's body the same way every time he or she drinks. Figure 3.2 presents this process. The dotted lines illustrate alcohol's passage through the body. The numbers indicate the order in which alcohol reaches the various parts of the body. Although alcohol reaches the brain last, it gets there within minutes after it has been drunk.

How Alcohol and the Person Interact

Even though alcohol passes through everyone's body the same way, drinking has very different effects on different people. Even when the same person drinks exactly the same amount of alcohol on two different occasions, it can have very different effects.

Alcohol's effects are governed by the person's drinking behavior and patterns and both the physical and psychological state of the drinker.

Seven different factors may be distinguished that determine how alcohol affects people:

1. how much they drink
2. how fast they drink
3. what kind of beverage they drink
4. how much they weigh
5. how much they have eaten
6. the state or condition of their body
7. how they think and feel about drinking
8. where a person drinks—the setting

1. Amount of Alcohol. Of course, the most important influence on how alcohol affects people is how much alcohol they drink. The more alcohol, the stronger the effects. And the key word here is *alcohol*. A person may be drinking beer, wine, or whiskey but what matters is how much alcohol there is in each of these drinks.

Most people think that whiskey is "stronger" than beer or wine. However, this isn't necessarily true. As the illustration in Figure 3.3 indicates, a 5-ounce glass of wine and a 12-ounce can of beer have about the same amount of alcohol in them as a 1-1/2-ounce shot glass of hard liquor.* The reason *mixed drinks* (alcohol plus soda, orange juice, etc.) are often "stronger" than beer or wine is that the host or drinker has put a lot *more* than one shot of alcohol into the glass—perhaps two or three shots.

2. Speed of Drinking. Our livers can metabolize alcohol (convert it to carbon dioxide and water) at a steady rate of approximately 3/4 ounce of alcohol per hour. At this speed, the body burns up the alcohol at the same rate as our bloodstreams absorb it. This amount of alcohol, as we saw above, equates roughly with one mixed drink containing one shot (1-1/2 ounces) hard liquor, one 5-ounce glass of wine, or one 12-ounce can of beer consumed over the period of about an hour. If alcohol is consumed more rapidly than this, it circulates in the bloodstream until the liver can metabolize it. During this process of circulation, the alcohol keeps on

*The so-called "light" beers have slightly less actual alcohol than regular beer.

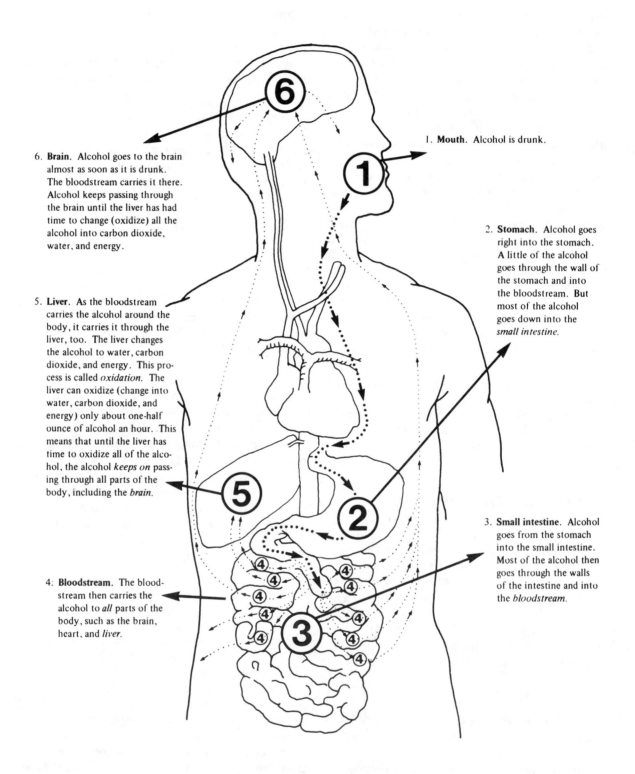

6. **Brain**. Alcohol goes to the brain almost as soon as it is drunk. The bloodstream carries it there. Alcohol keeps passing through the brain until the liver has had time to change (oxidize) all the alcohol into carbon dioxide, water, and energy.

5. **Liver**. As the bloodstream carries the alcohol around the body, it carries it through the liver, too. The liver changes the alcohol to water, carbon dioxide, and energy. This process is called *oxidation*. The liver can oxidize (change into water, carbon dioxide, and energy) only about one-half ounce of alcohol an hour. This means that until the liver has time to oxidize all of the alcohol, the alcohol *keeps on* passing through all parts of the body, including the *brain*.

4. **Bloodstream**. The bloodstream then carries the alcohol to *all* parts of the body, such as the brain, heart, and *liver*.

1. **Mouth**. Alcohol is drunk.

2. **Stomach**. Alcohol goes right into the stomach. A little of the alcohol goes through the wall of the stomach and into the bloodstream. But most of the alcohol goes down into the *small intestine*.

3. **Small intestine**. Alcohol goes from the stomach into the small intestine. Most of the alcohol then goes through the walls of the intestine and into the *bloodstream*.

FIGURE 3.2.   Alcohol's Passage through the Body. Reprinted from Peter Finn and Jane Lawson, *Alcohol: Pleasures and Problems* (Washington, D.C.: U.S. Government Printing Office, 1976) pp. 6–7. Illustration by Linda Clement.

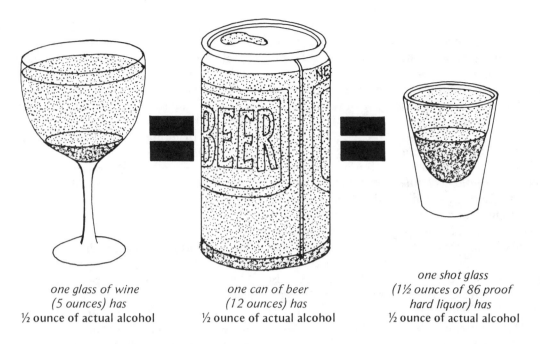

one glass of wine
(5 ounces) has
½ ounce of actual alcohol

one can of beer
(12 ounces) has
½ ounce of actual alcohol

one shot glass
(1½ ounces of 86 proof
hard liquor) has
½ ounce of actual alcohol

FIGURE 3.3.   Amount of Alcohol in Different Alcoholic Beverages. Reprinted from Peter Finn and Jane Lawson, *Alcohol: Pleasures and Problems* (Washington, D.C.: U.S. Government Printing Office, 1976) pp. 6–7. Illustration by Linda Clement.

passing through the brain. As a result, the faster alcohol is drunk, the more alcohol reaches the brain (and other body organs), producing quicker and more potent results for the drinker.

3. Type of Beverage Consumed. Distilled spirits are usually absorbed more readily than either wine or beer, and combining distilled spirits with carbonated drinks will speed up the action of the alcohol still further, because the carbon dioxide quickly opens the pyloric valve, which separates the stomach from the small intestine, allowing the alcohol to pass immediately into the intestine from which it is absorbed into the bloodstream. (This process partly explains why champagne "hits" people so quickly.) Water on the other hand dilutes the amount of alcohol thus slowing down the rate of absorption.

4. Body Weight. People who weigh a lot are less affected by the same amount of alcohol than lighter people. That is because alcohol is diffused throughout the body, and since heavier people have more blood and water in their bodies, the same amount of alcohol will be diluted and not affect them as much (See the discussion of blood alcohol concentration [BAC] later in the chapter.)

5. Food. Alcohol "goes to your head" more slowly if a person has just eaten or eats while he or she drinks. Food slows down the passage of the alcohol from the stomach to the small intestine. It is from the small intestine, not the stomach, that most of the alcohol is absorbed into the bloodstream and carried to the brain (look at the body diagram again in Figure 3.2).

6. Body Condition. A drinker who is tired when he or she drinks may be more influenced by alcohol than someone who is alert. A person who has an illness may also be affected more strongly than a person who is healthy. Finally, the presence of other drugs in the bloodstream can dramatically change the way alcohol affects a drinker. Taken in combination with certain other drugs, alcohol can have double or triple its normal sedative effects (see the discussion later in the chapter on death under "Bodily Damage").

All these reasons—amount of alcohol, weight, food, body condition—are *physical* reasons alcohol affects people differently. But, as we noted, the same person may be affected differently when he or she drinks on different occasions even though the *same* amount of alcohol has been drunk and the person is in the *same* physical condition on each drinking occasion. Usually, these different reactions occur because there is a seventh influence that determines how alcohol affects us which has nothing to do with alcohol as such or with our bodies. This seventh influence is how we think and feel about alcohol.

7. Thoughts and Feelings about Drinking. First of all, experienced drinkers often develop what is called *psychological tolerance.* On the basis of many drinking experiences, they have learned what alcohol does to them and can *compensate* or make up for its effects. Just as a sailor eventually learns to walk across the deck of a rolling ship, the experienced drinker learns to stand up very slowly or reach for the salt very carefully after he or she has had several drinks. In fact, people who frequently get drunk sometimes practice walking in a straight line or touching their noses so they can make the police think they are sober if they are arrested. However, just as the experienced sailor does not stop a ship from rolling but learns to make up for the tilting, the experienced drinker cannot prevent alcohol from affecting him; he or she can only attempt to learn to *cope with* some of the effects of the alcohol.*

Second, alcohol may affect someone differently depending on what a person *expects* to happen after drinking. When drinkers expect to get "high," they are more likely to do so. In fact, in careful studies when experienced college drinkers were given phony alcohol but told it was the real thing, most of them got high! (The same study has been done with marijuana; experienced smokers got high even though they weren't smoking the real thing.)

Third, people's *mood* when they're drinking affects what alcohol does to them. Alcohol may simply make someone who is already feeling unhappy more depressed; or it may enable someone who feels cheerful to become even happier.

---

*We often think we can tell when somebody is drunk or "high," but because of psychological tolerance, we may be fooled into thinking a drinker is sober when that may not be the case. It is very difficult to know how seriously alcohol has affected a drinker's ability to perform complex tasks simply by watching his or her behavior in familiar and routine activities. Therefore, it is important to watch how much *alcohol* has been drunk (not alcoholic *beverages,* that may vary in alcoholic content), especially if someone expects to engage in a potentially dangerous activity, like driving, mowing the lawn, swimming, or even changing a light bulb.

Finally, *where* people drink—the *setting*—may affect how much they drink and how they react to alcohol. A person drinking moderately at a party among close friends is more likely to feel good after drinking than if he or she drinks alone at home or attends a tense business function and has one too many.

While drinking has different effects on different people and sometimes on the same person at various times, we do know what some of the major effects are that alcohol will have on *many* if not most people.

Alcohol's Most Common Effects

1. Pleasure. (For most people, alcohol heightens pleasure and enthusiasm.) It enables them to let go, to be friendly, to experience feelings more strongly, to relax, and to have a good time. While drinking often heightens pleasant feelings, it also may help people to feel good by making them less aware of unpleasant feelings and events.

2. Inhibitions. (Alcohol tends to reduce people's inhibitions or shyness and loosen self-control.) Although they may feel this effect as stimulation, alcohol is a depressant. Some of the feelings that may be released include anger, hostility, feelings of inferiority or superiority, overconfidence, love, generosity, tenderness, and jealousy. All of these feelings may result in unusual (for the drinker) behavior, such as crying, fighting, yelling, hugging, laughing, nagging, and taking risks. However, people who have no major "hang-ups" may experience no important emotional changes in behavior when they drink.

3. Thinking. (While small amounts of alcohol with food will not normally affect most people's ability to think clearly, increasing amounts tend to make it harder for people to make judgments, concentrate, and understand.) In particular, alcohol may prevent inexperienced drinkers from realizing that their ability to think clearly and act normally isn't very good. *They* think they're "sober as a judge." However, experienced and mature drinkers often know very well when they can't think clearly or act sensibly.

4. Performance. (Generally speaking, the more alcohol a person drinks, the more difficulty he or she will have doing physical tasks.) However, moderate amounts of alcohol (one or two drinks drunk during a 1-2 hour time period) do not seem to interfere with an experienced drinker's ability to act sensibly. For some people and some tasks (for example, playing the piano), small amounts of alcohol may help them to do things better, perhaps because it relaxes them by removing tension or nervousness which sometimes inhibits behavior. For example, a couple of drinks can make sexual activity easier for some people—but larger amounts of alcohol make sex more difficult and often impossible. However, even moderate amounts of alcohol may increase anxiety in people who are already tense, and this anxiety, as well as the physiological effects of the alcohol, may cause deteriorated performance.

5. *Body Temperature.* People who drink usually feel warmer because alcohol increases the blood supply to the skin. However, although a drinker may feel warmer, body temperature has actually gone down.

6. *Energizer.* While alcohol helps some people sleep, it seems to act as a stimulant for others so that they don't feel as tired. In fact, alcohol is a depressant that makes some people *feel* more energetic by dulling the part of the brain that tells us when we are tired.

7. *Hangovers.* A hangover is the awful feeling someone gets from having drunk too much the day before. People may feel nauseous, tired, thirsty, or have a terrible headache. Some drinkers never get hangovers, while others get them all the time. A few people get them after only one or two drinks. No one knows for sure, yet, what causes hangovers, but there is some speculation that they may represent the effects of impurities in the alcoholic beverages (congeners) that are still in the body or be a response to guilt or anxiety over what happened or was said when the person was drinking the previous evening. Hangovers may also be initiated as a form of withdrawal from alcohol. All we know for sure is that hangovers can occur or continue *after* alcohol has left the body and that there are no ways to cure them. Taking vitamins or having a big breakfast won't help. Taking another drink may help a person to feel better, but this is a high risk cure that "works" for only a short while. Only time and rest will allow the body to eliminate any remaining alcohol, congeners, or

upsetting emotions and thereby enable a hangover to go away.

8. *Physical Tolerance.* Moderate or heavy drinking over a period of several years usually reduces many effects of alcohol on the body, so that more alcohol is required to produce the same effects. A marked increase in physical tolerance may be an early sign of alcoholism.

9. *Diseases and Bodily Damage.*

   a. *Liver.* Most people who die from cirrhosis (scar tissue replacing liver cells) are heavy drinkers, because large quantities of alcohol consumed over a period of time directly damage the liver. However, a small percentage of people who develop cirrhosis are not abusive drinkers.

   b. *Brain.* Alcohol seems to permanently destroy brain cells. The question then becomes how many extra brain cells a person has that can take over the work of those cells destroyed by alcohol during a human lifetime. At present, it appears that moderate drinking does not cause significant brain damage. However, advanced alcoholism can result in debilitating and irreparable damage to the brain.

   c. *Delirium Tremens.* Alcoholics who stop drinking may have the "DTs." They shake, have convulsions, and may see and hear things. This condition occasionally leads to death. The DTs are the body's response to suddenly being without alcohol ("stopping cold turkey") when it has become used to regular, heavy amounts. It is a violent form of withdrawal that requires medical attention.

   d. *Fetal Alcohol Syndrome* (FAS). There is increasing evidence that many of the birth defects found in offspring of women who drank heavily during pregnancy are alcohol related. This finding has raised the question of just what is a safe amount of alcohol, if any, to drink during pregnancy. (See chapter 2 for more details on FAS.) What is also unknown is the effect that a man's drinking may have on his ability to promote a healthy conception.

   e. *Death.* Very large amounts of alcohol (for example, a quart drunk in 5–30 minutes) may cause death by anesthetizing the brain center which "tells" us to breathe. People who drink enough alcohol can die from its anesthetizing effects on the brain. Alcohol, when combined with certain other drugs, particularly barbiturates and heroin, acts synergistically to create an even more depressing effect on the brain. The two drugs combined do not simply add their effects. Rather, each drug makes the other even stronger, so that the effect is like 1 + 1 = 4. For example, many people, like Janis Joplin, John Coltrane, and Marilyn Monroe, who supposedly died from overdoses of heroin or barbiturates, had also been drinking heavily at the time. Even one or two average drinks of alcohol, when taken with common medicines, can have very powerful effects. Cold medicines taken before or after a drink can make people very sleepy; aspirin and alcohol combine to eat away the stomach lining; and drinking and taking tranquilizers can cause dizziness, clumsiness, and death.

DRINKING AND DRIVING

The combination of drinking and driving is an extremely serious problem in America. About 25,000 traffic deaths each year involve a drinking driver, or nearly seventy deaths *every day*.[6] More people have been killed in alcohol-related traffic accidents in this country than have died in all our foreign wars. Drinking may be the most frequent single cause of automobile accidents.

How Many Drinks Make Driving a Car Dangerous?

Drinking and driving *can* mix when the drinking is very moderate or when enough time passes between the time people drink and the time they drive so that they are completely sober again. But just how many drinks does it take to make driving a car dangerous?

Automobile driving experts have scientifically tested the driving ability of skilled racing drivers before and after giving them alcohol. They learned that for someone who weighs 150 pounds, has not eaten before drinking, and drives within an hour after drinking, three or four average drinks (cans of beer, shots of whiskey, glasses of wine) make driving much more dangerous *even for very skilled* drivers.

---

[6] U.S. Department of Health, Education, and Welfare, *Preventing Disease/Promoting Health: Objectives for the Nation.* (Washington, D.C.: U.S. Government Printing Office, 1979), page 55.

Four normal drinks (or two or three extra strong drinks) taken an hour before driving make it about six times more likely a person will have an accident than if he or she were sober. For some people, driving after drinking only one or two average drinks can be dangerous, too.

What Effects Can Alcohol Have on Driving?

Below is a list of some of the effects drinking *may* produce on experienced, as well as novice, drivers after three or four average drinks and *will* produce on drivers after five or more average drinks.

1. *Reduced ability to judge things*, such as distances, speeds, and angles.
2. *Reduced ability to judge one's own abilities* and therefore reduced awareness of one's poor performance: even though the motorist is driving poorly, *he* or *she* may not think so.
3. *Greater tendency to take risks*, such as passing on a curve, because of feeling overconfident.
4. *Forgetfulness*, such as not turning lights on at night, leaving high beams on, and not signaling turns.
5. *Impaired reflexes*, such as reduced ability to deal with the unexpected, like skidding, blinding by oncoming high beams, sudden appearance of other cars or pedestrians, changing signal lights, road construction, and faulty or wet brakes.
6. *Sleepiness*, because alcohol combined with the natural fatigue of a late evening makes a person even more sleepy and unable to concentrate.
7. *Impaired vision*, such as reduced peripheral vision and loss of ability to refocus quickly after blinding by oncoming headlights.

Blood Alcohol Concentration

As we've seen, counting how many drinks people have had isn't a very good way to learn how much alcohol they've drunk. A beer may have 8 to 16 ounces; a mixed drink may have one 1-ounce shot of 86 proof whiskey or three 1-1/2-ounce shots of 120 proof vodka; wine may have 12 percent alcohol or 20 percent.

Because of this problem, alcohol specialists and the police use blood or breath tests to learn how much alcohol *is in a person's bloodstream*. This is essential because alcohol affects people only when it enters their bloodstream. This amount of alcohol in the blood is called *blood alcohol content* or *BAC* for short.

Only four factors affect the amount of alcohol in a person's blood—that is, his or her BAC:

1. The *amount of alcohol* a person drinks, not the number of drinks.
2. Whether the person has *eaten* before drinking or eats while drinking.
3. How much a person *weighs*.
4. How much *time goes by* after drinking or between drinks.

Nothing else affects a person's BAC. Mixing different types of alcoholic drinks will not make someone drunker nor will cold showers or drinking hot coffee make someone more sober because none of these things changes the amount of alcohol in a person's blood—his or her BAC.*

In most states there is a law that says that anyone caught driving who has a BAC of .10 percent or higher is presumed to be driving while intoxicated (DWI). Four average drinks taken within one hour (or five or six drinks in two hours) would give a person who weighs 150–175 pounds a BAC of .10 percent. This doesn't mean it's safe to drive with a BAC of under .10 percent; it only means that *legally* a person is not considered to be driving under the influence unless his or her BAC reaches .10 percent. We all know that some people drive legally but dangerously at times.

Activity #11 provides a Blood Alcohol Content Wheel you (and your students) can cut out and experiment with. You can figure out how many average drinks you would have to take to reach a BAC of .10 percent. Instructions for putting the BAC Wheel together are provided on the first page of the wheel.

PROBLEM DRINKING AND ALCOHOLISM

You have probably heard of the terms problem drinker and alcoholic and may have been con-

fused by the loose way in which both have been used. However, there are clear-cut and very important distinctions between the two terms even though all alcohol use can be seen as on the following continuum from abstinence through alcoholism:

Abstinence–Social drinking–Problem drinking–Alcoholism

On the simplest level, a problem drinker is anyone for whom the use of alcohol creates a problem. The problem may be medical—for example, drinking when expressly advised not to because of an ulcer, or driving home every Friday after work while intoxicated after celebrating payday. There are also problem drinkers who drink to maintain a frequent or constant euphoria. The key is that these individuals are not physically or psychologically dependent on alcohol and therefore can sometimes *stop* drinking if they so choose. Because they can often control their drinking, they may be able to abstain or drink socially if they feel the situation calls for not drinking or drinking in moderation.

Alcoholics, on the other hand, are individuals who once they *begin* to drink cannot normally predict or control how long or how much they will drink because they are dependent on alcohol. While they can sometimes go without alcohol for long periods of time, as little as one drink (even if it is the first drink in several hours, days or months*) will almost always result in loss of control and drinking to the point of intoxication.

Because some alcoholics appear to be able to control their drinking, it is often difficult in practice to distinguish between problem drinkers and alcoholics. Another difficulty in telling these two groups of alcohol abusers apart is that problem drinkers may be on their way to developing alcoholism and thus be showing some of the early signs of alcoholism such as:

- drinking to calm nerves or because of unhappiness
- lying about how much has been consumed
- showing marked personality changes when drinking
- becoming neglectful of health
- having unexplained cuts and bruises

---

*However, the *time* that passes while taking a shower or drinking coffee (or tea or cocoa) will give the body a chance to get rid of more alcohol from the bloodstream.

*Sometimes alcoholics stop drinking just to "prove" to their families or themselves that they aren't alcoholics.

To help clarify these differences between problem drinking and alcoholism, the American Medical Society on Alcoholism has defined alcoholism as follows: Alcoholism is a chronic, progressive and potentially fatal disease. It is characterized by tolerance, physical dependency or dangerous changes to body organs, all of which are the direct or indirect consequences of the alcohol ingested.

1. *Chronic* and *progressive* indicates the presence of physical, emotional or social changes which are cumulative and worsen with the continuation of drinking.
2. *Tolerance* means that the brain has adapted to the presence of high concentrations of alcohol. As a result, more alcohol is needed to achieve the same high than before.
3. *Physical dependency* means that there are withdrawal symptoms upon decreasing or ceasing consumption of alcohol. In addition, the individual with alcoholism cannot consistently predict on any drinking occasion *how long* he or she will continue to drink or *how much* alcohol he or she will drink.
4. *Dangerous changes to organs* of the body can be found in almost any organ, but most often involve the liver, brain, nervous system and the gastrointestinal tract.
5. The drinking pattern is generally *continuous* but may be intermittent with periods of abstinence between drinking episodes.
6. The social, emotional and behavioral symptoms and consequences result from the effect of alcohol on the function of the brain. However, the degree to which these symptoms and signs are considered *deviant* will depend upon the *cultural norms* of the society or group in which the individual operates.*

The Typical Person with Alcoholism

There are an estimated 10 million people with alcohol problems and alcoholism. Although alcoholism shows no preference for color, race, creed, or socioeconomic level, most alcoholics are middle aged, middle class, fully employed,

*Reprinted with the permission of the *Annals of Internal Medicine* 85 (6), December 1976.

and married with children. The stereotype of alcoholics as skid row residents is a myth. Less than 5 percent of those with this disorder are on skid row. In fact, many of our skid row population do not have true problems with alcohol but have major social and psychological problems, of which an alcohol component is minor.

One reason for the concentration of those with alcoholism among employed, married people is that it usually takes 10-20 years of progressively heavier drinking before a diagnosis of alcoholism is warranted. By the time people are beginning to have full-blown symptoms of alcoholism, they are usually economically, socially, and maritally well established.

Alcoholism: Theories of Causation

Recent research in alcoholism is beginning to confirm earlier theories that stated there are essentially two types of alcoholics: (1) Primary—alcoholics with both a psychological and a physical dependence on alcohol; and, (2) Secondary—alcoholics with only a psychological dependence on alcohol. The reasoning behind these two types of alcoholism is not as clear as the fact that they exist.

Some researchers indicate physiology is important since alcoholics may either lack a certain enzyme or have another genetic abnormality that makes them more vulnerable to the development of alcoholism.

Another set of theories attributes the development of alcoholism to psychological difficulties. These theories, which do not necessarily contradict the physiological theories, explain another dimension of human interaction—the individual needs of the person. The psychological theories specify that the development of a dependence on alcohol is due to factors such as having a low tolerance for frustration; having a marked conflict between feelings of dependence and independence; using alcohol when depressed to produce a temporary euphoric state; and being essentially self-destructive by using alcohol as a way of actually harming oneself.

A set of theories that adds yet another dimension are the sociological theories. One theory states that the development of alcoholism is due to the inexpensive cost and wide availability of alcohol. Another states that since the use of alcohol is a learned behavior, those who have not learned to use it properly develop problems. A third theory points to the fact that society widely accepts alcohol problems and, therefore, these problems exist. This sociological theory indicates that in societies where there is less tolerance for alcohol-related problems—in fact, those with alcohol problems are "shamed" and made to feel outside the main societal group—there are actually fewer alcohol problems.

Each theory expands the puzzle. Apparently, there is no single answer.

What Can Be Done to Help the Alcoholic?

Many people with alcoholism find help in *Alcoholics Anonymous*. Here, through the fellowship of others who have this same stigmatized disease, people with alcoholism can begin to reorient their lives and obtain the strength they need to stop drinking. Alcoholics Anonymous (AA) seems to be the most successful source of help for alcoholics. AA has 13,000 local groups composed of recovered alcoholics who get together one or more times a week to help each other get sober and stay sober. It has over a half million members worldwide. At AA meetings, members discuss why they used to drink so much, what their drinking did to them, how they have managed to stop drinking, and what life has been like since they stopped.

AA believes that people are never cured of alcoholism—just as people are never cured of diabetes. AA stresses that "once an alcoholic, always an alcoholic," in the sense that alcoholics must never drink at all again if they hope to live a normal life. This belief in abstinence as a lifelong goal is not limited only to AA but also reflects the belief of the majority of doctors and others who treat alcoholics and some of the researchers who have investigated this field. However, other researchers believe that a few alcoholics can learn to drink again socially. Unfortunately, some alcoholics may try to drink again under the mistaken notion that they are among those few recovered alcoholics who can drink in moderation and simply lapse back into uncontrollable drinking.

Alcoholism has been called the family disease because its impact, like that of other problems, is felt throughout the family unit. Help is therefore needed for the whole family. Two organizations have used the AA model for helping the relatives of alcoholics. Al-Anon is available to husbands and wives and other relatives of alcoholics, whether or not the alcoholic family member is in AA. Assistance is usually needed for the entire family when one lives with or loves someone acting in a destructive way, for it is easy to begin to blame him or her for all the problems in one's own life and not take responsibility for one's own happiness. The support given in Al-Anon and Alateen can be very important in overcoming these and other problems involved in living with an alcoholic.

Alateen is an organization for 12–19-year-old children of alcoholic parents, Al-Atots exists for younger children, and Young People's Al-Anon is available for the young adult. In some ways, alcoholism's most devastating effect is on the children. Children of alcoholics tend to grow up isolated and alienated because their fear that people may learn of their "secret" at home discourages them from maintaining normal social contacts with schoolmates and friends.

In both Alateen and Al-Anon, members talk less about helping the alcoholic than about how they can help *themselves* to avoid being "dragged down" by the alcoholism in their family. The value of membership in both Alateen and Al-Anon lies in learning that one is not alone in this predicament and in taking advantage of others' trial-and-error attempts at better adjustment. Chapter 4 discusses the problems of children of alcoholics in more detail.

A second major type of help for both alcoholics and problem drinkers is *counseling or psychotherapy*. With this form of treatment, abusive drinkers talk with psychiatrists, psychologists, social workers, or group discussion leaders about their problems. While talking things over with a friend or relative can be very helpful, often someone trained to help people with their problems can be more effective.

Drugs are sometimes used, with careful medical supervision, to help alcoholics to stop drinking. The best known such drug is Antabuse (disulfiram). People who take Antabuse every day get violently ill if they then have a drink with any alcohol in it. (Even being around alcohol fumes or eating food containing uncooked alcohol can make them sick.) If alcoholics have the motivation to take their Antabuse every morning, they have "solved" their drinking problems for at least that day. Usually Antabuse is used not only under medical supervision but also with counseling—the drug serving to keep the alcoholic sober so that he or she can benefit from psychotherapy.

Places where alcoholics can get these kinds of assistance include day hospitals, therapeutic communities, detoxification centers, in-patient and out-patient rehabilitation clinics, and after-care facilities. The whereabouts and services of these institutions may be learned from the local or state department of alcohol abuse and alcoholism, or from the state or local mental or public health department.

In addition to getting help from other people to stop their abusive drinking, many alcoholics and problem drinkers cut down on their drinking *on their own*. For unknown reasons, they often just drink less as they get older. (The same thing happens with some heroin addicts, too.) Perhaps they come to terms with life's problems; maybe they have more responsibilities with which heavy drinking interferes; or possibly alcohol has stronger effects on them as they age, so they need less of it.

Finally, some alcoholics and problem drinkers stop drinking when they have to face something that they feel is even *more* painful than giving up alcohol. Sometimes a husband (or wife) will stop drinking when his wife (or the husband) is ready to get a divorce or when a boss threatens to fire him or her. Making the problem drinker "shape up or ship out" has been called "tough love" and "supportive confrontation." It involves telling the problem drinker that you care for him or her but won't put up with the drinking because you come first.

If there is a person with alcoholism on the faculty in your school, in your family, or in your circle of friends, the following key points emphasized by most programs are worth remembering:

1. Detach with caring—this concept calls for maintaining a loving and respectful distance and not interacting with the alcoholic while he or she is intoxicated.
2. Don't cover up their mistakes—covering up for the mistakes of alcoholics deprives them of the opportunity of learning from their errors. Covering up also deprives them of their responsibility for their own lives. This can prolong their illness.
3. Don't be manipulated into doing things that you feel are counterproductive—being manipulated in the long run will only make you angry and therefore less available to the person with alcoholism.
4. Learn more about alcoholism.
5. If you're close to the alcoholic, perhaps join

Al-Anon and get counseling yourself—go to Al-Anon or a local alcoholism treatment facility and help yourself before you try to help the alcoholic.

DRINKING AND THE LAW

The relationship between alcohol use and the law can be approached from numerous perspectives, but we will consider only four such interactions: (1) public intoxication, detoxification, and civil commitment; (2) drinking and driving legislation; (3) the relationship between alcohol abuse and crime, and (4) laws regulating the sale and consumption of alcoholic beverages.

Laws regulating public intoxication vary considerably from state to state—and their enforcement may also vary considerably across jurisdictions within a given state. Although several states have decriminalized public intoxication in part or whole, being drunk in public remains illegal in the majority of states. (Attempts to have the courts rule that public intoxication by alcoholics cannot be considered a crime because alcoholics have a disease have been unsuccessful.) Over two million arrests are made annually in states where public intoxication is still a crime. In most states, an intoxicated person may be (1) arrested and kept in detention until he or she is sober and can be released to return home or face criminal charges or (2) taken to a detoxification center and detained for a specified number of days. Under most state laws, civil commitment for alcoholism is permissible. In some instances, a separate alcoholism commitment procedure has been established. In others, the procedure is included within the general mental health commitment provisions. The provisions often require hospitalization and permit long terms of detention, but in some instances they reflect more modern concepts of voluntary community-based treatment.

The other major piece of legislation regulating drinking behavior focuses on drunk driving. Most states have at least two relevant driving while intoxicated (DWI) statutes. Local variations can be learned from your State Department of Motor Vehicles or local police station. These two basic statutes are:

1. *An implied consent law* which stipulates that as a condition of the privilege of driving a car, every motorist is deemed to have automatically given his or her consent to a test to determine his or her blood

alcohol concentration (BAC) if charged (but not before) with DWI. The driver may refuse to take the test. If he or she does, no test is given, but the driver's license is revoked for a specified period of time.

2. *A presumptive level of intoxication law* which, in most states, stipulates that a driver whose BAC is found to have been .10 percent or over is presumed, but not proven, to have been driving under the influence of alcohol. The prosecution must still convince a jury or judge that the driver was, in fact, driving under the influence of alcohol; the defense lawyer and defendant, in turn, can attempt to rebut this presumption.

A few states have *per se* laws which stipulate that a driver whose BAC is found to be over a certain percentage, usually .15 percent, is automatically guilty of DWI. No further proof or argument in court is needed.

The penalties for driving while intoxicated vary greatly from state to state but usually involve some combination of license suspension and fine, and often mandatory participation in alcohol education programs. Where fatalities occur, penalties also typically involve jail sentences. *Enforcement* of these laws, however, tends in most states to be very lenient for a combination of reasons. Police do not like to arrest for DWI because such cases are usually plea bargained down to reckless driving charges, and judges and juries do not like to convict people for DWI for a variety of reasons, including the attitude that "there but for the grace of God go I," and the feeling that the loss of a driver's license would impose too great a hardship on a breadwinner who must drive to work every day to support a family.

So far we have been discussing acts that are illegal because they involve the abuse of alcohol—appearing in public or driving an automobile are not normally against the law when conducted by pedestrians or motor vehicle operators in a sober state. However, there is convincing evidence that alcohol abuse contributes to the commission of a number of major activities that are illegal whether performed sober or drunk. Several studies, for example, have indicated that over half of all homicide perpetrators, their victims, or both have been drinking. Other crimes with which alcohol abuse is significantly associated include car theft, assault, and rape. Alcohol use in these instances may con-

tribute to the commission of these crimes by reducing inhibitions and allowing people to release pent-up aggressions, experience a false sense of courage, or ignore the potential consequences of their acts.

Because of the effects alcohol abuse may have on people's health and the welfare of their families, as well as its impact on crime, every state regulates the purchase and sale of alcoholic beverages. These laws vary a great deal from community to community, as does their enforcement. Characteristically, there are laws that regulate:

- the hours and days of sale (for example, not after 2 a.m.; not on holidays; not before 1 p.m. on Sundays)
- where alcohol may be sold (in hotels; restaurants; package stores; bars; etc.)
- in what form alcohol may be sold (by the drink; by the bottle only; etc.)
- what kinds and concentrations of alcohol, if any, may be sold (wine, beer, hard liquor, "3.2" beer); and
- who may sell bottled alcoholic beverages (state monopoly vs. private owners)

Countless combinations of the above laws may be found throughout the country. One town may be completely "dry" (no alcoholic beverages may be sold in any form), another allow the sale of only wine and beer on weekdays and Saturdays solely in restaurants, and a third permit bars, restaurants, and package stores to sell alcohol at any time except election days.

Finally, and most controversially, states regulate the age at which youngsters may legally purchase alcoholic beverages. In the late 1960s and early 1970s, many states lowered the legal purchase age from 21 to 18 in response to the apparent hypocrisy of drafting teenages for the adult job of fighting in Vietnam but prohibiting them from drinking (as well as voting and signing contracts). In the past few years, however, the trend has been to raise the age back to 19 or over as a result of concern that lowering the legal purchase age to 18 resulted in increased alcohol use and abuse by youngsters 14 to 18. Whether this legal reversal will result in reducing teenage drinking problems remains to be seen. (See chapter 4, "Alcohol and Youth.")

Given this patchwork quilt of alcohol legislation, you can learn exactly what the laws regulating drinking are in your state and community by contacting your Department of Motor Vehicles, Alcoholic Beverage Control Commission (or similar agency—usually found within the Department of Taxation), and Town or City Hall.

ADDITIONAL READING

Drinking Patterns/Epidemiology

Alcohol Problems in Canada: A Summary of Current Knowledge. Quebec City, Ontario: Department of Health and Welfare, 1976.

Cahalan, Don, and Cisin, Ira H. *American Drinking Practices: Summary of Findings from a National Probability Sample*, vol. I. New Brunswick, N.J.: Rutgers Center of Alcohol Studies, 1968.

Cahalan, Don; Cisin, Ira H.; and Crossley, Helen M. *American Drinking Practices.* New Brunswick, N.J.: Rutgers Center of Alcohol Studies, 1969.

Cahalan, Don, and Room, Robin. *Problem Drinking among American Men.* New Brunswick, N.J.: Rutgers Center of Alcohol Studies, 1974.

MacAndrew, Craig, and Edgerton, Robert B. *Drunken Comportment: A Social Explanation.* Chicago: Aldine Publishing Co., 1969.

Pernanen, Kai. "Validity of Survey Data on Alcohol Use." In *Research Advances in Alcohol and Drug Problems*, vol. 1, edited by Robert J. Gibbins et al. New York: John Wiley & Sons, 1974.

Sulkunen, Pekka. "Drinking Patterns and the Level of Alcohol Consumption: An International Overview." In *Research Advances in Alcohol and Drug Problems* vol. 3, edited by Robert J. Gibbins et al. New York: John Wiley and Sons, 1974.

U.S. Department of Health, Education, and Welfare. *Alcohol and Health.* Third Special Report to the U.S. Congress. Washington, D.C.: U.S. Government Printing Office, June, 1978.

Manufacture and History

Clark, Norman H. *Deliver Us from Evil: An Interpretation of American Prohibition.* New York: W. W. Norton, 1976.

Ewing, John A., and Rouse, Beatrice A. "Drinks, Drinkers, and Drinking." In *Drinking: Alcohol in American Society: Issues and Current Research*, edited by John A. Ewing and Beatrice A. Rouse. Chicago: Nelson-Hall, 1978.

Fleming, Alice. *Alcohol: The Delightful Poison: A History.* New York: Delacorte Press, 1975.

McCarthy, Raymond G., ed. *Drinking and Intoxication: Selected Readings in Social Attitudes and Controls.* Carbondale, Ill.: Southern Illinois University Press, 1962.

Merz, Charles. *The Dry Decade.* Seattle: University of Washington Press, 1969.

Pittman, David J., and Snyder, Charles R., eds. *Society, Culture, and Drinking Patterns.* Carbondale, Ill.: Southern Illinois University Press, 1962.

Tongue, Archer. "5,000 Years of Drinking." In *Drinking: Alcohol in American Society: Issues and Current Research*, edited by John A. Ewing and Beatrice A. Rouse. Chicago: Nelson-Hall, 1978.

Physical and Behavioral Effects

Block, Marvin A. *Alcohol and Alcoholism.* Belmont, Calif.: Wadsworth Press, 1970.

Carroll, Charles R. *Alcohol: Use, Nonuse and Abuse.* Dubuque, Iowa: William C. Brown, 1970.

Chafetz, Morris. *Liquor: The Servant of Man.* Boston: Little, Brown, 1976.

——. *How Drinking Can Be Good for You.* New York: Stein and Day, 1978.

Trice, Harrison M., and Roman, Paul M. *Spirits and Demons at Work: Alcohol and Other Drugs on the Job.* Ithaca, N.Y.: New York State School of Industrial and Labor Relations, 1972.

U.S. Department of Health, Education, and Welfare. *Alcohol and Health.* Washington, D.C.: U.S. Government Printing Office, 1971.

——. *Alcohol and Health: New Knowledge.* Washington, D.C.: U.S. Government Printing Office, 1974.

Waller, Julian A. "Alcohol and Unintentional Injury." In *The Biology of Alcoholism*, vol. 4, edited by Benjamin Kissin and Henri Begleiter. New York: Plenum Press, 1976.

Alcoholism and Problem Drinking

Cramer, Jerome. "The Alcoholics on Your Staff." *The American School Board Journal* (August 1977): 49–52.

Criteria for the Diagnosis of Alcoholism. New York: National Council on Alcoholism, 1972.

DeLint, Jan, and Schmidt, Wolfgang. "The Epidemiology of Alcoholism." In *The Biological Basis of Alcoholism*, edited by Yedy Israel and Jorge Mardones, New York: John Wiley & Sons, 1971.

Edwards, Patricia; Harvey, Cheryl; and Whitehead, Paul C. "Wives of Alcoholics: A Critical Review and Analysis." *Quarterly Journal of Studies on Alcohol* 34 (1973):112–132.

Fox, Ruth. *The Alcoholic Spouse.* New York: National Council on Alcoholism, n.d.

Goodwin, Donald. *Is Alcoholism Hereditary?* New York: Oxford University Press, 1976.

Hoff, Ebbe Curtis. *Alcoholism: The Hidden Addiction.* New York: Seabury Press, 1974.

Jellinek, E. M. *The Disease Concept of Alcoholism.* New Haven: College and Univeristy Press, 1960.

Keller, Mark. "The Disease Concept of Alcoholism Revisited." *Journal of Studies on Alcohol* 37 (1976): 1694-1717.

Pattison, E. Mansell. "Nonabstinent Drinking Goals in the Treatment of Alcoholics." *Research Advances in Alcohol and Drug Problems*, vol. 3, edited by Robert J. Gibbins et al. New York: John Wiley & Sons, 1976.

Pomerleau, Ovide; Pertschuk, Michael; and Stinnett, James. "A Critical Examination of Some Current Assumptions in the Treatment of Alcoholism." *Journal of Studies on Alcohol* 37 (1976):849-867.

U.S. Department of Health, Education, and Welfare. *Alcohol and Health.* Washington, D.C.: U.S. Government Printing Office, 1971.

———.*Alcohol and Health: New Knowledge.* Washington, D.C.: U.S. Government Printing Office, 1974.

Laws

Grad, Frank. "Legal Controls of Drinking, Public Drunkenness, and Alcoholism Treatment." In *Drinking: Alcohol in American Society: Issues and Current Research*, edited by John A. Ewing and Beatrice A. Rouse. Chicago: Nelson-Hall, 1978.

Gusfield, Joseph R. "The Prevention of Drinking Problems." In *Alcohol and Alcohol Problems: New Thinking and New Directions*, edited by William J. Filstead, Jean J. Rossi, and Mark Keller. Cambridge, Mass.: Ballinger Publishing Co., 1976.

Pernanen, Kai. "Alcohol and Crimes of Violence. In *The Biology of Alcoholism*, vol. 4, edited by Benjamin Kissin and Henri Begleiter. New York: Plenum Press, 1976.

Popham, Robert E.; Schmidt, Wolfgang; and de Lint, Jan. "The Effects of Legal Restraint on Drinking." In *The Biology of Alcoholism*, vol. 4, edited by Benjamin Kissin and Henri Begleiter. New York: Plenum Press, 1976.

U.S. Department of Health, Education, and Welfare. "The Legal Status of Intoxication and Alcoholism." In *Alcohol and Health: New Knowledge.* Washington, D.C.: U.S. Government Printing Office, 1974.

Wilkinson, Rupert. *The Prevention of Drinking Problems: Alcohol Control and Cultural Influences.* New York: Oxford University Press, 1970.

Zylman, Richard. "Drinking Practices among Youth Are Changing Regardless of Legal Drinking Age." *Journal of Traffic Safety Education* 24 (1976):31-32, 37.

Drinking and Driving

American Automobile Association. *You . . . Alcohol and Driving.* Falls Church, Va., 1976.

Boyle, Bernard L., and Stern, Michael, I. *Myths about Drinking and Driving.* Toronto: Addiction Research Foundation, 1977.

Douglass, Richard, and Freedman, Jay. *Alcohol Related Casualties and Alcohol Beverage Market Response and Beverage Alcohol Availability Policies in Michigan*, vol. I. Ann Arbor, Michigan: University of Michigan Highway Safety Institute, 1977.

Israelstam, S., and Lambert, S., eds. *Alcohol, Drugs, and Traffic Safety.* Proceedings of the Sixth International Conference on Alcohol, Drugs, and Traffic Safety, Toronto, September 8-13, 1974. Toronto: Addiction Research Foundation, 1975.

Perrine, M. W., ed. *Alcohol, Drugs, and Driving.* Springfield, Va.: National Technical Information Service, 1974.

U.S. Department of Health, Education, and Welfare. "Alcohol and Highway Safety." In *Alcohol and Health: New Knowledge.* Washington, D.C.: U.S. Government Printing Office, 1974.

Waller, Patricia F. "Drinking and Highway Safety." In *Drinking: Alcohol in American Society: Issues and Current Research*, edited by John A. Ewing and Beatrice A. Rouse. Chicago: Nelson-Hall, 1978.

Alcohol and Special Groups

Minorities

Allen, Chaney. *I'm Black and I'm Sober.* Minneapolis: CompCare, 1978.

Davis, Fred T., Jr. *Alcoholism: Among American Blacks.* New York, National Council on Alcoholism, n.d.

Harper, Frederick D. *Alcohol and Blacks.* Alexandria, Va.: Douglass Publishers, 1976.

Melus, Antonio. "Culture and Language in the Treatment of Alcoholism: The Hispanic Perspective." *Alcohol Health and Research World* 4 (1980):19-20.

Indian Health Service Task Force on Alcoholism. *Alcoholism: A High Priority Health Problem.* Washington, D.C.: U.S. Department of Health, Education, and Welfare, 1977.

Women

Bourne, Peter G., and Light, Enid. "Alcohol Problems in Blacks and Women." In *The Diagnosis and Treatment of Alcoholism*, edited by Jack H. Mendelson and Nancy K. Mello. New York: McGraw-Hill, 1979.

Carrigan, Zoe Henderson. "Research Issues: Women and Alcohol Abuse." *Alcohol Health and Research World* 3 (1978):2-9.

Gomberg, Edith S. "Alcoholism in Women." In *The Biology of Alcoholism*, vol. 4, edited by Benjamin Kissin and Henri Begleiter. New York: Plenum Press, 1976.

Greenblatt, Milton, and Schuckit, Marc A., eds. *Alcoholism Problems in Women and Children.* New York: Grune and Stratton, 1976.

Lee, Essie E. "Female Adolescent Drinking Behavior: Potential Hazards." *Journal of School Health* 48 (1978):151–156.

Marden, Parker G., and Kolodner, Kenneth. *Alcohol Abuse among Women: Gender Differences and Their Implications for the Delivery of Services.* Springfield, Va.: National Technical Information Service, May 1979.

Wilsnack, Sharon C. "Prevention of Alcohol Problems in Women: Current Status." *Alcohol Health and Research World* 3 (1978):23–31.

Elderly

U.S. Department of Health, Education, and Welfare. "Alcohol and Older Persons." In *Alcohol and Health: New Knowledge.* Washington, D.C.: U.S. Government Printing Office, 1974.

4
Alcohol and Youth

Alcohol consumption by our youth is receiving greater and greater national attention, especially through the media. There is widespread concern about youthful alcohol-related problems despite the evidence that most teenagers drink socially and moderately just as most adults do.

Why the concern? Some see a trend toward teenage alcoholism, others a concern with the general permissiveness of society. The concern with teenage alcoholism, as we shall see, while it reflects the proverbial "kernel of truth," is not the major problem facing our youth. The major cause for apprehension should be the "acute" problems of youthful alcohol use, such as intoxication and traffic accidents. This is because most adolescents' problems with alcohol are one-time or short-term, as opposed to "chronic" or existing over a long period of time.

What We Know about Youthful Drinking

In 1978, the U.S. Department of Health, Education, and Welfare (HEW) estimated that there were 3.3 million problem drinkers in the 14 to 17-year-old group—19 percent of the 17 million persons in this age bracket. This calculation may be contrasted with the 9.3 to 10 million problem drinkers that the government believes are in the 18 and over population, or 7 percent of the 145 million found in this age group.[1] Why the significantly different proportions?

To begin to answer this question we must first look at the special criteria used to identify problem drinking in youth. In one major study, for example, youth were labeled as being problem drinkers if they either reported intoxication six or more times in one year *or* reported the

presence of negative consequences from drinking two or more times in at least 3 of 5 specified situations in the past year or both. The negative consequences that students acknowledged as a result of drinking were (1) getting into trouble with teachers or the principal, (2) getting into difficulties with friends, (3) driving when having had a "good bit" of drink, (4) being

[1] *Alcohol and Health*, Third Special Report to the U.S. Congress (Washington, D.C.: U.S. Government Printing Office, June 1978).

criticized by someone the student was dating, and (5) getting into trouble with the police. By this definition, nearly 19 percent of the students were problem drinkers—23 percent of the boys and 15 percent of the girls.[2]

Some have argued that if adults were judged by the same criteria, it would be interesting to see just what the numbers of adult problem drinkers would climb to! The fact remains, however, as we shall see presently, that there is cause for concern, not necessarily alarm, about our youth's consumption of alcohol. But first let us review what is known with certainty about youthful drinking behavior and trends.

1. A majority of youngsters experiment with drinking. Most Americans have had their first drink by the time they leave junior high school.
2. Most adolescents first drink at home, in their parents' presence, and with their parents' permission.
3. The average age of the first drinking experience has become younger. It is now no longer uncommon to see 12- and 13-year-olds initiate drinking experiences on their own, as well as be introduced to alcohol in the home.
4. In the past, the geographic regions with the heaviest proportions of youthful drinkers were the Northeast and Far West. Today, however, adolescents in the Midwest and South are drinking more often and at an earlier age than before, and their drinking patterns are beginning to look more like those of adolescents in the East and West. This change in the Midwest and South has been a major contributor to the increase in teenage drinking reported in national surveys.
5. A major change has occurred in the drinking patterns of females. It used to be that "good girls" didn't drink, unless "coerced" into doing so by their boyfriends. Now, girls congregate on their own, without boys necessarily present, for the purpose of drinking. In this and other ways their drinking pattern has become more like that of boys. However, while nearly as many girls now drink as do boys, girls, when they do drink, consume smaller amounts of alcohol than do boys.

[2] *Alcohol and Health*, p. 17.

6. Drinking by youngsters increased throughout the 1950s and 1960s but appears to have "peaked" around 1970 with no consistently documented increases since then.
7. About half of high school students report that at least once a month they are part of social occasions where alcohol is served and there is no adult supervision; as many as 40 percent are female.
8. Intoxication is increasing. Nineteen percent of our youth report becoming intoxicated at least once a month, a 10 percent increase in the last ten years.
9. The leading cause of death of adolescents is accidents. Single car traffic accidents where the driver has had one or more drinks are the most common.

PERSPECTIVE ON YOUTHFUL DRINKING

While the evidence appears clear that more girls are drinking and more boys and girls are becoming intoxicated than was true of prior generations, we need to place these behaviors in the perspective of both adolescence as a stage of growth and also the historical background of our relatively recent recognition of the increased use and abuse of alcohol by youngsters in the 1950s and 1960s.

First, we should remember that what may be more important than the frequency of drinking or intoxication in determining whether a given youngster is a problem drinker is the context in which it occurs—for example, relatively safely at home or prior to driving an automobile? If teenagers drink in cars, can this apparently hazardous behavior automatically be judged a problem, as one study does?[3] As one authority has suggested, "This may well be viewed as a problem by certain people, but this is a private view. For many youth this is not only normative behavior, but is clearly a situational response to adult attitudes and rulings and to drinking situation possibilities."[4] Even if drinking or drunken-

[3] J. Valley Rachal et al., *A National Study of Adolescent Drinking Behavior, Attitudes and Correlates* (Springfield, Va.: National Technical Information Service, April 1975), p. 154.

[4] Seldon D. Bacon, "Defining Adolescent Alcohol Use: Implications for a Definition of Adolescent Alcoholism," *Journal of Studies on Alcohol* 37 (July 1976): 1018.

ness leads to a clear-cut problem elsewhere in a youngster's life, before we can say the *youngster* has a drinking problem we must evaluate the severity of the problem, for whom it is a problem, and whether just because unpleasantness results this means the youngster should not drink or get drunk again. If a player on the high school basketball team gets into an argument with a parent over having gotten drunk when the team won the state basketball championship, is this necessarily a problem? Does the quarrel have to reach a certain level of acrimoniousness before it can be called a problem? How frequently must such altercations occur before the problem label is applied to the youngster's drinking behavior? Could the problem lie in the parent's inability to understand or tolerate what may be a reasonable and relatively harmless activity on the part of his or her child?

Given these complexities in the nature of teenage drinking and intoxication, it is not reasonable to routinely assume that all or most youngsters who drink or get drunk are heading for certain difficulties or already have a drinking problem. Attention to the nature, context, and pattern of each *individual* youngster's episodes of drinking and drunkenness is required before making such judgments rather than automatically labeling as problem drinkers those youths who get drunk an arbitrary number of times a year or who have an arbitrary number of so-called problems as a result of their use of alcohol.

Even admitting that a great deal of youthful drinking does take place in hazardous circumstances, it should be kept in mind that adolescence is a time when we encourage a certain level of experimentation. We value this testing for we want our youth to enter adulthood having made choices not only about educational career directions but also concerning an "adult" value system. The experimenting with different roles, different girlfriends and boyfriends, and different clothing and hairstyles often takes place in a context of experimenting with a variety of choices—alcohol being just one of them. Unfortunately, perhaps, experimenting sometimes involves taking risks, but, as one health educator has concluded:

WHAT IS HEALTHY? ... Probably taking some risks, even a few major ones now again. "Unhealthy" becomes the label when the individual takes too many risks or loses too often. And, of course, there are those fairly rare cases of taking too few risks.

Remember, though, healthy is traditionally a conservative value; the assumption underlying this value is that once you have it then you guard it by not taking risks. Being safe is being healthy ... What is health for? To function ... Risk-taking is necessary for healthy functioning ... the individual who takes a risk (with some caution perhaps) succeeds, and then more confidently faces the next set of life choices.[5]

Some of youth's use and abuse of alcohol can also be viewed as representing "light-hearted roistering" that "frequently dissipates with few remaining problems."[6] This attitude is not unlike the view that drunkenness, sexual experimentation, and pranks by young males are to be expected because "boys will be boys" —that is, any "red-blooded" youngster who doesn't engage in some rambunctiousness is a "sissy." The drinking parties of many college students can also be viewed as "a last fling. Those people who ... get to college know that they are enjoying the last years of childhood dependence. Drunken beer parties symbolize childhood's indulgence and freedom without responsibility."[7]

Furthermore, many teenagers who drink regularly or get drunk do *not* become problem drinkers as adults.[8] In one study of 200 college youth, 44 percent were problem drinkers while in college, but only 19 percent were twenty years later.[9] Other studies have indicated that

[5] Robert D. Russell, *Health Education* (Washington, D.C.: National Education Association, 1975), p. 115.

[6] Reginald D. Smart, *The New Drinkers: Teenage Use and Abuse of Alcohol* (Toronto: Addiction Research Foundation, 1976), p. 61.

[7] Morris Chafetz, *Why Drinking Can Be Good for You* (New York: Stein and Day, 1976), p. 91.

[8] Don Cahalan, "Implications of American Drinking Practices and Attitudes for Prevention and Treatment of Alcoholism." Paper prepared for presentation at conference on Behavioral Approaches to Alcohol and Drug Dependencies, University of Washington, Seattle, July 31, 1975, p. 22; Don Cahalan and Ira H. Cissin, "Drinking Behavior and Drinking Problems in the United States," in *The Biology of Alcoholism*, vol. 4, edited by Benjamin Kissin and Henri Begleiter (New York: Plenum Press, 1976), p. 96; Don Cahalan and Robin Room, *Problem Drinking among American Men* (New Brunswick, N.J.: Rutgers Center of Alcohol Studies, 1974), pp. 73–74; Smart, *The New Drinkers*, pp. 59, 61.

[9] Kay M. Fillmore, "Drinking and Problem Drinking in Early Adulthood and Middle Age: An Exploratory 20-year Follow-up Study," *Quarterly Journal of Studies on Alcohol* 35 (September 1974):819–840.

youngsters with a variety of apparently serious problems, including juvenile delinquency and drug abuse, "mature out" of their problems as they grow older and take on adult responsibilities.[10] For some teenagers, in short, what appears to be or actually is problem drinking is "part of the process of growing up and will decrease with age and maturity."[11]

Much is also made about the phenomenon of "peer pressure" in stimulating alcohol abuse among youngsters. This problem—and it *is* a problem—also needs to be clarified.

Most adolescents will initially develop the drinking practices of their parents, and many will have their first drinking experiences at home, usually under parental supervision—wine with a meal, champagne on a holiday, or a beer after a ball game. The value placed on alcohol use, like other values, is first learned in the home. So, if a parent drinks heavily, regularly, for pleasure, to escape, socially, or not at all, usually the adolescent will initially drink the same way.

Peers form a secondary influence. Adolescents choose friends based on their values, values derived from their home. As adolescents mature and move further from their parents' values, there is a greater likelihood that their drinking values and habits will be different from those of their parents. However, most youngsters who go through a phase of heavier drinking stimulated by peer pressures (for example, during high school, college, and military service) return to their parental drinking practices in later years.

Peer pressure seems to exert a significant influence motivating teenagers to continue as drinkers once they have already been exposed to drinking, usually in the home. Adolescent peer pressure to drink either responsibly or irresponsibly is similar to pressure adults exert on each

other to "be sociable," "be one of the guys," "be a man," "show you can hold it," and not be "different." Peer pressure also appears to be a major influence motivating nondrinkers to abstain: abstainers tend to congregate with other abstainers.

HISTORICAL PERSPECTIVE ON TEENAGE DRINKING

Our understanding of youthful drinking behavior can also be better understood if we place the use and abuse of alcohol by youngsters in historical perspective. The consumption of alcohol by adolescents is not a new phenomenon; in fact, adolescent drinking has demonstrated the same types of fluctuations as have adult drinking patterns. For example, one study found that in the 1880s and 1890s young teens were being admitted to hospitals due to drinking problems. However, the average age of admission gradually rose through the 1900s. Presently, there are indications that teenagers with drinking problems may again be entering hospitals at gradually lower ages. What accounts for these trends?

The rise in the age of admission during the twentieth century reflected the trend for children not to enter the work force—and with it the adult world of drinking—until later and later ages. Children began to stay in school longer and usually did not begin to incorporate the use of alcohol in their lifestyle until they left school. This pattern of not using alcohol until entering the work force is beginning to change, and this shift accounts in part for our recent heightened awareness of youthful drinking.

Another factor that has accounted for society's current awareness of youthful drinking behavior has been our growing knowledge of the behavior of our youth in general. Youth today are engaging in many activities at progressively younger and younger ages, including sex, organized athletics, voting, and unsupervised social activities. Youth today are simply spending less time as "children." As a society, we are also becoming just plain more aware. Things that we have not been aware of previously we are conscious of now, and so they may seem new, when all they were before was unnoticed. This may help account for our sudden "horror" at youth's drinking problems.

[10] J. R. Henley and L. D. Adams, "Marijuana Use in Post-collegiate Cohorts: Correlates of Use, Prevalence Patterns, and Factors Associated with Cessation," *Social Problems* 20 (1973):514–520; J. R. Williams, *Effects of Labeling the "Drug-Abuser": An Inquiry.* NIDA Research Monograph 6 (Springfield, Va.: National Technical Information Service, 1976), p. 13; James Q. Wilson, *Thinking about Crime* (New York: Vintage, 1975), p. 224.

[11] Gerald Globetti, quoted in Patricia A. O'Gorman, Sharon Stringfield, and Iris Smith, eds., *Defining Adolescent Alcohol Use: Implications toward a Definition of Adolescent Alcoholism.* Proceedings, National Council on Alcoholism 1976 Conference, Washington, D.C. (New York: National Council on Alcoholism, 1976), p. 9.

Along with this new awareness has also come a new perspective in viewing behaviors right under our eyes. Youth have always had a problem with alcohol, but as far back as the 1940s, we paid more attention to the behaviors that the alcohol helped facilitate rather than the alcohol itself. In the 1940s, deaths at fraternity "hazings" were well publicized, but the fact that many of these youngsters had been drinking to excess (usually on a dare) went largely unreported. In the 1950s, we had gang warfare. This made front page news, but the untold story was the heavy drinking that preceded most "rumbles." It was only when the abuse of other drugs became prevalent among white, middle-class youth in the 1960s that many of us began to see the behavior that drug taking produces as *drug caused*. With this new awareness, the alcohol problem that had been around all the time appeared startling.

CAUSE FOR CONCERN NONETHELESS

While it is essential not to exaggerate or overdramatize the problem of youthful drinking, it is clear that an unknown but significant number of youngsters experience mild to severe problems related to their drinking behavior, from hangovers to alcohol-highway traffic fatalities. It does a teenager little good to get drunk in a spirit of youthful exuberance—which he or she might normally be expected to outgrow—if the youth is killed (or kills others) in a drunk-driving accident. The adolescents who switch from periods of acute alcohol abuse to a pattern in adulthood of sustained heavy drinking are not likely to be consoled by the fact that most of their peers toned down their use of alcohol as they took on adult responsibilities. In particular, it is important to recognize—and for youngsters to realize—that drinking has a stronger effect on teenagers than it does on older people regardless of what youthful drinking practices bode for the future of these individuals as adults.

There are five reasons alcohol has a more powerful impact on youngsters than it does on most adults. First, most teenagers weigh less than older people. As we saw in chapter 3, the less people weigh, the more effect alcohol has on them. (You and your students can experiment with the effects of different body weights using the Blood Alcohol Content Wheel in Activity #11.)

Drinking also can have a greater effect on teenagers because they have not yet learned to compensate or make up for what alcohol does to them. It takes years for baseball outfielders to learn how to compensate for the wind when a fly ball is hit their way. Just as outfielders have to tell themselves, "Slow down because the wind is going to hold up the ball," so people who get clumsy after two or three drinks have to learn to say to themselves, "Don't grab for the salt; reach very slowly." This ability to compensate for alcohol's effects, we noted, is called *psychological tolerance*.

Third, teenagers are often in the process of learning new skills that, combined with alcohol use, make it exceptionally difficult to perform or behave appropriately and safely. The best example of this is youthful drinkers who drive when they are not yet experienced in how to handle a car. Perhaps this inexperience combined with alcohol use explains why teenagers have more accidents after only a couple of drinks than adults do.

In addition, teenagers often have more stresses than older people. The teen years for most people are a difficult time of life. Many new things happen to them that are often both exciting and frightening—for example, independence, a paying job, a rapidly changing body, sexual experimentation, a car, travel, and so on. When alcohol is added to something that we are not used to and that is also very exciting or somewhat frightening, it can make it harder for us to control how we feel and what we do while drinking.

Finally, drinking may affect adolescents more or differently than adults because there is the "expected" effect that alcohol has on a youngster. Some teenagers feel that a little alcohol is supposed to make you high. Therefore, when they drink a little, they act much higher than the actual physiological effect of the alcohol warrants. In a sense, teenagers may become psychologically intoxicated.

TEENAGE "ALCOHOLISM"

A particular cause for concern about youngsters who drink excessively is the possibility that they may be alcoholics. But what is teenage alcoholism? There has been considerable controversy as to just what teenage alcoholism is and how it is to be managed. Some experts feel that alcoholism in teenagers manifests itself differently than it does in adults. Some find that there is less dependence, less damage to the body, and more harm to social relationships.

There is no consensus about what constitutes adolescent alcoholism, or, if it is a distinct clinical entity, how prevalent it is. However, it is certain that recent claims of an "epidemic" of teenage alcoholism are grossly exaggerated if not totally inaccurate. To date, there have been no major studies of adolescent alcoholism. Recently, the National Council on Alcoholism (NCA) attempted to assess the level of alcoholism that our youth have developed. After reviewing a survey of 120 studies, NCA concluded that we are not witnessing a major increase in adolescent alcoholism but an increasing *potential* for alcoholism to develop. NCA's finding was based on the rising incidence of acute alcohol-related problems, such as intoxication, traffic fatalities, and accidental injuries.

Since a diagnosis of alcoholism needs to be performed by a qualified doctor or counselor, the best course of action with a teenager who is suspected of having alcoholism is to refer him or her to someone who specializes in treating drinking problems. Such signs as unexplained absences, especially Monday morning and Friday afternoons; erratic grades; erratic mood swings; alcohol on breath; concern by fellow classmates for girl- or boyfriend; drinking before exams; and problems with the law that are alcohol-involved are indications that there *may* be a serious alcohol problem in a youngster, such as alcoholism. A faculty conference with the appropriate school personnel would be a wise course of action if you find any of these symptoms among your students. For an adolescent with a drinking problem, as for an adult, there is help. Alcohol problems, including alcoholism, can be arrested.

CHILDREN OF ALCOHOLICS: A CASE OF SPECIAL EDUCATION NEED

Of all the aspects related to alcoholism, children of alcoholics are the most overlooked. There are an estimated 28 million offspring (adults and children) of those who have full-blown and developing alcoholism. Studies indicate that

upwards of 50 percent, or 12 million of these offspring, will become alcoholics themselves. It is important, therefore, not only to understand the dynamics of alcoholism (as reviewed in chapter 3) but also to be aware of the special problems experienced by any of your students who may have alcoholism in their family.

In the family with either developing alcoholism or with fully developed alcoholism the parents are usually more involved with each other than is best for the child. The spouse of the alcoholic becomes the alcoholic's caretaker and is often too drained to have much in reserve for the child. Furthermore, part of alcoholism's manifestations, even in its early stages, is a personality change on the part of the alcoholic, many times in the direction of greater aggression during periods of intoxication. The mood swings of the parent creates confusion for the child, because when the parent is sober he or she is probably gentle or passive. The child's responses to his or her parents must, therefore, adjust to widely varying behavior caused by the use of alcohol.

The alcoholic's family lives in anticipation of the next drinking event. Members of the family "walk on eggshells" around each other with little communication, hoping not to precipitate a drinking episode. This build-up of tension in the family usually results in a drinking episode during which time family members become involved with each other by yelling, even fighting, but definitely "communicating." The problem for the child in this atmosphere is that it is difficult to predict which mode of functioning on his or her part will be required. During periods of nondrinking the child will usually not attempt to engage the parents, for to engage them at the "wrong" moment would mean either to be blamed or to blame oneself for the onset of the next drinking episode. Yet to engage the parents during the drinking episode may mean to run the risk of physical assault or verbal abuse.

To function within this setting the child builds a wall around him- or herself. He or she begins to resent both parents. Interestingly enough, in many cases the nonalcoholic parent is the more resented parent as the child becomes angry about the amount of attention the alcoholic parent receives. The alcoholic parent is often feared. Consequently, the child begins not to interact freely with others outside, as well as inside, the home. This coping style is usually established by the time the child enters school.

A word of caution—sobriety in the alcoholic parent is not a panacea. Research has shown new problems often develop when sobriety is reached as the alcoholic parent tries to become the "perfect mother" or "perfect father" to compensate for his or her other lack of involvement—or inappropriate involvement—in the past. Many times this further confuses the child and may precipitate greater outward anger as he or she resists the parent's attempt to change his or her established coping style. This is often seen with the interaction of a parent recovered from alcoholism and a child who is becoming an adolescent. The parent may, for the first time, be attempting to play a positive role in the child's life and choose to regulate not only the adolescent's hours but also his or her friends. When this occurs at the same time an adolescent is attempting to move away from the family and establish his or her own values, major conflicts frequently occur.

But what does the child of an alcoholic look like? The child may well begin its life with the Fetal Alcohol Syndrome (FAS) (see chapter 2 for more information). This syndrome has been traced to the consuming of alcohol, not necessarily abusively, by the mother during her pregnancy. The impact of male drinking on conception has not yet been fully researched and so remains an open question.

Once a child starts preschool, there are a variety of markers that might signal concern on the part of the educator, the most obvious being any evidence of child abuse or child neglect. Research is just beginning to focus on child abuse or child neglect. Research is just beginning to focus on child abuse and neglect and its relationship to alcohol use and abuse. It appears that alcohol use may facilitate child abuse. For example, excessive drinking as seen in developing alcoholism, when there are frequent explosive alcohol-related outbursts, appears to be correlated with child abuse. One explanation of this is that the child has literally not learned to get out of the way of the prealcoholic parent. By the time the alcohol-related violent outbursts become more frequent, the child may learn the cues and go to his or her room, go to a neighbor, not come home at all, run away, or call the police. At this point the child may no longer be physically abused and the outstanding feature of this home may become child neglect, as the involvement of the parents with each other

escalates and time for the child diminishes. Thus, it appears that younger offspring may be more often abused and older offspring more often neglected. While this does not hold true for every child, it does provide a starting point for the identification of this group. However, because child abuse and neglect may result from a number of other family problems besides that of alcoholism, it is important to recognize the other indications of the presence of this disease in the home.

The following are warning signs indicating potential parental alcohol abuse and possible child neglect. When these signs are repeatedly found in a child, they represent a cause for concern:

- Destructiveness, obstructiveness, aggression, extreme shyness, withdrawal, excessive compliance, "super-coper," the child who rigidly does everything correctly.
- Unexplained absences, cuts, bruises, extreme mood swings, depression, extreme grade swings, learning difficulties, unkempt clothes, falling asleep in class, poor nourishment, difficulty in trusting authority, poor coping skills, lack of friends.

It is basically the extremes of behavior, including "rigid excellence," that warrant concern. Seeing these signs repeatedly in conjunction with such events as the child spontaneously telling of an explosive drinking episode at home, a parent appearing intoxicated for a school conference or at a PTA meeting, or jokes made by schoolmates about a child's parent's drinking behavior, would all warrant concern.

In teaching older children of alcoholics the same rule of being aware of extremes applies, with the added dimension of being sensitive to extremes in his or her drinking patterns. A quest for companionship plus a desire to either prove themselves different from—or like—their parent(s) may catapult adolescents from an alcoholic home into early experimentation and usually heavy use pattern of alcohol.

We may, therefore, roughly divide the salient warning signals by age as follows:

- Elementary—child's spontaneous remarks, signs of child abuse or neglect
- Intermediate school—child neglect, erratic school performance
- By junior and senior high school—the added dimension of actual alcohol abuse

WHAT YOU CAN DO

Although you may only observe these suggestive symptoms and not be sure whether any of your students have an alcoholic mother or father, children of alcoholics may also inadvertently identify themselves by withdrawing from the class discussions and other learning activities about drinking that you have initiated as part of your unit on alcohol because they find the topic frightens or embarrasses them. Some of these students may also seek you out after class once you have begun your unit to reveal their problem to you. They may simply want a sympathetic ear for sharing their problem or they may ask for help, with such questions as, "Should I run away from home? Should I drink? What can I do to make my mother or father stop drinking?"

What can you do about any students in your classes who you suspect or learn have an alcoholic parent? As we noted in chapter 2, your most important role is that of educating—not counseling. Teaching children from alcoholic homes, however, requires the full range of instructional skills in order to provide such children with the best opportunities and motivation to learn about alcohol use and abuse. In particular, you might consider including one or more activities in your unit that directly address the problems alcoholic mothers and fathers create for their children so that any such pupils in your classes can realize that they should not feel they are alone in their dilemma and so that they can have a structured learning environment in which to explore their concerns in more depth than they may have previously been able to do.

In addition, as an adult with whom these children not only spend a considerable amount of time but whom they may perceive as knowledgeable about alcohol problems and concerns, you end up in an excellent position to suspect or be told about family drinking problems and therefore be able to refer students to appropriate school or community resources for help. In general, you should not advise these students about their personal problems but direct them to sources of help. Potentially helpful school authorities include the nurse, principal, and guidance counselors. Community groups that may be of assistance are the local Council on Alcoholism, open Alcoholics Anonymous meetings, the Salvation Army, and, most of all, local

Alateen or Al-Anon groups. Alateen groups consist of teenagers who have an alcoholic parent, while Al-Anon groups are for the relatives of alcoholics. Some communities also have Al-Atot groups for the preteen children of alcoholics. Membership in these groups does not require the alcohol abusing parent to be in Alcoholics Anonymous or other form of treatment. Such groups can be located by phoning the number listed in the white pages under Alcoholics Anonymous.

The final crucial contribution you can offer is to help students from alcoholic homes develop social skills, as these children become social isolates due to the erratic nature of life in the family. They soon learn not to invite potential and actual friends home and this results in no longer being invited to their friends' homes. You can provide much needed continuity and social opportunity for these students by selecting them as class monitors, encouraging their participation in group educational activities, and, in particular, encouraging them to join after-school clubs or other social groups.

THE YOUTHFUL DRINKING SCENE

In this chapter we have described the current state of knowledge about how, why, and when youngsters drink. We have also focused on the severe problems most children have when their father or mother is an alcoholic. It is important, however, not to focus attention only on the abusive drinking practices of youngsters or the harmful effects an alcoholic parent can have on his or her children. Most adolescents do not currently experience problems around alcohol use, whether they abstain or drink. Many of those who do have drinking problems related to their own or their parents' abuse of alcohol will either "outgrow" them or, with the help of professional help or the assistance of family members and friends, learn to solve or cope positively with their troubles. However, as a classroom teacher, you are in a unique position to help ensure that those youngsters who are not experiencing problems related to alcohol use *continue* in their currently trouble-free mode of relating to alcohol. You can also assist some students who are experiencing such problems to begin to examine their feelings and behaviors related to the nonuse, use, and abuse of alcohol more closely than they may do without your assistance and thereby help them to resolve these problems sooner than they might otherwise do. In order to achieve these goals and to teach about alcohol in ways that are in touch with today's teenage drinking "scene," it is essential to maintain the balanced view of youthful alcohol use which this chapter has presented.

ADDITIONAL READING

Bacon, Margaret, and Jones, Mary Brush. *Teen-Age Drinking.* New York: Thomas Y. Crowell Company, 1968.

Blane, Howard T., and Chafetz, Morris E., eds. *Youth, Alcohol, and Social Policy.* New York: Plenum Press, 1979.

Blane, Howard T., and Hewitt, Linda E. *Alcohol and Youth: An Analysis of the Literature—1960-1975.* Springfield, Va.: National Technical Information Service, 1977.

Brown, James, and Finn, Peter. "Drinking to Get Drunk: Findings of a Survey of Junior and Senior High School Students." *Journal of Alcohol and Drug Education,* in press.

Demone, Harold W., Jr., and Wechsler, Henry. "Changing Drinking Patterns of Adolescents Since the 1960s." In *Alcoholism Problems in Women and Children,* edited by Milton Greenblatt and Marc Shuckit. New York: Grune and Stratton, 1976.

Engs, Ruth C. "Drinking Patterns and Drinking Problems of College Students." *Journal of Studies on Alcohol* 38 (1977):2144-2156.

Fillmore, Kaye M. "Drinking and Problem Drinking in Early Adulthood and Middle Age: An Exploratory 20-Year Follow-up Study." *Quarterly Journal of Studies on Alcohol* 36 (1974):819-840.

Finn, Peter. "Teenage Drunkenness: Warning Signal, Transient Boisterousness, or Symptom of Social Change?" *Adolescence* 14 (1979):819-834.

Jessor, Richard, and Jessor, Shirley L. "Adolescent Development and the Onset of Drinking." *Journal of Studies on Alcohol* 36 (1975):27-51.

Maddox, George L., and McCall, Bevode C. *Drinking among Teenagers.* New Brunswick, N.J.: Rutgers Center of Alcohol Studies, 1964.

Mandell, Wallace, and Ginzberg, Harold M. "Youthful Alcohol Use, Abuse, and Alcoholism." In *The Biology of Alcoholism,* vol. 4, edited by Benjamin Kissin and Henri Begleiter. New York: Plenum Press, 1976.

Marden, Philip; Zylman, Richard; Fillmore, Faye M.; and

Bacon, Selden D., "Comment on 'A National Study of Adolescent Drinking Behavior and Correlates.'" *Journal of Alcohol Studies* 37 (1976):1346-1358.

O'Gorman, Patricia A.; Springfield, Sharon; and Smith, Iris, eds. *'Defining Adolescent Alcohol Use': Implications toward a Definition of Adolescent Alcoholism.* New York: The National Council on Alcoholism, 1977.

——, and Lacks, Hazel. *Aspects of Youthful Drinking.* New York: The National Council on Alcoholism, 1979.

Rachal, J. Valley. *A National Study of Adolescent Drinking Behavior, Attitudes and Correlates.* Springfield, Va.: National Technical Information Service, 1977.

Rouse, Beatrice A., and Ewing, John A. "College Drinking and Other Drug Use." In *Drinking: Alcohol in American Society: Issues and Current Research,* edited by John A. Ewing and Beatrice A. Rouse. Chicago: Nelson-Hall, 1978.

Schuckit, Marc A.; Morrissey, Elizabeth, R.; Lewis, Nancy J.; and Buck, William T. "Adolescent Problem Drinkers," In *Currents in Alcoholism,* vol. 2, edited by Frank Seixas. New York: Grune and Stratton, 1977.

Smart, Reginald G. *The New Drinkers: Teenage Use and Abuse of Alcohol.* Toronto: The Addiction Research Foundation, 1976.

Wechsler, Harold, and McFadden, Mary. "Sex Differences in Adolescent Alcohol and Drug Use." *Journal of Studies on Alcohol* 37 (1976):1291-1301.

Wechsler, Harold, and McFadden, Mary. "Drinking among College Students in New England: Extent, Social Correlates and Consequences of Alcohol Use." *Journal of Studies on Alcohol* 40 (1979):969-996.

Wechsler, Harold, and Thum, Denise. "Teen-age Drinking, Drug Use, and Social Correlates." *Quarterly Journal of Studies on Alcohol* 34 (1973):1220-1227.

Wechsler, Harold, and Thum, Denise. "Alcohol Intoxication and Drug Use among Teen-agers." *Journal of Studies on Alcohol* 37 (1976): 1672-1677.

5

Selected Teaching Methods

ROLE PLAY

Role play is an activity in which one person pretends to be someone else and acts in the way he or she believes that other person would act. Thus, a student can act as if he or she were a parent, a problem drinker, or an automobile passenger—that is, he or she can play the *role* of these other persons.

When implementing a curriculum intended to alter students' behavior and attitudes, role play becomes almost indispensable.

Why Use Role Play

1. Role play offers an unusual opportunity to *promote understanding and empathy* between types of people who often have diffi-

Source: This chapter is adapted from Peter Finn and Judith Platt. *Alcohol and Alcohol Safety*, vol. 1. Washington, D.C.: U.S. Government Printing Office, 1972.

culty communicating effectively with one another, such as alcoholics and social drinkers, employers and employees, parents and children, and teachers and students. When students get involved in these roles by acting them out, they can gain considerable insight into these peoples' problems and feelings in a way that is difficult to achieve through more traditional teaching methods.

2. Role play allows students to *experiment with the drinking and nondrinking roles and personalities* that they may be unable to assume in real life (due to lack of confidence, peer pressure, etc.). For example, the youngster who would like to resist peer pressure to get drunk every Friday night may have an opportunity to forget momentarily his or her fear of rejection and experiment with refusing to drink abusively. Role playing allows students to "try on" personalities and roles in a nonthreatening situation.

3. Role play confronts participants with the necessity for *making decisions* and attempting to influence people about drinking and thereby enables them to see some of the possible repercussions these decisions and attempts to influence people may have without having to suffer the actual consequences.
4. Role play encourages the development and expression of *feelings* about alcohol use. This is particularly important in a curriculum dealing with an emotionally charged area such as alcohol.
5. Role play can be an effective means of *evaluating* alcohol education because it can indicate decision-making abilities and reveal attitudes.

Role play is most appropriately used to illustrate and explore conflicts between people about drinking issues. Some problem situations that lend themselves well to role play are the following:

- Parents discovering their children drinking and punishing them—or expressing relief that they are not taking "drugs"
- Youngsters (or adults) deciding what to do about being pressured at a party to drink
- Youngsters faced with decision of riding with a drunk driver
- Employers questioning employees who have been tardy or absent due to suspected drinking problems and deciding what to do
- Politicians or community workers deciding how to allocate funds for alcohol problems

Drawbacks to Role Play

There are a number of difficulties that role play can involve that must be considered along with its significant advantages. Most teachers are unfamiliar with the technique and therefore are not fully comfortable with it, convinced of its educational value, or able to implement it properly. In addition, many students find it is not easy to engage in role play. Role play can highlight relatively unimportant points or stray from the major topic at hand. It can at times become silly if students feel awkward playing the parts, or it can become overemotional if students end up taking parts which have intense personal meaning for them. Sometimes, role play can simply be dull and unrevealing.

How to Write Role Plays. The most important task in role play is getting people emotionally involved in their roles. To help achieve this, you must provide your students with a written "role profile" or description of the person whose role they will adopt. This role profile should be:

- As brief as possible
- Written in the second person ("You have just caught your son drinking vodka," not, "The person you are playing is a parent who has just caught his or her son drinking vodka")
- Given to students in advance of the actual role play if familiarity with the part is necessary.

The role profile should include enough concrete details so that the role is clearly structured and focused and students understand the character they are to portray. To ensure this, the role profile should provide the student with:

- The motives and goals of the role ("You want your son never to touch alcohol until he is 21")
- Obstacles in the way of achieving these goals ("Your son may try to get back at you by drinking again")
- Enough incidental information about the person to make him or her seem real to the student ("You are 42 years old and have other sons, aged . . .")
- A scenario or capsule history of the events that preceded the situation that is going to be role played. The scenario contains all the information that is common knowledge to all players.

The last sentence of each role profile should set the stage for the action of the role play ("You have just opened the door and seen your son try to put the bottle under the bed, what do you say or do?").

How to use Role Play

A good way to introduce role play is to have your students respond in writing to several scenarios such as those available in many of the learning activities in chapter 11. Another good way is to conduct "practice" role plays to familiarize them with the concepts and process involved. Practice with a sample role play in which your students play their parts from their seats, using dialogue and no action. In fact, if your students are unable to act out role plays even after several attempts, they can continue to conduct them from their seats. Younger students can use hand puppets if they are uncomfortable playing parts themselves.

When introducing an actual role-play activity, begin by passing out or explaining the general conflict (the "scenario") to the whole class. Then:

- Ask for volunteers to play the roles. Be careful about selecting students who volunteer to play parts that may be too emotionally upsetting for them—for example, a student with an alcoholic parent who asks to play the role of the son or daughter of an alcoholic.
- Pass out the appropriate role profiles only to each participant. Don't let the players see each other's role profile.
- Before any action takes place, instruct observers to save all their comments and questions until the role play is over. Instruct the rest of the class to think about how *they* would act were they in the role play.
- Before the action begins, instruct participants that they have the right to call a "cut" in the action at any time without having to say why. This allows participants who feel they are getting too emotionally involved an easy "out" from what may, on rare occasions, be an unpleasant situation. Be alert to the action and feelings of the role play and don't hesitate to call a "cut" yourself if you feel the role play is arousing too much anxiety.
- While action is in progress, don't inhibit it by commenting on or altering the action.
- The role play ends when the participants have reached a logical ending point or you decide to cut the action because it is dragging or has become irrelevant.
- Student observers can also act as "reporters" who write down or later verbally describe what they saw and heard, comparing their accounts with each other and with what the role players felt occurred.

How to Follow Up Role Play

Much of the learning from role play will be lost if you don't follow up each role play with additional learning exercises designed to build on the

experience. Among the follow-up exercises you can pursue are the following:

- Students can repeat the completed role play as it stands with different participants or with a new scenario or role profiles.
- Encourage your students to develop and use their own role plays and scenarios. Once attuned to the technique, students can often create role plays and scenarios about alcohol issues that contain a realism and relevance that you may find difficult to attain.
- When an individual role play or series of role plays is over, focus the ensuing discussion on what the participating students' feelings were as they role played; what their attitudes were toward the other players; what different actions the observers might have taken were they in the role play; and what the observers and participants feel they learned about alcohol.
- Avoid giving your opinion of whether the role played solution was "right" or "wrong" and concentrate instead of eliciting and having your students debate the advantages and drawbacks of *alternative* solutions.

Several activities in chapter 11 involve the use of role play, including #5, #18, #21, #22, #23, #27, #28, and #29.

SMALL GROUP DISCUSSION

One of the most useful teaching methods in an alcohol curriculum is to break your class into small discussion groups of three to five students per group. This instructional approach may be the single most effective teaching method for promoting student learning about alcohol because of the following considerations:

- Small groups offer a more receptive setting than class discussions for students to express their *feelings* about alcohol. For example, youngsters often feel freer to express anger in arguing with a peer than with a teacher (or any adult) and less inclined to hide their real feelings about alcohol since they know they can't "con" their friends.
- Small group discussions indicate to students that *their* opinions and information about alcohol are important and worth listening to—you are not the only, nor always the best,

source of information and opinion. Small groups present an opportunity for students to learn from each other and to realize that there is a lot that they can teach each other. This gets them involved as *deliverers* in the educational process and increases their commitment to learn.

- There is much more concern with sharing opinions than with impressing you or supplying you with the "right" answer.
- In small group discussion students can follow the natural flow of their concerns about alcohol—moving freely from one topic to another, unfettered by external restrictions or feelings that they must "stick to one topic." As a result, small group discussions are a good way for you to uncover the alcohol issues that concern your students so you can select and use other activities which address these concerns.
- Small groups offer a better medium for shy students to express themselves than in a large and possibly threatening classroom situation.
- Small group discussions develop several important skill areas needed to cope effectively with alcohol issues, including cognitive (describing, analyzing, questioning, evaluating), affective (feeling concerned, feeling responsible, accepting, empathizing), and communication skills (arguing, influencing, listening).
- Small group discussions can break up the monotony of spending every class either writing or listening to you.

Difficulties with Small Group Discussions

Small group discussions can focus on issues irrelevant or at best tangential to the topic under consideration. While they may be lively at times, at others they can involve long periods of silence. One or two members can dominate a small group discussion and either exert peer pressure to encourage the rest to accede to their views or simply ignore the presence of the other participants.

On the one hand, one or two forceful students can impart accurate but one-sided information to the other members of the group (for example, on the pleasures of moderate drinking); on the other hand, the entire group may engage in mutual sharing of ignorance (for example, on how to "cure" a hangover).

Simultaneous small group discussions can be difficult to supervise both in terms of preventing discipline problems and also of evaluating the amount of learning taking place. Also, to run smoothly and productively, small group discussions require extra preparation on your part to assign students carefully to different groups based on their ability to contribute to the discussion and their holding different views on the issue at hand.

Forming Small Groups

A useful approach to structuring small group discussions around alcohol issues is to present students with a scenario and have them record, on no more than a page, how they would respond and why. For example, rather than ask students to "write your opinion on whether or not the drinking age should be lowered to 16," tell your students, "You are a state legislator and a Bill to lower the drinking age to 16 has come to the floor for a vote. How do you vote? Why do you vote that way? Or if you don't vote, why not?"

Two other approaches to obtaining student positions on an alcohol issue are to place them in the position of a "Dear Abby" columnist for a newspaper or a staff member of a community hotline. Ask your students to respond to letters seeking advice, such as "Dear Abby, I have been going to parties with this swell guy, but every time we go he gets drunk. What shall I do? Signed, Bewildered."

These position papers should be written a day or two before the actual discussion so that you have time to assign your students carefully to small groups on the basis of the opinions they expressed in their position papers.

Several different considerations need to be balanced in forming the best possible combinations of small groups of students. One alternative is to let the students form their own groups. Often this creates more problems than it solves. Friends stick with friends, with the result that students may not be exposed to different points of view. In addition, introverted students may end up together, resulting in a low level of discussion in their groups.

If you decide to assign students to groups, try to address the following considerations:

- The sex composition should be so arranged that no one is embarrassed by being the only female or the only male in the group, except for students who don't mind (and even relish) this arrangement.

• All the talkative students should not be clustered in one group and all the silent students in another.

• Each group should be so balanced that conflicting points of view are represented about the alcohol issue being discussed.

Structuring the Discussion

When you have broken your class into small groups, return the position papers and pass out written instructions specifying what the students are to discuss in their groups or write the instructions on the blackboard.

The groups should be assigned to:

1. resolve their differences on the alcohol issue. (E.g., what should you do at a party if your date is drunk but wants to drive home?) The group's solution is recorded. If a group cannot agree, it can write down all the different positions represented.

2. discuss *why* they believe that their position on the alcohol issue is the "correct" one. These reasons should also be recorded. Normally, attempting to resolve different positions involves consideration of why these positions are maintained, but it is useful for students to be explicitly told to probe the reasons behind each student's position.

Spend a couple of minutes in each small group to get an idea of how well the discussion is progressing, but don't answer any questions a group asks; instead, require the students to address their questions to each other.

Following Up the Discussion

At the end of the period, or whenever discussion wanes, collect each group's papers. At this point, there are at least two alternatives you can pursue:

1. Continue the small group discussions during the following class period, either around the same alcohol issue or around some offshoot of that issue that seems to concern the students.

2. Hold a debate between two or more groups who came to different conclusions on the topic under discussion.

Following any small group discussion, each group should report its results to the rest of the class and then respond to questions and criticisms from the other students and you. At times it may be appropriate to reproduce the groups' conclusions and pass them to the class for future reference.

The success of small group discussion depends on many factors, some of which have been enumerated above. Perhaps the most important factor is the selection of alcohol issues for discussion that really do concern students. Students should, therefore, help decide what these should be.

Many of the activities in chapter 11 involve small group discussion, including #3, #16, #17, #20, #21, #22, #23, #25, #27, #29, #30, and #33.

CLASS DISCUSSION

Normally, if a class can profitably discuss a *controversial* alcohol-related issue as a class, it can discuss the issue more profitably in small groups. Furthermore, class discussion can end up as a lecture if students fail to participate or if you have a tendency to dominate the class. Even if you fervently want your students to carry the dialogue, only a few students may involve themselves, and these few may end up dominating the discussion. Therefore, whenever possible, small group discussions should be used.

Class discussion can be useful, however, when:

• the previous activity requires a follow-up discussion to synthesize what took place. For example, role play always needs follow-up discussion so that different students' perceptions, interpretations and feelings about what took place can be aired and summarized. Small group discussion also should be followed by class discussion so that students can learn and comment on what occurred in other small groups.

• you feel that the discussion topic is complex and needs guidance from you to assist students as they discuss it.

• there are not enough talkative students in the class to make small group discussion feasible.

When these conditions prevail, there is a type of class discussion that can be particularly effective in a curriculum that deals with controversial areas like alcohol and alcohol safety. This is *student-directed class discussion*. In this type of discussion, students are encouraged to address their comments to each other, rather than to you. When, for example, you ask whether the drinking age should be lowered to 16, and one student disapproves, the next student comment should be directed at this previous student. In this manner, but with initial constant reminders, you can moderate a discussion about alcohol so that students communicate with each other. If you adopt this approach, you should tell your students to direct their comments to each other before the discussion begins and, when necessary, keep reminding them to do so. You will soon be able to encourage direct student-to-student communication with forgetful pupils who want to direct their comments to you by a mere wave of the finger in the direction of the other student with whose opinion they are disagreeing.

Class discussions are also useful when there is a consensus among your students on what could or should be a controversial issue, or when most or all of them take a certain point of view for granted and have never examined its underlying rationale. Examples of such topics include the presumed "superiority" of monogamy, monotheism, capitalism, and the nuclear family. Examples in the field of alcohol studies include the "necessity" for having laws to limit drinking behavior, both for adults and minors; the belief that getting drunk is always unhealthy or dangerous; the idea that youngsters should not drink or not get drunk; and the theory that alcoholism is a disease.

When a consensus exists on an alcohol issue, you can provoke a stimulating class discussion by playing devil's advocate and telling your class, for example, "There should be no laws prohibiting minors from drinking." As students formulate their rationales—and different students may have very different rationales—you can stimulate them to probe deeper and deeper into the foundations of their beliefs. The purpose of this approach is not, of course, to create confusion in the minds of pupils but to require conscious and substantiated rationales for holding intelligent positions on alcohol issues. You may need to make clear to your students that you do not necessarily believe in the position you are defending to prevent misunderstandings that may result in parent complaints.

All of the small group discussion activities in chapter 11 that were listed at the end of the previous section on small group discussion can also be conducted as class discussions.

INDEPENDENT STUDY

Independent study activities involve students in selecting topics that concern them and then studying them within a structured framework of assistance and direction from you. Independent study activities can include interviews, field trips, polls, debates, reading, and other forms of research.

Independent study, when it flows from student concern, can be one of the best learning approaches in an alcohol curriculum because:

- since students are bound to have different concerns, *it enables different students to pursue alcohol subject areas that pertain specifically to their own various needs and concerns* and encourages them to learn the answers to their most urgent questions. Activities in which an entire class must participate may fail to address some pupils' needs.
- it enables different students with different resources to pursue their concerns about alcohol in ways that fit in with their own particular learning abilities.
- it frees you to devote more personal and in-depth attention to individual students.
- students can pursue their concerns about specific alcohol issues in greater depth than in classroom activities because they are free to do research using a variety of approaches (polls, reading, interviews, etc.).

While independent study methods offer considerable potential, students must be reasonably self-motivated, disciplined, and conscientious to engage effectively in this educational method. With inadequate supervision, students can flounder and not be productive, but if pupils are supervised too closely they may lose the opportunity to learn from their mistakes and the chance to follow their own curiosity and creative urges. Independent study can be a problem when some students in a class are equipped and motivated to engage in this approach to learning while others are not similarly capable or interested. How to teach these other students while the first group is engaged in independent study can present a dilemma.

The usual method for using independent study is to distribute a list of suggested research topics on alcohol and encourage students to add to it. Another method is to keep available in the classroom a file of activity sheets students can browse through, such as those provided in chapter 11. Students should ponder their preferences for a few days and then select one. Then break your students into small groups on the basis of their choices. Set aside class time for the groups to do the following:

- further refine the topic area
- determine their research methods, such as interviews, phone calls, polls, readings, field trips, letter writing, teaching, and volunteer work
- divide up responsibility for the research
- meet to discuss their progress and keep you informed of their progress and problems
- prepare reports to the class
- present their reports to the class and respond to its questions and comments
- write articles for submission to school and community newspapers, when time permits

You should function as a resource and guide who provides students with assistance on such matters as how to find needed materials, how to take notes, how to structure the research (read primary source materials before secondary, etc.), and how to verify controversial "facts." If students are left too much on their own, they may spend their time in unproductive ways and lose interest in their study.

In preparing their class reports, students should be encouraged to invite guest speakers, develop or borrow audiovisual aids, develop skits, and use other creative methods that are appropriate to the effective presentation of their research findings.

Chapter 11 provides several activities which students can engage in independently, including #4, #26, #31, and #33. In addition all of the activities that involve field trips, interviews, and polls, peer teaching, and volunteer work can also be conducted as independent study activities.

INTERVIEWS

Interviews can be an integral part of an alcohol and alcohol safety curriculum for the following reasons:

- There are many fascinating and informed people in this field of study who are very responsive to the inquiries of students (see list of potential interviewees at the end of this section).
- This is an excellent way to obtain firsthand information from people who have experienced alcohol problems or been in direct contact with those who have.
- There are a variety of opinions on a number of alcohol and alcohol safety issues with strong spokespersons for them all whom students can listen to and question about the bases for their beliefs.

Interviews can be difficult and time consuming to arrange—especially for an entire class. Moreover, interviewees can become upset at the questions being asked, especially in an area as "touchy" as alcohol use and abuse. Angry calls to the school principal are possible, although discussing the project in advance with school administrators can help them later to clarify the exercise in a calm manner to concerned interviewees who may complain. Interviews may also reveal to students only "canned" or superficial opinions of the people being questioned or one-sided views that leave a greater impression on the interviewing students than is warranted by the facts.

When conducting interviews, students should do the following things:

- First, study the appropriate alcohol literature about their chosen alcohol topic.
- Then draw up a list of critical questions to ask. Some of these questions may seek factual information, but questions, when possible, should deal with areas of controversy or difficult-to-obtain information. Neither the interviewee's nor the students' time should be wasted on questions that can be answered by glancing at an alcohol source book.
- Ask other students in the class what questions about alcohol *they* would like to see answered.
- Contact the interviewee, arrange for an appointment, and request permission to bring a tape recorder or, barring that, to take written notes or arrange for the interviewee to come to the school.
- Begin their interviews by asking the interviewees their exact title, position, and duties.

This information is useful to gain an idea of how much credence to place in the interviewees' statements and to help students through the nervous first few minutes.

- Take independent notes during or immediately after the interview since one "reporter" may not be able to write down everything that is said and different students may interpret what was said differently.
- Ask critical but polite questions that probe inconsistencies, hypocrisies, unaccounted for results, successes, and failures.

Upon completion of an interview, the students should:

- Evaluate the results in such terms as: What alcohol topics did the interviewee seem most informed about? Why? What new information and ideas about alcohol were learned?
- Report their findings and *critical interpretations* to the rest of the class.
- Prepare an article describing their findings for submission to the school and local community newspapers. Permission should first be obtained from any interviewees who will be identified in the article.

One other type of interview students can conduct is the telephone interview. If interviewees are too busy or inaccessible for in-person interviews, they may agree to answer questions over the telephone by an appointment secured in advance. Students who want to interview several respondents in order to compare opinions and attitudes can use telephone interviews for this purpose, too.

Individuals whom students may want to interview include doctors, police officers, judges, lawyers; local, state, and federal welfare officers; members of Alcoholics Anonymous, Al-Anon, and Alateen; alcoholism program directors and staff; insurance company employees; hospital alcoholism unit patients and staff; newspaper editors and reporters; parents and other adults; advertising monitors and writers; state and local tax officials; alcoholic beverage control commission officials; package store salespersons and owners and bartenders; and alcoholic beverage manufacturers.

Activities #4, #13, #26, #31, and #33 in chapter 11 involve students in conducting interviews.

POLLS

Polls and questionnaires can be extremely useful and exciting activities in an alcohol curriculum. By administering, collating, and interpreting polls on alcohol issues students can:

- learn about attitudes toward, beliefs about, and behaviors with alcohol in a realistic and meaningful way.
- learn about the difficulties in discovering and measuring alcohol attitudes, beliefs, and behaviors, and, as a result, be better able to evaluate the results of surveys that report on these issues.
- learn to make and understand correlations and thereby realize that alcohol opinions and behaviors may be dependent on socioeconomic status, age, sex, ethnicity, and other factors.
- learn about alcohol attitudes, beliefs, and behaviors that they might not previously have been aware existed.

Drawbacks to Polls

All of the difficulties attendant on interviews may also be true of polls. They can be difficult to arrange, provide misleading or unreliable information, and upset some of the individuals being questioned. In addition, polls can be time consuming to conduct, including not only the interviews themselves but also the tabulation of results, interpretation of findings, and preparation of a report on any conclusions that are drawn. Finally, whatever the results of a student-run poll and no matter how carefully it is conducted, analyzed, and reported, the findings must always be considered skeptically given both the complexities involved in professional polling techniques and interpretation and also the naiveté of the students in these areas.

Construction of Polls

Encourage your students to develop their own polls or questionnaires. Most students can formulate their own questions, but you should caution them to consider the following polling techniques:

- Phrase questions in the way most likely to get an honest response in this potentially "touchy" area.
- Avoid questions that require a written response (respondents are often pressed for time, lazy, or afraid of handwriting detection).
- Avoid too long a poll (for the same reasons).
- Assure respondents of anonymity and see to it that the poll in fact cannot reveal names.
- Investigate relationships, such as sex, race, age, economic status, political preference, and drinking experience and habits. These relationships, when tabulated after a poll has been taken, are called correlations (e.g., there is a positive correlation between economic position and social drinking; that is, more people in higher socioeconomic classes drink alcohol than do people in lower socioeconomic classes).
- Select the proper sample of people to be interviewed so that these correlations can be made. If students want to see if women tend to have different views about alcohol laws than men, they must be sure to include enough women in their poll to make it possible for them to learn this.
- Test the poll on the rest of the class to remove the "bugs," such as confusing questions or too limited a choice of possible responses to check.
- Learn what a "representative sample" is, such as 10% of the school body; or .01% of the town's parents—that is, a sample that is large enough to permit the poll taker to generalize about the attitudes toward alcohol or drinking behavior to the whole school or all of the town's parents.
- Decide how many people should be polled (conducting a poll and tabulating correlations by hand can take hours).

Administration of Polls

How honestly an alcohol poll is answered may depend on how it is administered. Some student respondents may be more honest and serious if the poll is administered by other students rather than by a teacher. On the other hand, faculty respondents may answer more honestly if you give them the poll at a staff meeting rather than if your students administer the questionnaire. Sometimes it is most effective to have a principal administer the poll to the faculty. Students

can also take polls home to their parents or go in teams to knock on doors.

Tabulation and Interpretation of Polls

Students may need help drawing up a matrix to record their correlations. You should see to this immediately before students have wasted much time doing unnecessary or useless tabulations. Sample matrices are provided in Table 5.1.

Students need to be reminded that polling statistics rarely explain *why* certain people hold certain attitudes and beliefs or act in certain ways. It is the researchers' job to interpret the findings and develop hypotheses to answer these questions.

Polling topics your students can consider using include the following:

- why, when, and how much people drink or abstain
- what people drink
- how alcohol affects people's thoughts and actions
- knowledge of alcohol's effects and alcohol laws
- how people learned about alcohol
- people's attitudes toward alcohol education
- people's attitudes toward alcoholics and drunkenness
- people's attitudes toward drinking age limits and laws
- what people feel is and is not responsible drinking behavior and why

Activities #1, #6, #14, and #24 in chapter 11 involve the taking, development, administration, or analysis of polls.

FIELD TRIPS

There are several kinds of field trips your students can take that involve alcohol, but they have enough points in common to warrant some general comments. These comments apply to solo, small group, and entire class trips.

Field trips are a useful learning experience when you teach about alcohol because they can do the following:

- Enable students to explore a part of the real world and thereby make explicit the relevance of the classroom activities on alcohol in chapter 11 to real-life alcohol issues.

Table 5.1

Question: How many people feel that alcohol abuse is a serious problem in their community?

Raw data

	Men		Women		
	Yes	No	Yes	No	Total
Age 10–18	3	1	4	2	10
Age 19–30	10	6	4	5	25
Age 31–	3	9	5	8	25
Total	16	16	13	15	60

Percent by age group

	Yes	No
Age 10–18	70%	30%
Age 19–30	56%	44%
Age 31–	32%	68%

Percent by sex and age group answering yes

	Men	Women
Age 10–18	75%	67%
Age 19–30	62%	44%
Age 31–	25%	38%

Percent by sex

	Yes	No
Men	50%	50%
Women	46%	54%

- Provide more accurate in-depth information about alcohol than many secondhand sources can supply.
- Put students in contact with alcohol information sources that may arouse or reinforce an interest or concern.

Drawbacks to Field Trips

It can take considerable effort and time on your part or that of your students to arrange field trips, especially when different small groups of students plan to visit different sites. Depending on the ages and levels of maturity of the students, adult supervision and transportation may be a problem to arrange and time consuming to provide. Legal issues may be involved in the provision of transportation. Large groups of students of field trips can present discipline problems. Finally, students may be able to view only part of the site they are visiting because the hosts limit the field trip on grounds of safety, time, or self-interest. As a result, what is viewed

may be atypical or only part of the complete operation, leaving students with an incorrect or incomplete understanding of the issue being studied.

Before a Field Trip Is Taken

Before a field trip is taken, certain things should be taken care of:

- The decisions should be made early, on consultation with students, to ensure adequate student motivation and time to make the necessary arrangements, including written parental permission, financial matters and transportation.
- Students must be given adequate background information about where they are going, why they are going, what they can expect to see and/or hear about alcohol, and what they can expect to learn about alcohol.
- Students need to be familiar with enough of what they will be seeing and/or hearing,

either through personal knowledge or second-hand information, so they can prepare questions in advance that will be answered either through observation during the field trip or by the tour guide or other "on-site" people.

- Authorities at the field trip site must be aware of how many students are coming, their ages, and prior information level and experience so they can gear the tour to the students' specific needs.

During a field trip students should be encouraged to ask questions, observe and listen carefully, and take notes if necessary.

Where to go on field trips depends largely on the availability of community resources, adult supervision for minors, transportation and time. Some good field trips your students can go on include town hall, city hall, state house to talk with local legislators and officials, including staff in the Divisions or Departments of Alcohol, Mental Health, and Education; nonprofit alcoholism agencies, such as local councils on alcoholism; breweries, wineries, and distilleries; police stations and courts; open Alcoholics Anonymous, Al-Anon, and Alateen meetings;* hospital alcoholism treatment units, half-way houses, drop-in centers, and hotlines; "skid row," bars and college pubs; and package stores.

Many cities and school districts provide a list of companies and agencies that encourage field trips, including times of availability and number of students desired. It is worth contacting your State Department of Education, local superintendent of schools, or state or local audio-visual department to see if such a list has been compiled.

A variation of field trips that dispenses with both teacher supervision and extra travel arrangements is observation. Students can be given weekend or overnight assignments to observe a variety of phenomena that relate to different alcohol issues, such as alcohol advertisements on television, radio, billboards, trucks, etc.; adult and juvenile drinking behavior at parties, restaurants, etc.; and types of people who patronize package stores, bars, and restaurants that serve liquor.

After a field trip, students must compare and review what they learned, since different students will have drawn different conclusions that can profitably be shared. In addition, many things that were learned will be quickly forgotten or distorted over time if they are not reinforced immediately. Follow-up activities should therefore involve students in *sharing* what they learned, *applying* what they learned, and *exploring* new alcohol issues that their learnings may have stimulated them to pursue.

Activity #31 in chapter 11 suggests a field trip students can take that will increase their understanding of alcohol issues and problems.

VOLUNTEER WORK

Learning by doing is a potent educational approach. One way to "do" is to engage in volunteer work. Particularly in areas of human behavior such as alcohol use and abuse, classroom learning is made more real and meaningful if it is accompanied by actual experiences in the area. You can encourage students to engage in volunteer work and tell them

1. that volunteer work, in addition to its altruistic dimension, can be personally useful as a learning experience about human nature and problems; an opportunity to learn an enormous amount about oneself; and a way to make classroom learning about alcohol more meaningful.
2. that volunteer work is desperately needed by individuals with alcohol problems and by agencies seeking to help these people.
3. which public and private agencies in the community dealing with alcohol problems need student volunteers and what kind of work is involved with each.
4. the type of work they can expect to do. The work available to them may often be menial, but there will still be plenty of opportunity for students to learn about and observe alcohol problems.

You should also

1. give your students some form of academic credit for volunteer work, such as less homework, a grade, or free class time.

---

*These visitations may require careful advance preparation to avoid or mitigate potential embarrassment if the students see someone they know. Be sure to discuss what should be said in such a circumstance and the importance of maintaining confidences. When possible, students can restrict themselves to visiting meetings held outside their own communities to minimize the risk of running into someone they know.

2. require your students to keep a log of their activities and thoughts about their volunteer work, but not require that it be turned in if the student feels it is a personal document.
3. ask your students to report to the class on their work at least once.
4. ask your students to write articles about their work for submission to the school and community newspapers.

Some types of institutions that deal with alcohol problems and may welcome volunteers are alcoholism units of public and private hospitals, big brother and sister programs, halfway houses, student youth centers, and councils on alcoholism.

Despite the existence of a number of agencies and organizations, which may accept volunteers, it is well to realize that it can be time consuming for both an instructor and students to arrange for volunteer work arrangements. Even with the most sustained effort, it may be difficult to find opportunities because of the age of the students, legal constraints, transportation problems, and a shortage of volunteer positions available in a particular community.

PEER TEACHING

Definition and Value of Peer Teaching

Peer education is an amorphous concept that connotes different things to different people. Generally, it involves the sharing of information, attitudes, or behaviors by people who are not professionally trained educators but whose goal is nonetheless to educate. Peer educators may have special expertise in a particular subject or skill or have received training in how to be peer teachers, but they do not have the experience or credentials of professionals in the content area that they are communicating and their occupation does not involve teaching in this field.

Peer teaching can be a highly productive and exciting learning process. Most teachers at one time or another have noticed students and their own children helping each other with homework and other academic problems. In an effective classroom, some peer teaching and learning is always going on, usually in the form of discussions. This approach can be deliberately built into an alcohol education program where it can

become a valuable teaching strategy. Most commonly such structured approaches to peer education involve older students teaching younger students, and the remainder of this discussion of peer teaching as a method in alcohol education is presented with this particular perspective in mind.

Peer teaching can be useful in an alcohol education course for the following reasons:

1. The students being taught often learn more efficiently than they otherwise might.
   - They often trust other students' opinions and statements in controversial areas like alcohol use and abuse more than they trust those of adults. They are often more willing to express their own opinions more candidly in front of each other than to a teacher.
   - They can sometimes understand other students' explanations better than they can those given by adults, since other students speak the same language and, more important, have recently gone through the learning process themselves.
2. The students doing the teaching gain new insights into the issues involved and are prompted frequently to do further research and thinking in response to questions and comments from their peers.
3. Students involved come to realize that they all have resources that they can tap and skills they can share.

Problems with Peer Teaching. It takes time to arrange for peer teaching on the parts of both the instructor and the peer teachers. Careful and ongoing supervision by the instructor is necessary to ensure that the peer teachers are performing adequately. This educational approach also requires identifying and training students who are highly motivated and capable of conducting this kind of interpersonal effort in an effective manner. Even when capable students are found, adequately trained, and thoroughly supervised, peer teaching can become peer pressure as younger students simply accept what their peer teachers have to say on the basis of "superior" age, rank, or experience. Furthermore, when older youngsters teach younger ones, there are scheduling, administration, and sometimes parent concerns about this approach that need to be dealt with to make it successful.

These concerns and how they are handled will vary according to each particular school and community. However, in general parents should be brought into the school to form a dialogue as soon as the program is being considered. They must be supportive of not only the program in the abstract but also of their children's possible involvement in it. If this is not the case, the program is likely to put both the child and the school in a "no-win" situation.

Training Peer Teachers

In selecting and training peer teachers, several considerations must be addressed:

1. The peer leaders must volunteer for the assignments. Compulsory teaching assignments usually produce poor results. Volunteers must then be "screened" for appropriateness to the assignment.
2. The peer leaders must have a clear idea of
   - what they are going to teach about alcohol. This should involve questioning the younger students to discover *their* concerns about alcohol.
   - how they are going to teach. Options include:
     - one-to-one tutoring
     - small group discussions
     - team teaching to a class
     - use of written materials, homework, etc.
   - what their relationship to the younger students should and should not be. Options include authority figure, *primus inter pares* (first among equals), pal, older brother or sister, and counselor.
   - what the alternatives are to coping with and assisting younger students who ask for help with personal drinking problems or problems in their families.
3. The students must have a reasonable grasp of the alcohol content area and issues involved prior to teaching, but they should not feel they have to be "experts" in order to help others to learn.
4. If the students will be expected to run small group discussions, they must be helped to develop active listening skills along with conflict management skills and small group leadership skills such as agenda setting.

WRITING

It is important for students to write frequently in an alcohol curriculum for two reasons:

1. Writing stimulates intensive, creative, and critical thinking about alcohol issues in a way that for some people is difficult through verbal interchange.
2. Writing creates an opportunity for students to read what their classmates have written about alcohol and this in turn helps make them aware that *youngsters* have important, interesting, and informative ideas to communicate.

Nonetheless, many students have difficulty writing and may become defensive or discouraged by their inarticulateness on paper. Writing assignments may thereby create an atmosphere of reticence that may carry over into the other instructional methods used in your course. When students are able to write effectively, you must devote time to evaluating what has been written and to providing individual students with helpful assessments of their written work.

In an alcohol curriculum there are several useful writing modes for students to engage in, such as the following:

1. position papers stating and defending their stand on an alcohol issue
2. "handbooks" that offer guidelines and opinions on laws, suggest advice to parents, teenagers, drinkers, and abstainers, or indicate desirable courses of action to agencies and institutions
3. imaginary dialogues and interviews between individuals with opposing points of view on alcohol issues
4. autobiographical and biographical narratives
5. story beginnings, middles and endings.

Since the major objective of this type of writing is to elicit feelings and opinions, you should avoid commenting on students' opinions on alcohol issues in such terms as "that's a good idea," "good," "I agree," "I think you're wrong." When this is done, students become accustomed to writing opinions and ideas they think you want to read, rather than what they truly believe. However, students do need to be commended and corrected in terms of their *techniques*. Students should be criticized on the basis of:

1. whether they *supported* their opinions with logic and facts, or at least said their position could not be logically or factually defended
2. whether they took into account and "disposed of" arguments and considerations that *run counter* to their contentions
3. whether they have made *untrue* statements.

Student writing is most productive when your attention is focused on whether opinions have been adequately defended rather than on whether you agree or disagree with them.

In chapter 11, Activities #15, #19, #21, #23, #29, and #30 involve writing.

AND IN CONCLUSION . . .

It is clear that there are a variety of teaching methods you can implement in your alcohol curriculum including not only the innovative and student-centered ones described in this chapter but also the more traditional techniques of lectures, demonstrations, audiovisual presentations, and guest speakers. In addition, while the methods presented here are to be preferred over the more typical approaches, these student-centered strategies have drawbacks on their own, which we have also fully presented. Most serious of all, perhaps, is that these approaches all require extra time and sensitivity to implement successfully and that in many instances students who engage in them must be relatively well motivated, self-directed, and conscientious. *However, the additional time required to implement these teaching methods will be more than compensated by the additional learning they are likely to achieve with most students. Furthermore, many students who initially appear to be poorly suited to engage in them can develop the incentive and ability to undertake them effectively if given the chance to do so.*

In selecting the mix of methods you will use in your particular course, you will of course want to choose teaching approaches which are best suited to both your own abilities and time constraints and also to the needs and competencies of your particular students. Additional suggestions for selecting appropriate teaching methods are provided in chapter 10.

ADDITIONAL READING

Finn, Peter. "Developing Critical Television Viewing Skills." *Educational Forum* 44 (1980):473–482.

_____. "Teaching Students to Be Lifelong Peer Educators." *Health Education*, 12 (1981), in press.

Gray Advertising. *Communications Strategies on Alcohol and Highway Safety*, Vol. 2. Springfield, Va.: National Technical Information Service, 1975.

Kunkle-Miller, Carole, and Blane, Howard T. "A Small Group Approach to Youth Education about Alcohol." *Journal of Drug Education* 7 (1977):381–386.

Miles, M. B. *Learning to Work in Groups*. New York: Teachers College, 1959.

Russell, Robert D. *Health Education*. Washington, D.C.: National Education Association, 1975.

Samuels, M. and Samuels, S. *The Complete Handbook of Peer Counseling*. Miami: Fiesta Publishing Co., 1975.

Schamuck, P. A., and Schamuck, D. *Group Processes in the Classroom*. Dubuque, Iowa: William C. Brown, 1971.

Todd, Frances. *Teaching about Alcohol*. New York: McGraw-Hill Book Co., 1964.

U.S. Department of Health, Education, and Welfare. "Peer Approach to Prevention." *Alcohol Health and Research World* (Spring 1974):10–14.

Witherill, Jerome W. *Group Process in Alcohol Education, with Strategies for the Classroom*. Washington, D.C.: American Driver and Traffic Safety Education Association, 1978.

Alcohol Education
at the Elementary Level

Preadolescence is the time when most young-sters are first confronted with the opportunity to drink and faced (albeit in embryonic form) with many of the consequent feelings and behaviors that accompany the use of alcohol. Most Americans have had their first drink by the time they turn fourteen.[1] Twenty-five percent of all seventh graders report having been drunk one or more times during the past year.[2] Many young-sters must also learn to cope at an early age with relatives who abuse alcohol, a serious "drinking" problem for these children who themselves may not drink at all. Thus, there are many children at the elementary school level who will have a personal interest in learning about alcohol use and abuse. In addition, good attitudes toward drinking are best established at an early age. By the time some youngsters enter high school and even junior high school, many of their feelings about drinking have "hardened" and are less amenable to change in response to new information and insights than when these youths were younger.

Clearly, then, there are sound reasons for teaching about alcohol prior to the junior high or middle school level. However, instruction in alcohol use and abuse with smaller children

[1] Howard T. Blane and Linda E. Hewitt, *Alcohol and Youth: An Analysis of the Literature, 1960–1975* (Springfield, Va.: National Technical Information Service, 1977), pp. II-17–II-18; J. Valley Rachal et al., *A National Study of Adolescent Drinking Behavior Attitudes and Correlates* (Springfield, Va.: National Technical Information Service, 1975), p. 45.

[2] U.S. Department of Health, Education, and Welfare, *Alcohol and Health: Second Special Report to the U.S. Congress* (Washington, D.C.: U.S. Government Printing Office, 1974), p. 28; Harold Wechsler and Mary McFadden, "Sex Differences in Adolescent Alcohol and Drug Use," *Journal of Studies on Alcohol* 37 (September 1976):1291–1301.

This chapter is adapted from *Instructor*, November 1975. Copyright © November 1975 by The Instructor Publications, Inc. used by permission.

requires special goals, approaches, and sensitivity. We have therefore included this separate chapter devoted exclusively to alcohol education at the elementary school level.

What can alcohol education realistically do for children at the elementary level? While schools—elementary or secondary—can do little for pupils who are well on the way to becoming problem drinkers and need professional help, you can, if you are an elementary school teacher, effectively help your students in a number of ways.

1. You can help them make wise decisions about whether or not to drink alcoholic beverages by doing the following:
    a. discussing the reasons people drink or abstain
    b. suggesting several acceptable drinking patterns
    c. helping them to understand how drinking abusively can undermine their own or other people's physical or mental health, family life, employment, or freedom
    d. describing what many people feel are the positive effects of moderate drinking and abstention
2. You can help your students to:
    a. define what constitutes nonabusive and abusive drinking by discussing different cultural drinking practices in America and the variety of social attitudes toward drinking and abstention.
    b. decide when and how to resist peer pressure by discussing its strength and nature.
    c. decide how to respond to and help people who abuse alcohol.

Even when alcohol is not a salient issue for youngsters, particularly at the lower elementary grades, you can still do much to help your students develop or preserve constructive attitudes toward fundamental issues, such as risk-taking and peer relationships, that will play a significant role in influencing how they will ultimately make drinking decisions. In fact, the elementary school level is the ideal place to begin alcohol education because some student attitudes have solidified by the time pupils reach secondary school, at which time it may be too late for you or their parents to alter them. Primary school youngsters still have relatively open minds and

flexible attitudes toward alcohol and often can be helped to develop personally and socially acceptable attitudes about drinking and abstention from drinking that will stand them in good stead the rest of their lives.

There are two simple ways you can introduce alcohol education into your classes. The first is to raise for brief discussion alcohol issues as they arise spontaneously on the part of students. The second is to integrate on occasion a study of alcohol into existing subject areas.

1. THE SPONTANEOUS INTEREST APPROACH

Opportunities for cultivating responsible attitudes toward and providing basic information about alcohol exist in several areas of student interest. You should look for cues in what students talk about in class that indicate an interest in alcohol-related issues, and then, in the context of that interest, discuss the alcohol issues broached by the children. This is a particularly good approach to use in grades 1–3 when fears and questions about alcohol are raised more often in informal or free-time situations.

These issues raised by children tend to range from specific questions about alcohol and alcoholism themselves through related questions on safety and health, to general issues, such as risk-taking, peer pressures, and the handling of emotions. Alcohol may be treated as one of several relevant examples or applications within all of these questions and issues.

Here are some examples of issues that students might raise:

(a) If they joke about a drunk character seen on television, in the street, or at a party, the class can discuss why he might be drunk, why he seems funny, what it might feel like to be drunk, and what might happen if he crossed the street, drove a car, or climbed a ladder.

(b) If students talk about poisons, the discussion can include references to denatured and methyl alcohol as part of a larger discussion of poisonous substances.

(c) In a discussion of other drugs, such as heroin or marijuana, alcohol can be introduced as a drug that may be used socially or addictively. If smoking is brought up as a health risk or decision-making issue, drinking also can be raised.

(d) Whenever you or your students talk about avoiding accidents—in crossing streets, riding bicycles, using playground equipment, and riding in cars—you can discuss alcohol and its effects on reflexes and its role in accidents.

(e) If students mention advertisements, discussion can follow on the nature and goals of advertising in general and alcohol advertisements in particular. The class can analyze the appeals of advertisements for cereals, toys, and alcohol, and go on to discuss how these appeals may be misleading or how any claims made may be unproven. Students can identify some of the characteristics alcohol advertisements seem to associate with drinking, such as being "grown up," athletic, fun-loving, and part of the gang. And they can discuss whether some people might be influenced by advertisements to drink more than they otherwise would.

(f) Students may also want to discuss the role that alcohol plays in many movie and TV programs, such as westerns, detective stories, and situation comedies. Such questions can be pondered as: Does alcohol use make you braver? Is it really so thirst quenching to have whiskey when you come off the prairie? What is the effect of having three drinks and then riding off on a high-speed chase to catch the "bad guy"?

(g) Ethnic, regional, and national eating habits and tastes in food and drink can be used to introduce various patterns of alcohol use. The issue of youngsters in other countries who regularly drink alcoholic beverages with meals can be discussed to demonstrate the variations in eating and drinking patterns and raise the issue of different attitudes toward drinking.

(h) Handling emotions is a general topic under which the use of alcohol may be introduced as a method of coping with anger, fear, frustration, and unhappiness. Students can discuss what makes people—in particular, them—happy, sad, angry, or afraid. They can list constructive and destructive ways of coping with emotions. For example, constructive methods of handling sadness might include engaging in a carefree activity, like bicycling, playing ball, or going to the movies, making an effort to understand the causes of one's unhappiness, or talking things over with a friend. Destructive methods might be brooding and feeling sorry for oneself, or making nasty comments to people. Use of alcohol for different reasons and to different degrees might represent either a constructive or destructive way to handle emotions. Some people might view occasional and moderate drinking as a constructive way to meet a need to share feelings of

solemnity or joy, or as a method for reducing minor feelings of tension, while other people might see habitual or heavy drinking used as an escape from such feelings as shyness or to meet a need to feel grown up as a destructive way of coping with emotions.

(i) Emulation of older youths and adults is a broad area of interest under which you may introduce the use of alcohol in terms of why and when youngsters begin to try alcoholic beverages. Students can discuss real or fictional people they admire and want to be like and why and whether their feelings about these people would—or should—change if the pupils knew these people abstained, drank moderately, or abused alcohol. The class can discuss how children (and adults) often pattern their behavior on that of specific adults. Students can then discuss what particular behaviors would make them feel more mature, such as overcoming obstacles, solving problems, drinking coffee, staying up late at night, living through hard times, drinking alcohol, smoking, coping successfully with unpleasant feelings, not giving in to harmful temptations, or helping someone in need.

(j) Awareness of peer relationships is a good area in which to raise the issue of experimenting with alcohol, cigarettes, and such, in order to "go along with the group." Introductory activities about peer relationships can include making collages that illustrate what students do and do not value in friendships and discussing things the students might do with friends that they would not do alone.

(k) Motives and consequences of risk-taking can be discussed in terms of alcohol. What is a risk? Why do we take risks? How do we know whether to take a risk? Short-term risks, such as walking across thin ice and driving under the influence of alcohol, may be compared with longer term risks (that is, where consequences may not be known for a long time) such as smoking and heavy drinking.

2. THE SUBJECT AREA INTEGRATION APPROACH

Alcohol education also can be introduced effectively by integrating it with health education, social studies, English, and art. (This approach is more appropriate in the upper elementary levels.) There are several logical points of entree within each of these disciplines where a part or all of a period could be devoted to a study of alcohol issues. For example, during or after a discussion in social studies about the family and the responsibility of various family members to each other, you can raise for discussion what the individual's responsibility should be toward family members (and friends and strangers) who drink excessively, drive, cross streets, or perform other potentially dangerous activities when impaired by alcohol use, or make drinks available to others, particularly when these recipients may drive or engage in other activities which are potentially dangerous to themselves or to other people.

As part of English classes, you can assign books that describe alcohol use or abuse, or take a few moments out whenever your students are engaged in a reading assignment that involves drinking to raise for discussion such issues as how drinking might relate to personality (characterization) and how in literary terms the author goes about describing the drinking behavior (exposition, allusion, symbolism, and so on). You can look through the books in your school library for appropriate novels and short stories for students to read, such as *Emily's Runaway Imagination* by Beverly Cleary, in which pigs who eat fermented apples become intoxicated; *The Outsiders* by S. E. Hinton, in which a group of adolescents gets drunk and starts a fight with another gang; *The Cool World* by Warren Miller, in which a gang gets "high" to boost its courage for a fight; *Jennifer* by Zoa Sherburne, and *You Can't Get There From Here* by Earl Hammer, Jr., both of which describe attempts by teenagers to cope with an alcoholic parent. Other reading materials are suggested in the Resources section at the end of the book.

Art classes can involve students in the creation of collages, mobiles, models, and paintings around alcohol themes such as behavioral and physical effects, safety hazards of excessive drinking, and reasons people drink. If students raise the question of handling emotions, or an emotionally charged situation arises either between two students in class or in a story or movie, you can develop an art exercise in which students draw pictures expressing different responses to being sad, angry, or happy.

Some responses to look for and suggest, if your students have not themselves raised them, include discussing the problem with a friend or with the person who caused the anger; looking for company; engaging in physical activity, such as playing ball, cleaning house, or bicycling to expend physical energy; driving a car very fast; having a drink or getting drunk; locking oneself in one's room; picking on a younger brother or sister, or pet; crying; throwing things and slamming doors; eating ice cream and cake; and refusing to eat.

By using one or both of these approaches to integrating alcohol education into the classroom, you can unobtrusively yet effectively contribute to your students' understanding of the use, nonuse, and abuse of alcohol, and promote the development of healthy attitudes toward drinking and abstention. At the same time, occasional discussion of drinking at the elementary level will encourage youngsters to realize that alcohol issues and problems are amenable to rational discussion, rather than shameful areas that are best kept hidden until they become insupportable or highly destructive. To the extent that we promote a dialogue about alcohol at an early age, we will be assisting future adults to think about their drinking attitudes and behaviors before serious problems develop.

Many learning activities appropriate to the elementary grade levels have been included in the Instructional Activities section at the end of this book.

ADDITIONAL READING

Bloom, Gaston E., and Snoddy, James E. "The Child, the Teacher, and the Drinking Society: A Conceptual Framework for Alcohol Education in the Elementary School." In *Adolescence and Alcohol*, edited by John E. Mayer and William J. Filstead. Cambridge, Mass.: Ballinger Publishing Co., 1980.

Byler, Ruth; Lewis, Gertrude; and Totman, Ruth. *Teach Us What We Want to Know*. New York: Mental Health Materials Center, 1969.

Finn, Peter. "Alcohol: You Can Help Your Kids Cope." *Instructor* 85 (1975):76-78, 83-84.

Jahodah, G., and Crammond, J. *Children and Alcohol: A Developmental Study in Glasgow*, vol. 1. London: Her Majesty's Stationery Office, 1972.

Lee, Essie E. "Alcohol Education and the Elementary School Teacher." *Journal of School Health* 46 (1976):271-272.

7

How to Teach Objectively about Alcohol

To help your students learn to abstain or use alcohol in acceptable ways, it is essential that you teach them about alcohol in an objective manner, without moralizing or "preaching." This means you need to become familiar with your own attitudes and feelings about alcohol and then be alert to instances where your personal attitudes and feelings about drinking may be influencing your teaching.

HOW ATTITUDES MAY INTERFERE WITH TEACHING ABOUT ALCOHOL

How may your attitudes intrude into the classroom? The most common example is when a teacher advocates abstinence for youngsters until they reach a certain age—usually the legal purchase age. While this is a common teacher attitude in the classroom, it may be less harmful than other more subtly expressed feelings because its very openness allows students to compensate for it—usually by dismissing it out of hand. More subtle teacher attitudes that may filter into alcohol education instruction include feelings of hostility, resentment, jealousy, fear, or admiration regarding students who drink. Teachers may experience these emotions because possibly they:

- are not at ease with their own drinking behavior
- regret not having "sown their wild oats" when they were young
- want to recapture their lost youth
- would like to emulate the apparent freedom and lack of inhibition their students seem to exhibit
- are concerned that some of their pupils know more about drinking from an experiential point of view than they do

Many teachers also allow an attitude to influence their teaching that suggests that "moderate" drinking is all right as long as students accept the teacher's definition of moderate—which may be a glass of wine with lunch, three cocktails before dinner, getting drunk every Friday night, or any number of other drinking patterns.

These are just a few of the diverse attitudes that you, like everyone else in our society, may have about drinking. Having such attitudes and feelings, of course, is perfectly appropriate—the person in our society who has no opinions about drinking is rare indeed. However, a problem arises if you allow your attitudes to become part of your teaching, either in the form of (1) recommending how your students should or should not drink or (2) presenting alcohol education information and issues in a biased manner.

WHY NOT TO OFFER ADVICE

There are a number of reasons why attempts on your part to produce specific drinking or abstention behaviors in your students or to teach about alcohol in a way that reflects your personal feelings about drinking will seriously hamper your efforts to be an effective alcohol educator.

First, many students who are concerned about good grades in school may express only those opinions about controversial issues like drinking that they feel represent what their teachers want to hear. Students often become adept at supplying the expected responses and in the process may spend more time exercising talents of flattery and mimicry than examining their own real feelings about alcohol. As a result, trying to encourage students to adopt your drinking philosophy may only result in their agreeing with you for the sake of good grades.

A second reason direct inculcation of drinking attitudes may not succeed with some students is that today's youth often disrespect and "tune out" the teacher who tells them what is right and wrong, because youngsters are extremely sensitive to the hypocrisy of how adult behavior belies adult precepts. They know that many teachers admonish them to behave one way but fail to live up to their own advice. Students hear teachers warn them of the dangers of driving after drinking knowing full well that many such

instructors cannot wait until the class period ends to hasten to the teacher's room to puff on a desperately needed cigarette. Pupils know that many teachers who admonish them not to get drunk did so themselves as youngsters and often continue to do so as adults. Students see overweight teachers offer instruction about nutrition and hear about the hazards of risk taking from instructors who never wear safety belts. In short, most youth have seen what they feel is too much adult hypocrisy to accept advice from teachers on how they should conduct their own lives. Adults have lost their unquestioned powers on command and moral suasion for a good part of the younger generation: The age of the teacher as preceptor and moral exemplar is over.

A third reason many students may not respond to your advice on how to drink is that they may be offended by your implicit assumption that youngsters, given the facts and the opportunity to discuss their feelings, are too "dumb" to come to their own intelligent conclusions about whether and how to drink—especially when, given the facts about seat belts, most adults are evidently unqualified to come to their own conclusions about *their* personal safety habits. Many youngsters, given accurate information and a chance to discuss their attitudes toward drinking, can, in fact, come to their own conclusions about whether and how they should drink as well (or poorly) as adults can.

A biased presentation of alcohol education or any attempt on your part to promote your personal views about drinking with your students will be unsuccessful because, given the wide diversity in our society regarding what is felt to be responsible drinking behavior, most students will wonder why your drinking advice is any better than the other recommendations to which they are exposed from parents, peers, advertisements, and the media.

In addition, students should be encouraged to come to their own conclusions about drinking so that they learn the process of independent thinking—a skill that can then, hopefully, be transferred to other critical problems where responsible decision making is important. Trying to make up your students' minds about drinking for them defeats this important skill building goal.

Finally, and perhaps most importantly, by allowing your attitudes toward drinking to be expressed in your teaching you may inhibit your students from surfacing and exploring *their* attitudes about alcohol because their attention has been drawn to you and not to their own mental state. And it is primarily through the examination of their own feelings about drinking that most students will come to understand the role alcohol plays in their lives and be able to make responsible decisions about drinking and abstaining.

TWO APPROACHES TO TEACHING OBJECTIVELY

There are two approaches you can adopt in order to teach objectively about alcohol and avoid giving your students advice about what their current or future drinking practices should be. The first is to be honest about your attitudes and feelings toward drinking by informing your students what they are but also indicate that they are only your opinions and that you will not allow these feelings to bias your teaching or attempt to have your students adopt them as their own. The second approach is to refrain consistently from stating your opinions about drinking at all when you teach about alcohol but make clear to your pupils why you are refusing to do so. Let us examine both the educational advantages and drawbacks to each of these approaches and also the practical implications of how to implement them in the classroom. Keep in mind, however, that while you may decide that you will be most effective in the classroom if you consistently follow only one of these approaches, you may also find it useful to express complete frankness at some points in your teaching and withhold your opinions entirely at others.

The Candor Approach

There are a number of arguments for expressing with candor your attitudes toward drinking and your drinking experience to your students—with the proviso that you do not allow these feelings and practices to bias your teaching.

1. You are being hypocritical if you expect your students to express *their* opinions and feelings about alcohol but refuse to do so yourself. You may even inhibit your students from being open and honest if you

refuse to set a good example of openness. By being honest about your own feelings and experiences, you provide a role model for how your students should also approach the study of alcohol. A vigorous give-and-take can be encouraged in the classroom where everyone shares and compares his or her opinions and experiences and learns to evaluate the attitudes and practices of others in the class—including yours.

2. By being honest about your feelings and practices, your students can be alert for evidences of bias in your teaching. Trying to hide your attitudes may not work—one way or another they may creep into and bias your teaching. Therefore, if you forewarn your students about your biases, they can evaluate what you say about alcohol in light of your acknowledged feelings on the topic.

3. Keeping your feelings about alcohol to yourself and not telling your students about your drinking experiences may continue to place alcohol in the taboo realm of illicit use and thereby reinforce the mystique about drinking that appears to promote youthful (and adult) alcohol abuse. "Hiding" one's feelings about drinking and one's drinking practices may encourage your students to feel that they too should not subject their attitudes and behaviors to the scrutiny of others because they should be ashamed or feel guilty about them. By disclosing, comparing, and evaluating our drinking or abstention practices in an educational setting, students and teachers alike can consider modifying any unhealthy habits they may have.

If you choose to implement this "candor" approach to teaching about alcohol objectively and consistently throughout your alcohol education unit, begin your unit by describing your feelings about alcohol and your drinking practices to your students and explain why you are doing so. Indicate that while you hold these opinions and have had these experiences you will do your best to teach them alcohol as objectively as possible. During your unit, you may wish to periodically or consistently state your opinion on the issue under consideration to let your students know where you stand on the topic. The important consideration in implementing the candor approach is to make sure that your purpose in expressing your opinions and describing your drinking practices is one or more of the ones described above and not one of trying to influence your students to adopt your attitudes or practices.

The Nonopinion Approach

There are also cogent reasons for *not* describing your drinking practices or feelings about alcohol to your students.

1. If you don't drink, you may be concerned that if your students know this they may discount everything you have to say about alcohol as coming from someone whose knowledge comes secondhand from books and is therefore inadequate or inaccurate. It is sometimes possible to prevent students from feeling this way if they are unaware of an abstaining teacher's personal drinking or current practices.

   Contrariwise, if you are an instructor who got drunk or drove after drinking as a youngster or do so now as an adult, you may be concerned that if your students become aware of these facts they may find justification for their own drinking behaviors in your use of alcohol. Unfortunately, many of us still engage in the practice of telling youth to "Do as I say, not as I do," and the instructor who puts himself or herself in this position is going to lose all credibility with his or her students. This dilemma can be resolved by not telling students anything about your feelings about alcohol or your drinking experience.

2. A second argument in favor of not revealing your drinking attitudes and practices to students is that parents, school committee persons, or others in the community may disapprove of your opinions or behavior and become concerned about "what is going on in the classroom." Given that our society has no consensus regarding appropriate drinking attitudes or behaviors, you may wish to keep your opinions and experiences to yourself rather than risk antagonizing any segment of the local community.

3. Finally, you may, as many other people do, feel that your drinking practices and experiences, like your sex life, are personal matters that are nobody else's business—or at least not everybody else's business. Or

you may simply feel that these habits are no *student's* business.

How can you implement the nonopinion approach in the classroom? What should you say if your students ask you if you drink or have ever been drunk? What if they want to know your opinion about teenagers getting drunk?

If you plan to consistently withold your attitudes about alcohol use and abuse, one way to respond to these and similar questions is to inform your students *before* you embark on your alcohol education unit that you have certain opinions and feelings about drinking and not drinking but that since they are of no concern to what your students need to learn about alcohol you will not be expressing them. Present honestly any of the reasons given above to which you subscribe as to why you will not be indicating how you personally feel about alcohol and what your drinking practices are and have been. If, during the unit, students ask for your opinions or drinking history, reiterate the reasons you will not answer their questions. If you wish, you can indicate that when the unit is over you will be happy to answer such questions because such information at that time will not interfere with your teaching efforts and your students' study of alcohol.

A final point needs stressing in terms of teaching about alcohol. Whether you choose to reveal your opinions and practices regarding alcohol or not, lying about them is the worst possible course of action. Few of us can lie convincingly with most youngsters, and attempting to do so and failing will make everything you have to teach them suspect, if not completely worthless, in their eyes. Better to relate your drinking experiences and opinions honestly or else indicate candidly why you won't talk about them rather than to fib.

HOW TO TEACH OBJECTIVELY ABOUT ALCOHOL

Whether you decide to adopt the "candor" approach or the "nonopinion" approach to alcohol education on a given topic of discussion or consistently throughout your teaching, your success in either approach will depend in large part on *the extent to which you are aware of, understand, and are comfortable with your own drinking practices and feelings about alcohol.* If you haven't carefully examined them, you will not be able to keep your biases from influencing how you teach about alcohol. On the one hand, if you decide to tell your students your attitudes and drinking experiences, you will have difficulty doing so if you haven't clarified your feelings to yourself to the point where you can communicate them in an understandable manner. On the other hand, if you keep your opinions and practices to yourself, they are likely to be revealed despite your best efforts at concealment because you can't hide attitudes that you haven't taken the time to identify in yourself.

Being knowledgeable about and secure in your own attitudes and opinions about drinking will not by itself enable you to remain unbiased about alcohol if you remain unaware of how others regard questions of alcohol use and abuse differently from you. It is therefore essential that you become familiar with, understand, and be able to express objectively several *alternative* views about alcohol issues as well as your own opinions.

Because it is so important that you become familiar with and comfortable with your feelings about alcohol and your drinking practices—and those of other people—a major section of chapter 9 is devoted to ways you can explore these attitudes and behaviors as a part of in-service education or teacher training programs. You can also address many of the issues discussed in that chapter by yourself or independently with one or two other teachers or family members. You should also be prepared to admit that if you have mixed feelings or misgivings about your attitudes toward alcohol or the way you drink or abstain, you probably shouldn't be teaching this topic. But if you can spend time exploring your feelings and practices with regard to drinking, you may develop two of the major prerequisites to being able to teach objectively about alcohol: self-insight and self-acceptance.

Guidelines for Teaching Objectively

As we mentioned earlier, whether you choose to adopt the "candor" or the "nonopinion" approach, you will want to be careful always to present alcohol education issues and facts without bias. How can you do this successfully and consistently?

1. Welcome all student opinions nonjudgmentally. This does not mean simply tolerating divergent views; it means actively soliciting them by adhering to the following guidelines:
   - Indicate that on most issues related to alcohol use there are no "right" or "wrong" answers
   - Explicitly ask your students to express their views and feelings and indicate that while you of course have opinions and feelings of your own you will not express any *judgments* of what the students say.
   - Ask open-ended questions, such as, "Is it all right to get drunk or not?" rather than, "Why is it wrong (or right) to get drunk?"
   - Insist that when a student answers an open-ended question, that other students, not you, respond to his or her opinions and feelings.
   - Avoid making moral judgments about alcohol, such as, "It's *wrong* to drive while under the influence." Say "It's *dangerous* to drive while under the influence."
   - Include in quizzes and tests, opinion questions that are not graded on the basis of what opinions students express but are either ungraded or graded on the basis of how well the opinions were substantiated and argued.

2. Repeatedly encourage your students to address their opinions to each other and continually urge students to respond to each other's comments and to avoid directing their discussion to you.

3. Have your students discuss issue-oriented questions in small groups where emphasis is placed on the expression and substantiation of opinions and not on trying to please you.

4. Ignore occasions when your students seem to "get off the track" in a discussion and talk about feelings that seem unrelated to the alcohol issue at hand. Often these so-called "irrelevant" opinions and feelings are the basis for students' (and adults') feelings about alcohol. For example, a discussion of whether man has free will can be significant in shaping one's feelings about whether alcoholics and problem drinkers are morally "debased" or ill people.

5. Know the major facts about alcohol—such as those presented in chapters 3 and 4 of this book. For example, it is easy to express a bias against alcohol use by saying that it's

dangerous to drive after drinking. For many people, a drink or two before driving, depending on whether they've eaten first and how much time elapses between the drinking and the driving, will have no significant effect on their ability to drive. Don't claim, "Getting drunk always involves serious risks," unless you can document your assertion (you probably can't!). Don't say that alcoholics can learn to drink again socially—the evidence is conflicting. When in doubt about the facts, admit your ignorance and postpone saying *anything* until you've had a chance to do some more research into the answers. Even better, help your students to research the answer for themselves. Otherwise, your answer may reflect your biases about drinking and abstaining more than it reflects the facts.

6. Point out the positive uses alcohol fills for a majority of people and stress the enjoyment most people derive from drinking. This guideline for teaching objectively about alcohol is so important that it merits further discussion.

Stressing the Pleasures of Drinking

Most youngsters know very well that a majority of people find drinking pleasurable. As a result, if you fail to discuss this enjoyment, you risk losing your students' confidence in the trustworthiness of what you have to say about alcohol *abuse*. If you can ignore the delights of drinking, your students may assume that you are liable to exaggerate the dangers. Therefore, very early in your unit on alcohol you should focus on the enjoyment of drinking in order to gain your students' immediate confidence that you will be teaching objectively about drinking. The pleasures of drinking are different for different people. Some of them include the following:

- creating a feeling of relaxation
- savoring the taste
- getting high and feeling happy
- getting drunk and losing some control
- sharing a meaningful social ritual with friends, family, or strangers
- improving the taste of food
- relating to other people better
- forgetting minor worries
- increasing the fun of an already enjoyable event

- signifying the importance of a special occasion

Objectively presenting the pleasures of drinking not only requires devoting adequate time to their study, it also necessitates your approaching the topic with a positive frame of mind. Many instructors discuss the enjoyment of drinking begrudgingly or with considerable hedging—"Drinking can help some people to relax, *but* ...." They may feel that it is important to qualify their descriptions of the enjoyment of drinking because they are concerned about possible parental objections to any straightforward presentation of the positive functions alcohol serves in our society. Some teachers also feel that their students are too young to be drinking or too suggestible to know how to set limits on an enjoyable activity whose abuse is dangerous. Another more complex problem from an educational point of view is that presenting drinking as normal and beneficial for a majority of adults may cause some students who are abstainers to assume that something is "wrong" with them and their families for failing to participate in such an apparently desirable activity.

There are two educational strategies you can adopt that will help avoid any potential community repercussions, student misinterpretations, and student alienation resulting from a study of drinking's pleasures. (1) Choose your words carefully in talking about the enjoyment of drinking. Use such phrasing as, "*Many* people find that drinking . . ." and "Alcohol use has the pleasurable effect for *some* drinkers of . . ." Over time, the cumulative effect of such consistently guarded statements can help clarify that drinking is not an enjoyable or acceptable practice to millions of people, nor should we expect it to be. (2) After conducting class activities focusing on the pleasures of drinking, discuss why 20–30 million teenagers and adults in the United States have chosen *not* to drink at all and another several million have decided to drink less than once a month. The reasons for abstaining or drinking infrequently must be presented as being as sensible and acceptable as those given for why most people do drink.

Activity #4 (at the end of the book) is devoted to studying the reasons people drink and abstain and why a majority of Americans find the use of alcohol pleasurable. The activity contains a number of exercises that you can have your students engage in early in your unit so that they realize as soon as possible that you will be presenting alcohol education to them with complete objectivity. This combination of an objective presentation on your part and appropriate followup activities on the pleasures of drinking can help ensure that your students will move on to study alcohol's dangers, ready to accept open-mindedly whatever negative conclusions the evidence warrants.

Using Alcohol Education Materials

A final point with regard to objectively teaching about drinking or abstaining relates to the fact that many alcohol education materials—films, booklets, fact sheets, etc.—are themselves biased in their presentation of alcohol use, nonuse, and abuse. Many of the materials we have recommended in the Resources section contain some bias. This partiality is unavoidable largely because of the many misconceptions most people have about drinking and because many publishers of educational materials are reluctant to portray the enjoyment of drinking in an honestly favorable light. The question arises, how can you use these materials without hampering your efforts to develop an objective alcohol education unit?

With any material you use (including materials from this book and ones you develop yourself), ask your students to see if *they* can detect any instances of bias in the publication or film. Point out some lapses in objectivity that you have noticed. Then ask the class why it thinks these biases appear in the material. A useful exercise might be to have your students read two different accounts or view two different audiovisual presentations about the same alcohol topic and have them compare the different treatments of drinking. Which treatment was the more objective? Why? Such an analysis can lead naturally into a discussion or study of whom we *can* rely on for accurate information about alcohol. The very lack of objectivity in so many alcohol education materials can thus be turned to positive educational use if you capitalize on the biases to help students to become critical users of all alcohol-related materials. This approach will be most successful if you encourage your students to be alert for instances of bias not only in what they read and view, but also in what you have to say about alcohol.*

*As a curious but worthwhile exercise in detecting bias, you might consider which position—candor or nonopinion—the authors actually favor. While we have tried to adopt the nonopinion approach in writing this chapter, our preference for how to teach about alcohol in the classroom may nonetheless have seeped through.

ADDITIONAL READING

Finn, Peter. "The Role of Attitudes in Public School Alcohol Education." *Journal of Alcohol and Drug Education* 20 (1975):23–42.
———. "Alcohol Education and the Pleasures of Drinking." *Health Education* 8 (1977):17–19.

U.S. Department of Health, Education, and Welfare. *The Drinking Question: Honest Answers to Questions Teenagers Ask about Drinking.* Washington, D.C.: U.S. Government Printing Office, 1976.

Working with Parents
and the Community

Education about alcohol, as with education about many "nonacademic" subjects, has historically been a function of the home and the religious congregation of the student. In the past, this approach presented no problem to the school since most adolescents drank in small numbers in a manner that did not disrupt the school's functioning or did not drink at all until they completed high school (see chapters 3 and 4).

The school has, over the last ten years, become more concerned with alcohol education as the drinking practices of students have changed, with students drinking at an earlier age, girls drinking more, and students becoming intoxicated more often—or at least more visibly (see chapter 4). These changes in our youth's drinking patterns have occurred at a time when there is a growing consensus that "the nuclear family is in danger" and "individuals have fallen away from their traditional religious beliefs." The school, as an apparently stable institution amidst

this climate of change, has therefore sought to fill the gap left by shrinking or ineffective parental and religious control over youth's drinking practices, just as it has intervened in such areas as sex education and career education.

THE MERITS AND DRAWBACKS
OF PARENTAL INVOLVEMENT

An analogy is also often made between alcohol education and drug education. However, in order to understand the reaction of local parents and the community to alcohol education, sex education is a more appropriate comparison, because whereas most parents agree that illicit drug use is clearly to be discouraged, they disagree over what constitutes acceptable drinking and sexual behavior and therefore over what kinds of drinking and sexual practices the schools should promote or discourage. Furthermore, parental sensitivity to what their children are taught about alcohol (and sex) is heightened in many cases by their own uncertainty regarding the appropriateness of their own personal use of alcohol (and sexual activities), whereas most parents feel secure that they are not abusers of heroin, LSD, or marijuana. In short, alcohol education in the schools can become an unwelcome (although positive) stimulus for parents to examine and question their own drinking behavior. Further, alcohol education may make some parents initially or continuously uncomfortable due to problems they, a family member, or close friend may have with alcohol abuse.

For all these reasons, parents in the local community may have serious objections to your teaching about alcohol to their children or reservations about how you are offering instruction in this area. It is therefore important that any school that plans to introduce this topic initiate and maintain a dialogue with parents regarding the instructional content and approaches it plans to develop so that any relevant parental concerns can be addressed before the unit is taught rather than later when the community's concerns can no longer be accommodated.

There are other cogent reasons, as well, for involving parents and the community in your alcohol education efforts. Many parents have considerable experience with adolescent alcohol use and abuse and possess significant insight into the phenomenon of adolescent drinking. These parents can help improve any alcohol education program that a school plans to offer. Involving interested agencies in the community, as well as parents, can strengthen support for school instruction in this area. Parent-teacher associations, civic groups (Chambers of Commerce, Rotary Clubs, Lions, Elks, Jaycees), religious organizations, treatment agencies, councils on alcoholism, preventive health clinics, business associations, and various professional groups can not only provide public support for your instructional efforts but also supply concrete resources and guidance for the implementation of your program.

Finally, failure to coordinate alcohol education approaches with community values may lead to instances in which youngsters are told or taught one thing about drinking in the schools and something different or even contrary in the home. This can result in placing the child in the middle of a painful and unproductive parent-school power struggle for his or her allegiance.

While the reasons for informing the local community about your alcohol education efforts are compelling on practical, educational, and ethical grounds, there can be drawbacks to such consultation. First, there is always the possibility that you will only be "stirring up a hornet's nest" when you should have "let sleeping dogs lie." Teaching about drinking without informing the community of your plans may simplify your task because parents may never conceive of the topic as controversial if you do not identify it as such by introducing it to them. Drawing community attention to the unit might thus create a concern in the community where none existed or needed to exist.

This objection to consulting with the community is not one that can be glibly rejected. If schools conferred with parents regarding everything they taught, there would be no time in which to teach. Moreover, instructors might create unnecessary apprehensions among parents by constantly soliciting their opinions and approval. On balance, however, we feel that this is an attitude that is patronizing toward parents because it assumes they do not have the intelligence or experience to distinguish between when they should leave educational matters to the discretion of the school and when they are qualified and entitled to offer their suggestions. Further, as we noted earlier, alcohol use and abuse is a field of study that, unlike mathematics, English, or social studies, many parents may feel should not be taught in the schools at all. Parents deserve to be consulted on a matter that they may believe is not the prerogative of the educational system to address.

Finally, on purely "tactical" grounds, it is usually better in the long run to anticipate and address potential parental concerns on this issue before you teach about alcohol, while there is still time to resolve any problems that may arise, rather than go ahead and teach your unit and potentially be faced with the community's ire after the fact. Often the simple courtesy of offering to involve parents in your plans is more than sufficient to satisfy the concerns of the average parent. Rather than stirring up a hornet's nest, you will probably be giving honey to bumble bees.

A second potential drawback to involving the community in an alcohol education program is that parents may express a number of *different* opinions regarding how the topic should be taught—or whether it should be taught at all. These disparate recommendations could create confusion and result in the conclusion that nothing can be taught about alcohol use and abuse that will not upset some segment of the community.

This outcome of parental involvement is a definite possibility. However, if the community itself is seriously divided over drinking issues, it may indeed be best not to offer alcohol education in the schools (although this may be precisely the type of community whose youngsters need it most). More likely is the eventuality that if diverse views result from your community contacts you will still be able to find some common ground on which to develop your curriculum. Even if you can't, it is well to remember that *consulting with parents does not necessarily mean acceding to their wishes in every or even most respects*. It may be sufficient to indicate that you appreciate their views but that on educational grounds you will have to teach about alcohol use and abuse in the way you originally planned. At least you will have met the important duty of both informing parents of what you will be doing in the classroom with their children and also providing them with at least the opportunity to offer their opinions of your plans.

ESSENTIAL CONSIDERATIONS IN COMMUNICATING WITH PARENTS

Five considerations should guide the efforts of you and your school to stimulate parent participation in your alcohol education plans.

1. The school has the right to take *an educational leadership role* in the community and to propose an approach to alcohol instruction that it feels is appropriate.
2. It is impossible to *predict* what the attitudes of the parents in your community may be toward alcohol education in the school. What opinions are held and how strongly they are maintained may be influenced by the race, sex, age, socioeconomic status, religion, and ethnic origins of the residents, as well as their personal experiences with alcohol use and abuse. Community feelings may also vary depending on the grade level or levels at which you propose to offer instruction about alcohol.
3. Be alert for attitudes on the part of both parents and community groups that may be at odds with your approaches, and *be prepared with sound, reasonable explanations for why your methods are valid*. In addition, secure the support of your school administration for your plans before you talk with any parents or community groups.
4. Realize that *parents may react differently to you* depending on how well they already know you, your age, your teaching experience, what grade level you teach, what they know or suspect about your drinking behavior—or that of members of your family—and even your sex. There may be ways to buttress the impression you make on parents, for example by having a better known, older, or more experienced teacher than yourself join you in cosponsoring the alcohol education unit and in meeting with parents in order to provide you with a "seal" of approval. You should also consider carefully what you may want to tell parents who may ask about your personal attitudes toward alcohol use and abuse and whether and in what fashion you drink. You may wish to volunteer some or all of this information and not wait for parents to inquire about it.

There are several ways in which you or your school can work with parents in the development of an alcohol education program. Realistically speaking, however, you and your school administrators may feel you do not have the time to involve the community. Many teachers and school administrators are already overburdened with work, and adding the task of facilitating parental participation in what will probably be a relatively small part of your curriculum may be an unrealistic and unwelcome responsibility to add. However, there are ways to involve the community which are not time consuming or complicated, as we will describe below.

Lack of time on the part of parents to become involved with the schools, or just plain apathy, may render your most conscientious efforts to communicate with the community fruitless. In a National Education Association (NEA) nationwide survey of 1,500 teachers who were members of the NEA, parental indifference was selected as their first choice from among thirty instruction-related problems. However, anticipation of lack of time or interest among parents in alcohol education should not deter you from attempting to stimulate their participation. It may turn out that there are a few parents who are able or motivated to get involved, and this limited participation may prove very beneficial in terms of the assistance they provide to your teaching efforts and the positive reactions to your instruction which they may share with other parents in the community.

METHODS FOR INVOLVING PARENTS

Approaches to involving parents can be quick and simple or time consuming and complex. On the easy end of the spectrum, you can, after consultation with your department head or principal, send a letter to your students' parents explaining why you will be teaching about alcohol use and abuse, what topics you will be covering, and how you will assure objectivity in your instruction. You can solicit parental reactions and suggestions by inviting them to telephone you, meet with you after school or during free periods, or write to you.

In conjunction with letter writing, or instead of it, you can present the suggested contents of the letter described above to your school committee and to relevant community groups, such as religious organizations, business associations (Rotary, Chamber of Commerce), and fraternal, sororal, and civic groups (League of Women Voters, Elks). One particularly productive form of school-community collaboration may involve working with local Parent-Teacher Associations (PTAs) where these exist. The National PTA has developed several alcohol education guides under grants from the National Institute on Alcohol Abuse and Alcoholism. This national commitment in PTA can provide a helpful entree for working on alcohol education programs with local PTAs.

Another approach to securing parent opinions and participation lies in asking randomly selected parents or key parent leaders in the community to respond to a brief questionnaire that solicits their views on alcohol education in the schools. At the end of this chapter we have provided a sample questionnaire that you can use as is or that you can adapt for this purpose. The questions were developed in conjunction with a small group of parents and then pilot tested on a larger group of parents. By implementing the questionnaire, you can apply what you learn to the task of tailoring your alcohol education course to meet reasonable expectations and demands of the local community. You can also use the questionnaire to inform parents about your alcohol education plans in a positive manner that might garner support for and reduce opposition to it. Used this way, the survey would enable you to adapt your teaching to accommodate concerns of the parents and at the same time educate them to the rationale for the instructional approaches you plan to implement.

You can use the questionnaire for other purposes, as well. You can use it to assess changes in the attitudes toward alcohol education of parents whose children participate in your alcohol education course. In this way, you can learn what the effects of your teaching are on parents if your students are encouraged to share at home what they learn in your classroom. You can also use the questionnaire to determine changes in your students' attitudes toward alcohol education as a result of their having participated in your course. This purpose becomes especially important when we consider that today's students will become tomorrow's school board members, teachers, and taxpayers who will exert a major influence on what kind of alcohol education schools provide for the next generation of youngsters.

Yet another use for the survey is to assess the attitudes of teachers toward alcohol education in the schools. Before teachers engage in alcohol education, a department head or curriculum coordinator can have them complete the questionnaire as a means of identifying inappropriate attitudes toward alcohol education that need attention in teacher training workshops (see chapter 9). Used in this manner, the questionnaire becomes a diagnostic tool for bringing to light areas in which future alcohol educators may need help in order to become effective instructors in this field. For example, responses to questions 1–3 on whether teachers feel alcohol education in the schools is important can be used to determine what kind of effort is needed to help instructors to understand the rationale for alcohol education so that they can teach about drinking knowing that their instruction will be worthwhile. Question 6 can provide information regarding the instructional methods that teachers feel should be used for alcohol education. If teachers select methods that a cur- riculum coordinator or department head feels are inappropriate or not useful, efforts can be made to help them appreciate the value of and learn how to implement other instructional strategies.

ADDITIONAL READING

Finn, Peter. "The Development of Attitudinal Measures toward Alcohol Education in the School and in the Home." *Journal of Drug Education* 8 (1978): 203-219.

——. *Alcohol Education for Parents: A Report of an Alcohol Education Study*. Chicago: The National Parent Teacher Association, 1978.

Globetti, Gerald, and Pomeroy, Grace. "Characteristics of Community Residents Who Are Favorable toward Alcohol Education." *Mental Hygiene* 54 (1970): 411-415.

National Parent Teacher Association. *How to Talk to Your Teenager about Drinking and Driving*. Rockville, Md.: National Clearinghouse for Alcohol Information, n.d.

O'Gorman, Patricia A., and Stringfield, Sharon, eds. *Alcohol Education: What It Is and How to Do It*. New York: National Council on Alcoholism, 1978.

Ryan, Charlotte. *The Open Partnership: Equality in Running the Schools*. New York: McGraw-Hill Book Co., 1976.

Sayler, Mary Lou. *Parents: Active Partners in Education*. Washington, D.C.: National Education Association, 1971.

A Survey

ALCOHOL EDUCATION IN THE SCHOOLS

The following questions describe many opinions about alcohol education in the public schools and ask you what yours are.

1. How important is it that alcohol education be taught at the *elementary school* level?
    ☐ not important   ☐ very important
    ☐ somewhat important

2. How important is it that alcohol education be taught at the *junior high school* level?
    ☐ not important   ☐ very important
    ☐ somewhat important

3. How important is it that alcohol education be taught at the *senior high school* level?
    ☐ not important   ☐ very important
    ☐ somewhat important

4. The following list presents reasons why you may feel schools should *not* be teaching alcohol education *at any grade level*. After reading through the list, place a "1" next to all the reasons you agree with *very strongly* and a "2" next to all the reasons you agree with *moderately*. Leave the other reasons blank.
    __ Only parents or the church should teach about alcohol.
    __ Teachers aren't trained to teach about alcohol effectively.
    __ Kids don't learn attitudes or behaviors from teachers.
    __ Teachers might say things about drinking which parents don't agree with.
    __ Teachers might tell students to make up their own minds about whether and how to drink.
    __ There are more important things that the schools should be teaching.
    __ Alcohol education in the schools will create conflict between students and parents.
    __ Teaching youngsters about alcohol may make them curious about trying it.
    __ Alcohol might be discussed in ways which force parents to justify or defend their drinking behavior to their children.
    __ Students might reveal personal family drinking behaviors to the teacher or to other students.
    What are other reasons, if any, why alcohol education should not be taught in the schools?
    _____
    _____
    _____

5. How much can a good alcohol education course in the schools help students to avoid drinking problems now or in the future?
    ☐ not at all   ☐ some
    ☐ a little   ☐ a lot

6. Assuming that alcohol education were taught in school, *how* do you think it should be taught? After reading through the list of possible methods which follows, place a "1" next to all the *very important* methods and a "2" next to all the *somewhat important* methods. Leave the other methods blank.
    __ by stressing that it is dangerous for adolescents to drink at all
    __ by stressing that adolescents should not drink at all except with their parents

(continued)

Source: Adapted from Peter Finn, "The Development of Attitudinal Measures toward Alcohol Education in the School and in the Home," *Journal of Drug Education* 8(3), 1978, 203–219. © 1978, Baywood Publishing Co., Inc. Reprinted by permission. Developed in conjunction with the Massachusetts Parent-Teacher-Student Association and with the assistance of Dr. Charlotte Ryan and Vincent Scardino.

___ by helping students to make up their own mind about whether and how they drink
___ by presenting the facts about alcohol's potentially harmful effects
___ by presenting what many people feel are the useful functions drinking serves as well as the dangers
___ by having students explore alcohol issues in small discussion groups
___ by having members of Alcoholics Anonymous talk with students
___ by taking a field trip to Skid Row
___ by suggesting a variety of strategies for coping with peer and other pressures to drink
What other ways, if any, should alcohol education be taught?
_____
_____
_____

7. Should parents become involved in alcohol education in schools? ☐ Yes ☐ No
If you answered "No" skip to question 8. If you answered "Yes," *how* should parents get involved with alcohol education in the schools? After reading through the list of ways parents might get involved with alcohol education suggested below, place a "1" next to all the *very important* ways and a "2" next to all the *somewhat important* ways. Leave the others blank.
___ by joining a panel of parents and teachers to help plan an alcohol education program
___ by evaluating and modifying an existing alcohol education program
___ by asking their children what went on during the alcohol education course each day
___ by meeting with teachers who will be teaching about alcohol to ask questions and offer suggestions
___ by participating in class if teacher and students approve
___ by finding community resources (speakers, films, booklets, etc.) which will help teachers
___ by helping teachers take students on field trips to breweries, alcoholism treatment clinincs, etc.
___ by helping children with their homework
___ by expressing support for an alcohol education program (attending school committee meetings, expressing approval to the principal, etc.)
What are other ways, if any, in which parents might get involved with alcohol education in the schools?
_____
_____
_____

8. The following list includes some of the reasons you might have for *not* wanting to get involved with alcohol education in the schools. After reading through the list, place a "1" next to the *very important* reasons and a "2" next to all the *somewhat important* reasons. Leave the other reasons blank.
___ Alcohol isn't that much of a problem for students.
___ Parents don't have enough information to help out.
___ Parents are too busy to help out.
___ Parents will just try to have their own point of view about drinking adopted by the school.
___ Education should be left up to the schools.
___ Teachers don't welcome assistance or suggestions from parents.
___ Youngsters would be upset if they knew their parents were involved in a school program.

(continued)

_ Parents might be afraid their personal drinking habits would be discussed.

_ Parent assistance wouldn't be taken seriously by teachers — it would be a token exercise.

What other reasons, if any, might motivate you not to want to get involved with alcohol education in the schools?

_____

_____

9. What would *encourage* you to get involved with alcohol education in the schools? After reading through the list of possible things which might motivate you, place a "1" next to all the *very important* things which would encourage you to get involved with alcohol education in the schools and a "2" next to all the *somewhat important* things. Leave the other ideas blank.

_ seminars or workshops

_ notices sent home by the school

_ special all-school meetings for parents

_ having students involve their parents as part of their homework assignments

_ making literature on alcohol available to parents in the school and town libraries

_ sending pamphlets on alcohol to parents and including articles on alcohol in the town newspaper(s)

_ word-of-mouth support from other parents

_ request from your children to get involved

What other things, if any, might encourage you to get involved with alcohol education in the schools?

_____

_____

_____

9

Teacher Training in Alcohol Education

The importance of training teachers to be effective alcohol educators cannot be overstressed. Because alcohol education deals with strongly held values and feelings, and because its ultimate goal is to fashion or change attitudes and behavior, instructors need special skills to be able to teach effectively in this field.

The training of educators in alcohol education occurs in several settings including:

- in-service and continuing education programs
- schools of education
- summer schools of alcohol studies

In this chapter, we suggest in detail the issues teacher training in alcohol education should treat and the training methods most likely to help teachers to address these issues successfully. The chapter concludes with an illustration of a training program that focuses on these issues and incorporates these training methods.

GOALS AND ISSUES IN TEACHER TRAINING

Training teachers to be effective alcohol educators should attempt to achieve four principal goals. It should promote in teachers the development of:

1. *attitudes and values* that are conducive to effective alcohol education
2. the ability to teach *objectively* about alcohol
3. *information* about alcohol use, nonuse, and abuse
4. the ability to implement effective *teaching approaches* and communicate effectively with students.

Let us examine each of these goals in detail.

1. Developing Attitudes and Values that Are Conducive to Effective Alcohol Education

People who plan to teach about alcohol need to identify, clarify, and explore their own attitudes and feelings about drinking and their own drinking or abstention behavior if they are to be able to help others successfully do the same. This analysis of attitudes should help them appreciate the appropriateness of many of the disparate drinking practices and attitudes toward alcohol that are prevalent in our society so they can avoid imposing—deliberately or unwittingly—their own personal opinions on their students. Teachers also need to become comfortable with their own attitudes and drinking practices in order to respond constructively when students query them about their own use of alcohol, and in order to role model positive attitudes toward alcohol for their pupils.

Teachers can move on from an examination of their own attitudes to discuss (1) what they feel are effective means for stimulating students to explore their own attitudes toward drinking; (2) why it is essential that students do so; and (3) how teachers can promote appropriate attitudes toward drinking on the part of their students.

A list of key attitudinal issues which teachers need to address follows.* A few of these discussion points appear to be matters of fact, not attitude. However, the very process of trying to reach a consensus on them will surface many teacher attitudes toward drinking. The attitudes which are revealed during these discussions can then be identified and further explored.

- Should alcohol be viewed as a drug, food, beverage, or all three?
- Should youngsters drink? If so, at what age and under what conditions?
- What should the legal drinking age be?

*The discussion points are presented in this section largely in the form of questions. This approach has been used because for many alcohol education issues there are no "right" or "wrong" answers (for example, the way a teacher should respond to a student who reveals that his father has a drinking problem). In addition, it is hoped that teacher trainers will implement this same open-ended approach when they discuss these issues with the teachers who are being trained, placing the responsibility on *them* to formulate functional answers to the many unresolved issues involved in teaching about alcohol.

- Why do some people abstain and others drink? Are there inappropriate reasons for not drinking and appropriate ones for drinking in moderation? Are there ever defensible reasons for drinking to excess (e.g., getting drunk)?
- How are women who drink and men who abstain viewed by different segments of our society?
- How strong is peer pressure among adolescents to drink and drink abusively? How is it exerted?
- How should youngsters and adults respond to peer pressure to drink, drink abusively, or abstain?
- Should people encourage each other to adopt their own drinking or abstention practices?
- Are there risks adults can take when they drink that youngsters should not? Is the reverse ever the case?
- Why do people take risks? How can we decide which risks are "worth" taking and which are not?
- How should teachers react to teenage intoxication? Should it be viewed as a problem or as a warning signal of a future problem? If not, should it be seen as a benign example of youthful boisterousness? Or—something else?
- Is there peer pressure among adults to use or abuse alcohol? If so, why and how is it exerted? Is it different from peer pressure among adolescents?
- Are there ways people with drinking problems can be identified?
- Is there a difference between problem drinking and alcoholism?
- Why do some people develop drinking problems?
- How should people feel about teenagers who have drinking problems?
- Can teenagers become alcoholics?
- How should people feel toward adults with drinking problems? Should they be viewed differently from teenagers with drinking problems?
- How do and should we feel about people who deny that they have or that someone they know has a drinking problem?
- What behaviors would influence how one evaluates intoxication by a youngster?
- How should adults react to moderate teenage use of alcohol?
- What constitutes moderate drinking and what is abusive drinking?

- Are problem drinking and alcoholism treatable?
- What methods, if any, are effective in treating problem drinkers and alcoholics?
- Should people give advice on how to handle personal drinking problems? Should people try to help friends who come to them with drinking problems? Should they volunteer help? What if they are not sure the friend has a drinking problem?
- How should family members respond to a parent, sibling, or child who has a drinking problem?
- How do and should we feel about people who drive after moderate drinking or after drinking to excess?
- Are there health consequences of even moderate alcohol use?
- Should people be responsible for friends (or strangers) who are about to drive while impaired or who are about to ride with an impaired driver?
- What role, if any, should parents take in educating their children regarding alcohol?

The following are several learning activities that may be found in the Instructional Activities section at the end of the book that will help teachers to surface, clarify, compare, and, if appropriate, modify their attitudes and values with regard to alcohol.

- Teachers role play and react to scenarios in which parents find their children drinking, drunk, or high, or driving after drinking. (Activity #18)
- Teachers complete unfinished stories about drinking conflicts between youngsters and their parents and discuss the completions. (Activity #19)
- Teachers discuss what restrictions they would or do set for their children on drinking and why. (Activity #20)
- Teachers engage in one or more activities revolving around issues of responsibility for other people's drinking behavior. (Activity #22)
- Teachers design, take, and administer one or more questionnaires regarding drinking experience and attitudes toward drinking. (Activity #24)
- Teachers discuss whether and when it may be appropriate to get drunk. (Activity #3)

- Teachers role play a town council meeting discussing local option. (Activity #5)
- Teachers discuss what they think constitutes excessive and problem drinking. (Activity #25)
- Teachers discuss giving money to alcoholic panhandlers and examine the attitudes toward alcoholism that surface during their discussion. (Activity #27)
- Teachers role play scenes in which a parent is concerned about his or her child's friendship with the child of an alcoholic and then discuss the attitudes toward alcoholics revealed in the simulation. (Activity #28)
- Teachers role play scenes in which non-alcoholics and alcoholics must interact; teachers then discuss their feelings about alcoholics and how best to help such persons. (Activity #29)

2. Developing Ability to Teach Objectively about Alcohol

Learning to teach objectively about drinking is one of the most subtle skills alcohol educators must develop.* However, before deciding *how* to teach without bias in this emotion-laden area of human behavior, teachers need to *define* "objectivity" in terms they can comfortably embrace and easily put into practice. For example, objectivity in alcohol education can mean:

a. remaining publicly neutral about one's personal opinions regarding alcohol in order to avoid encouraging students to parrot back what they think the teacher wants to hear and in order to stimulate students to express and explore their own attitudes toward drinking

b. presenting information and posing questions about drinking in ways that enable students to make up their own minds about the many unresolved issues related to alcohol use, abuse, and nonuse

c. understanding one's own feelings about drinking and being true to oneself in teaching about alcohol—that is, expressing one's

*Complete objectivity is probably impossible for most of us. The point is to become objective enough so that our biases do not interfere with achieving our teaching objectives.

opinions openly and honestly and encouraging students to do the same.

Having arrived at their own definition of objectivity, teachers need to decide how they can present or respond to the following facets of alcohol use and abuse in an objective manner:

- moderate drinking by youngsters
- youthful intoxication
- moderate drinking by adults
- intoxication by adults
- the physical, behavioral, and social effects of alcohol
- the physical, behavioral, and social effects of alcohol on a drinker who drinks (a) in moderation and (b) to excess
- the effects of alcohol use, nonuse, and abuse on other family members
- the legal drinking age.

Other questions related to objectivity that teachers can address include the following:

- How can teachers present to students in a balanced manner the reasons some people drink and others abstain?
- How can the attitudes of different religious denominations toward alcohol use be discussed in an objective manner? Should they be raised at all?
- How can teachers explain the differences between social drinking and problem drinking without moralizing or seeking to impose their own views?
- How can the dangers of driving after excessive drinking be described without sounding "preachy"?
- Should teachers present, agree with, or have students research the pleasure many people derive from alcohol? If so, how?
- How can a teacher point out an error or bias in a curriculum material or piece of literature without having students conclude that the entire book, pamphlet, or film is worthless?
- How can misinformation or poor advice a student has been given by a parent or peer be corrected convincingly without criticizing the source?
- How can students be helped to sort out the many conflicting opinions about alcohol expressed by lay persons and experts alike? Whom can students be told to seek out for reliable information?

- What stereotypes related to drinking and sex, ethnicity, and age may students have? Should teachers respond if students express any of these stereotypes? If so, how?
- Will teachers compromise their objectivity if they voluntarily or in response to questions from students express their opinions about drinking? Are there certain opinions that should not be expressed or others which should be?
- May the drinking attitudes and practices of teachers facilitate or impair their ability to teach objectively about alcohol? How? What impact may a teacher with a drinking problem have on his or her own students or on other students in the school if pupils know about the problem?

A more detailed discussion of objectivity in alcohol education has been provided in chapter 7. In addition, teachers can fruitfully engage in the following activities taken from the activities at the end of the book and use the exercises to examine how they can offer instruction about drinking and not drinking that does not moralize or present biases.

- Students evaluate "great" and "dumb" things they have done after getting high or drunk or have observed others do after drinking. (Activity #16)
- Students discuss experimenting with drinking. (Activity #17)
- Students role play and react to scenarios in which parents find their children drinking, drunk, or high, or driving after drinking. (Activity #18)
- Students discuss whether and when it may be appropriate to get drunk. (Activity #3)
- Students discuss what they think constitutes excessive and problem drinking. (Activity #25)
- Students role play scenes in which a parent is concerned about his or her child's friendship with the child of an alcoholic and then discuss the attitudes toward alcoholics revealed in the simulation. (Activity #28)

3. Providing Information about Alcohol Use, Nonuse, and Abuse

Teachers need to know basically the same information about drinking that youngsters should learn. Studies have demonstrated that most adults and teenagers share the same misconceptions about alcohol. The "facts" about alcohol that teachers need to become familiar with before teaching about alcohol have been presented in chapters 2, 3, and 4. However, of more significance than what the facts are is how teachers learn these facts and are taught to present them to their students. As we indicated before, teachers should learn about alcohol in the same manner that they will be expected to teach alcohol information to their students: Their own learning process should model the future learning approaches of their students. Information about alcohol should therefore be provided to teachers in the following manner:

- in small doses
- with reinforcement
- in the context of realistic life situations
- through methods that show the teacher trainers as facilitators of learning rather than imparters of information
- through methods that require the teachers to learn about alcohol as much as possible through independent study.

Two other considerations must be addressed with regard to providing teachers with basic background information about alcohol use and abuse. The first is that there are several key areas of study with regard to drinking that are still subject to considerable and at time bitter dispute. Teacher training must help instructors to become familiar with these unresolved issues and decide from among three alternatives how they will approach them. Teachers can choose to:

1. form independent judgements about them
2. rely on the judgement of an "expert" whose opinions they have come to trust
3. suspend judgement about the issue pending the publication of more conclusive findings.

The major issues in the field of alcohol studies that to date are unresolved include the following:

- whether recovered alcoholics can learn to drink again socially and, if so, whether they should experiment to find out
- how much alcohol, if any, a healthy individual can drink on a regular basis without suffering physical damage

- how many drinks a day create risks for the fetus of a pregnant woman
- whether alcoholism can be inherited
- whether alcoholism should be considered a disease
- how to communicate effectively to the public that moderate alcohol use can be hazardous under certain conditions.

Most of these issues have been discussed in chapter 2.

A second consideration in familiarizing teachers with information about alcohol relates to the role knowledge about drinking plays in shaping students' drinking attitudes and behaviors. How much do youngsters at different grade levels need to know? What, exactly, do they need to know? Furthermore, teachers need to consider how much *they* need to know about alcohol in order to teach about it effectively. In general, teacher attitudes and behaviors about alcohol are probably much more important in effecting responsible attitudes toward drinking among students than is knowledge of the facts about alcohol.

Teachers will find it helpful to engage in several of the activities at the end of the book for learning background information about drinking, including the following:

- Students answer an alcohol questionnaire to determine their level of knowledge. (Activity #6)
- Students answer questions about drinking and driving and discuss the answers. (Activity #14)
- Students complete a story involving drinking and driving and discuss whether and how they can tell if someone is too impaired to drive safely. (Activity #15)
- Students trace the passage of alcohol through the body on a specially prepared body chart. (Activity #8)
- Students interview friends (parents in the original activity) regarding the effects of alcohol they experience when they drink. (Activity #13).

In addition, chapters 3 and 4 of this book, as well as the references cited at the ends of these chapters, provide considerable information about alcohol.

4. Promoting the Ability to Implement Effective Teaching Approaches and Communicate Effectively with Students

Providing education regarding alcohol involves the selection of communication strategies with which teachers are comfortable and that are pedagogically sound. However, there is no single technique that alone is effective; many appropriate and productive alternatives are available. Teachers need to become familiar with the wide range of possible approaches and, through discussion and eventually practice, discard those that do not "work" for them or create uneasiness.

Below is a series of questions addressing the multiplicity of teaching approaches to alcohol education that teachers should address in their quest for personally satisfying and effective education techniques. You may also find it helpful to administer the questionnaire provided at the end of chapter 8 as a tool for identifying teachers' attitudes toward alcohol education and which of these attitudes may need to be modified through teacher training.

- At what age level should alcohol education be taught?
- Which alcohol education concepts can be introduced and explored at what age levels?
- What can education around drinking issues be reasonably expected to accomplish at each grade level? What should its goals be?
- What attitudes should youngsters and adults have toward alcohol if they are to abstain or drink in appropriate ways? How can teachers promote these attitudes?
- How can goal achievement be evaluated in an alcohol education course?
- To what extent should teaching about alcohol focus on alcoholism or problem drinking as opposed to alcohol?
- Most learning that takes place is the result of reinforcement, not "one-shot" experiences, or it comes from learning principles that can be applied to various specific instances. How can alcohol concepts be reinforced with students and how can students be helped to apply these concepts to different situations?
- What role, if any, do "scare tactics" have in education regarding alcohol—for example, stories of drunk driving crashes, diseased livers, or family strife?

- How can teachers create an open atmosphere in which students feel free to express their real concerns about alcohol and ask pressing questions they may have?
- Should teachers focus primarily on alcohol issues (e.g., drunk driving), on general, underlying issues of concern to students that relate indirectly to drinking (e.g., peer pressure, risk-taking behavior, curiosity), or on some combination of the two approaches?
- Some people feel that alcohol education may stimulate students to experiment with drinking. Is this true? If so, it is necessarily bad?
- Should alcohol education be combined with an exploration of other drugs?
- In what subject area(s) should alcohol education be taught?
- Should students be involved in the development of an alcohol education course in which they will be participating? If so, how?
- Should teachers exercise extra sensitivity with students who may come from abstinent homes or problem drinking families? If so, how should they address these people's feelings and views?
- Should teachers try to learn the drinking attitudes of their students' families? How can alcohol education be provided in ways that will avoid or minimize causing such students embarrassment and at the same time offer them help?
- What should a teacher do if a student reports that a member of his or her family has a serious drinking problem?
- How should teachers respond to the widespread teenage practice of drinking in order to get drunk?
- Should students be asked in class to answer questions about drinking issues, or should their opinions be considered a private matter until they voluntarily express them?
- How should teachers handle personal questions about their own drinking behavior which students may ask (e.g., "Have you ever been drunk?" "Have you ever driven after one or two drinks?")? Will not answering such questions, or answering them dishonestly or equivocally, place alcohol in the taboo realm of illicit use and thereby reinforce the mystique about drinking which appears to promote youthful and adult alcohol abuse?
- How should teachers handle questions from students about guidance personnel or other

faculty members who are known to have drinking problems?

- How can teachers ensure that their inevitable role modeling effects, in terms of their own attitudes toward drinking and abstention and their own drinking practices, can be positive ones for students to emulate?
- How can teachers realistically present the erratic enforcement of drunk driving laws and yet help students to obey the DWI laws?
- What role, if any, should parents play in a school or community alcohol education program?
- How may the drinking practices and attitudes of parents toward alcohol affect their children's attitudes toward drinking? Do parents and teachers have different or similar opportunities to influence and provide role models for the attitudes of youngsters toward drinking?

In designing a training program for teachers, each of the four goals discussed above—attitudes, objectivity, information, and teaching strategies—should receive adequate attention. However, in order to determine which goals require the most attention and which particular issues within each goal to focus on, teacher trainers should conduct a simple needs assessment study of the teachers to be trained. This assessment should involve administering a questionnaire, such as the one provided in Activity #1 in the back of the book, designed to discover how much the teachers *already* know about alcohol, what their *current* attitudes and values are about drinking, and which alcohol education teaching methods they *presently* feel competent to implement. The training program which is then developed can be designed to devote relatively more time to those areas in which the teachers do not yet have the requisite skills, attitudes, or knowledge.

One additional consideration in determining the content of a training program needs to be mentioned. There is often a tendency in teacher training programs in alcohol education to focus primarily on the third goal—providing teachers with information about alcohol—to the relative neglect of the other three areas. It is especially important to focus adequate attention on these other three goals because if teachers have not achieved them, they will only become knowledgeable experts about alcohol who are unable to put their information in the service of helping youngsters to become similarly informed. Training programs should, in particular, spend time helping teachers to surface, examine, and where appropriate, change their attitudes and values with regard to drinking. Most students will probably be more influenced by an instructor's feelings about drinking and his or her ability to help them explore their own feelings about drinking than by any factual information about alcohol that the teacher provides. In addition, exploring attitudes and feelings about drinking simply takes time—it cannot be done in a brief discussion. A training program must allocate as much time as possible to allowing teachers to attend to this essential component of effective alcohol education.

TRAINING METHODS

We noted earlier that the techniques used to train teachers in alcohol education should be the same instructional approaches teachers will be expected to implement with their students. As a result, instructors can replicate and use as a role model their own "student days" in alcohol education when they come to teaching students.

Teacher training methods in alcohol education fall into four broad categories:

1. small group discussion
2. independent study activities
3. simulation and role play
4. practice teaching and curriculum development*

Small Group Discussion. Teachers can discuss all the issues related to the four teacher training goals presented above in small groups where there will be ample opportunity for the free and thorough exchange of ideas. A detailed discussion of this training approach may be found in chapter 5 while practical applications of the method can be reviewed in Activities #3, #20, and #21 in the back of the book.

Independent Study. Activities in which teachers can engage on their own include field trips,

---

*Of course, there will be times when lecture and class discussion approaches may be necessary, but these should be used sparingly—just as teachers should minimize their use when they come to providing alcohol education for their students.

interviews, polls, and volunteer work. These approaches have been fully discussed in chapter 6. Teachers can engage in many of the independent study activities described in the Learning Activities including the following:

- Interview friends and others in the local community regarding the effects of alcohol they experience when they drink. (Activity #13)
- Design, take, and administer to others one or more questionnaires regarding drinking experience and attitudes toward drinking. (Activity #1)
- Deprive themselves of a highly desirable activity in order to experience some of the feelings alcoholics may have with regard to alcohol. (Activity #26)
- Engage in various activities designed to help them learn about and evaluate different treatment approaches for alcoholics. (Activity #31)

In addition, teachers can observe and interview experienced alcohol educators in terms of effective techniques, attitudes, and information in teaching about alcohol. Teachers should also make a special effort to talk with youngsters about student perceptions regarding alcohol education. Instructors can benefit immeasurably from discussing alcohol education with students before teaching about it because they will get first-hand information regarding the concerns students have about drinking that need to be addressed and how students themselves feel alcohol education should be conducted if it is to be effective in helping them to avoid alcohol abuse.

Simulation and Role Play. Teachers can engage in many of the role play activities provided in the Instructional Activities, including the following:

- Students role play and react to scenarios in which parents find their children drinking, drunk, or high, or driving after drinking. (Activity #18)
- Students role play ("engage in one or more activities," in the original activity) activities revolving around peer pressure to abstain, drink, or drink abusively. (Activity #21)
- Students role play ("engage in one or more activities," in the original activity) activities revolving around issues of responsibility for

other people's drinking behavior. (Activity #22)
- Students role play scenes in which a parent is concerned about his or her child's friendship with the child of an alcoholic. (Activity #28)
- Students role play scenes in which non-alcoholics and alcoholics must interact. (Activity #29)
- Students role play a town council meeting discussing local option. (Activity #32)

Teachers can also simulate how they might handle a variety of common teaching dilemmas that may confront alcohol educators, such as the following:

- A student asks you whether you have ever been drunk.
- A student accuses you of advocating abstention.
- A student wonders how you can teach about alcohol if you don't drink or have never been drunk.
- A student asks if you believe it's wrong for teenagers to drink or get drunk.
- A student asks you a question about alcohol that you don't know the answer to.
- A student finds out that you provided the class with incorrect information or firm conclusions about an alcohol issue about which there is still disagreement.
- A student says that he or she already knows everything there is to know about alcohol.
- A student says his or her parent has a drinking problem.
- A student hints that he or she has a drinking problem.
- Students start telling stories about how they have gotten drunk or been drinking and driving.
- A student starts to make fun of someone he or she saw who was drunk.
- Students make jokes about another faculty member who is known to have a drinking problem.

Practice Teaching and Curriculum Development. When possible, teachers should practice what they learn during their alcohol education training and share their experiences during subsequent training sessions. When possible, and if the approach does not arouse too much anxiety, one teacher can observe another teacher instructing in alcohol education and the two can share their impressions of the effort and identify areas for improvement. Every teacher training program should also involve teachers in some form of curriculum development, whether it be lesson plans for a week, an audiovisual material, or a student handout. Even though there is a great deal of high quality educational material currently available (see the Resources), teachers who develop their own curriculum designs and materials are not engaging in "reinventing the wheel." It is often only through such "hands-on" learning activities that instructors come to grips with the many teaching issues involved in alcohol education in a meaningful way.

ILLUSTRATIVE TRAINING CURRICULUM

It is impossible to recommend a specific training program in alcohol education given the varying amounts of time different teacher trainers may have at their disposal for training purposes and the different settings in which the training may take place. However, we can illustrate what an effective training program would look like if trainers had, let us say, sixteen hours of training time available spread out over a period of seven to fourteen weeks in an in-service context. The training design provided at the end of the chapter assumes these parameters. It also indicates which of the four goals for alcohol education training which we discussed earlier are addressed in each training activity and what chapter and activities in this book may be used as resources by the trainer or teachers to supplement each training activity. As a final word of caution, we need to stress again that this training design is illustrative only; not only will your particular training design need to accommodate local time and setting constraints, it will also need to reflect the results of any needs assessment study you conduct. Finally, you should be prepared to modify any training design you develop to meet the concerns of teachers that surface during actual implementation of the training.

ADDITIONAL READING

Feinglass, Stanford J. "How to Plan a Drug Abuse Education Workshop." In *Resource Book for Drug Abuse Education*, 2nd ed. Rockville, Md.: National Clearinghouse for Drug Abuse Information, n.d.

Finn, Peter. *Teacher Training in Alcohol Education Using the Two Film Series JACKSON JUNIOR HIGH and DIAL A-L-C-O-H-O-L.* Washington, D.C.: U.S. Government Printing Office, 1977.

———. "Should Alcohol Education Be Taught with Drug Education?" *Journal of School Health* 47 (1977): 466–469.

———. "Empathizing with Addicts." *Health Education* 9 (1978):40–41.

———. "Surfacing and Exploring Attitudes toward Alcoholics: Approaches and Techniques." *Journal of Alcohol and Drug Education* 24 (1978):58–72.

———. "Alcohol Education in the School Curriculum: The Single Discipline vs. the Interdisciplinary Approach." *Journal of Alcohol and Drug Education* 24 (1979):41–57.

———. "Teaching Students to Be Lifelong Peer Educators." *Health Education* 12 (1981), in press.

———. "Institutionalizing Peer Education in the Health Education Classroom." *Journal of School Health* 51 (1981), in press.

Hames, Lee N. "Can Students Be Taught to Mix Alcohol and Gasoline—Safely?" *Journal of School Health* 41 (1971):481–487.

Miles, Samuel A. *Learning about Alcohol: A Resource Book for Teachers.* Alexandria, Va.: American Alliance for Health, Physical Education, Recreation, and Dance, 1976.

Rankin, William L.; Tarnai, John; Fegan, Nancy J.; Mauss, Armand L.; and Hopkins, Ronald H. "An Evaluation of Workshops Designed to Prepare Teachers in Alcohol Education." *Journal of Alcohol and Drug Education* 23 (1978):1–13.

Russell, Robert D. *The Last Bell Is Ringing: A Booklet about Booze and the Lives of Some Humans . . . Who Educate.* Chicago: Midwest Area Alcohol Education and Training Program, 1977.

Todd, Frances. *Teaching about Alcohol.* New York: McGraw-Hill Book Co., 1964.

U.S. Department of Health, Education, and Welfare. *Beyond the Three R's: Training Teachers for Affective Education.* Washington, D.C.: U.S. Government Printing Office, 1972.

U.S. Jaycees. *Understanding How We Teach and Influence Children about Alcohol.* Tulsa, Okla.: U.S. Jaycees, 1975.

	Activity: DAY ONE	*Training time*	*Training goal(s)*	*Training information*
(1)	In small groups, teachers discuss the topics they would teach and how they would sequence these topics if they had to develop a one-week unit on alcohol education. Groups report out their units and compare and evaluate them. Activity serves as "ice-breaker," sets tone of serious work for the training sessions, and stimulates immediate thinking about curriculum and teaching issues.	60 mins.	approaches	• chapter 10
(2)	Trainers present overview of training program including the following: (a) how the teachers will be taught as they will be expected to teach (b) objectives and training methods to be used (c) importance of focusing on attitudes toward drinking (d) review of the curriculum development process (e) flexibility to change training content and approaches to meet expressed concerns of the teachers. Question and answer section on the program follows.	30 mins.	approaches	• chapter 10 • chapter 9
(3)	Teachers discuss small group discussion as an instructional method for alcohol education referring back to their participation in the opening activity.	30 mins.	approaches	• chapter 5
(4)	Teachers: (a) write response to open-ended scenario on defining excessive drinking (b) are assigned to develop before the next session one small group discussion activity that they could use in their classes at a later date.	15 mins.	attitudes approaches	• Activity #25 • chapter 5

	Activity: DAY TWO	*Training time*	*Training goal(s)*	*Training information*
(5)	In small groups, teachers discuss definitions of excessive drinking based on their written comments from the last session.	30 mins.	attitudes	• Activity #25
(6)	Groups present conclusions to class and discuss lack of consensus regarding what constitutes social vs. excessive drinking. Relevance of this lack of agreement for alcohol education is explored.	30 mins.	attitudes objectivity	• chapter 3 • chapter 1
(7)	Any one of a number of short films on drinking that presents different attitudes toward drinking is shown. Using film as a discussion catalyst, group explores:	60 mins.	information attitudes approaches objectivity	• Resources • chapter 7

(a)   their own drinking experiences and feelings about them

(b)   what role their attitudes toward drinking may and should play in the classroom

(c)   why it is important for students to explore their own attitudes and feelings about drinking

(d)   how teachers can create an open class atmosphere in which students can feel free to explore their attitudes and feelings.

	Training time	Training goal(s)	Training information
(8) Teachers anonymously take and pass in questionnaire on facts about alcohol. Teachers are assigned to: (a) read literature on alcohol's physical and behavioral effects (b) refine the small group discussion activity that they prepared for this session in light of the small group activity they participated in at the beginning of this session and practice it in their classes. (c) select a curriculum development project to complete before the end of the training program, such as the development of a week's lesson plans, an audiovisual material, or a student handout. Prior to beginning work, the teachers must review their project with several students.	15 mins.	information approaches	• Activities #6 and #14 • Resources • chapter 3 • chapter 5 • chapter 10

Activity: DAY THREE	*Training time*	*Training goal(s)*	*Training information*
(9) Teachers discuss results of small group discussion activity they "tried out" in their classes and identify ways to improve their use of this teaching method.	30 mins.	approaches	• chapter 5
(10) Teachers tabulate results of two fact questionnaires they took the previous session and evaluate how much they know about alcohol. Correct answers are provided. Discussion follows on the role of alcohol information in alcohol education in terms of: (a) how much and what information teachers need to know in order to be effective alcohol educators (b) how much and what information students need to know in order to avoid alcohol abuse and help other people to do the same (c) how teachers and students can secure reliable information about alcohol (d) what aspects of alcohol use and abuse that are still subject to disagreement among the "experts."	45 mins.	information approaches	• Activities #6 and #14 • chapter 3 • chapter 1
(11) Teachers role play scenarios involving alcohol use, nonuse, and abuse and discuss: (a) what attitudes about drinking were revealed (b) the value of role play in alcohol education (c) how to implement role play with students	60 mins.	attitudes approaches	• Activities #21, #22, #23 • chapter 5

(12) Teachers are assigned to:
    (a)   read literature on why people drink and
           abstain
    (b)   conduct a poll among friends, neighbors,
           other faculty, or strangers about why they
           drink and/or what effects alcohol has on
           them.

- Resources
- chapter 5
- Activity #1

Activity: DAY FOUR	*Training time*	*Training goal(s)*	*Training information*
(13) Teachers present and compare results of their polls, discuss reasons given for adult drinking, and compare these reasons with what they read in their last reading assignment. Teachers debate "good" and "bad" reasons for drinking and abstaining and discuss societal ambivalence on this question.	60 mins.	information attitudes	• Activity #1 • chapter 3
(14) Teachers discuss polls as a teaching method for alcohol education and how to implement this instructional strategy in the classroom based on their own recent participation in a poll.	20 mins.	approaches	• chapter 5
(15) Teachers discuss their ongoing curriculum development projects in terms of: (a) problems they may be having (b) the principles of curriculum development (c) what influence their interview with students had on their curriculum development efforts (d) what role students should play in the development of an alcohol curriculum (e) independent study projects as a teaching method in alcohol education.	45 mins.	approaches	• chapter 10 • chapter 5
(16) Teachers write responses to scenario about whether it is ever appropriate for youngsters to get drunk and are assigned to read literature on the prevalence, context, and results of drinking and intoxication by youngsters.	10 mins.	attitudes	• Activity #3 • Resources • chapter 4

Activity: DAY FIVE	*Training time*	*Training goal(s)*	*Training information*
(17) Teachers in small groups discuss whether it is ever appropriate for youngsters to get drunk using the responses the teachers wrote last session to the scenario as discussion starters. Groups present conclusions to the class, compare conclusions and try to reconcile disagreements.	60 mins.	attitudes	• Activity #3 • chapter 4
(18) Teachers discuss how to deal with the issue of teenage drunkenness with students in an objective manner. Teachers then role play responses to hypothetical questions from students about: (a) what they believe about teenage drunkenness (b) whether they have ever been drunk (c) how a teacher can teach about alcohol if he or she has never been drunk or doesn't drink	45 mins.	objectivity approaches attitudes	• chapter 4 • chapter 7

(d) whether there's anything wrong with getting drunk.

	Training time	Training goal(s)	Training information
(19) Teachers discuss their own drinking and abstaining experience and practices in relation to alcohol education considering: (a) how their experience may influence their attitudes toward drinking (b) how their attitudes may provide role models for their students (c) whether and what to tell their students about their own drinking experience and practices.	30 mins.	attitudes approaches	• chapter 1 • chapter 7
(20) Teachers are assigned to: (a) read literature on alcoholism (b) implement one role play activity with their students before the next session			• Resources • chapter 5

Activity: DAY SIX	Training time	Training goal(s)	Training information
(21) Teachers discuss their use of role play in their classroom during the previous week and identify ways to improve their use of this instructional strategy.	30 mins.	approaches	• chapter 5
(22) Teachers view short film on alcoholism and discuss a variety of issues related to alcohol abuse, such as: (a) distinctions between alcoholism and problem drinking (b) theories regarding the causes of alcoholism and most effective methods of treatment (c) the disease concept of alcoholism (d) the importance of engaging in alcohol education, not alcoholism education.	75 mins.	information attitudes approaches	• chapter 3 • chapter 1
(23) Teachers discuss the use of films as a teaching method in alcohol education, recalling the film from session two as well as the film they just viewed.	20 mins.	approaches	• Resources
(24) Teachers are assigned to conduct an alcohol education activity of their choice before the next session and to develop a method for evaluating its success. Brief discussion is held to identify some effective evaluation techniques that can be implemented.	10 mins.	approaches	• chapter 5 • chapter 10

Activity: DAY SEVEN	Training time	Training goal(s)	Training information
(25) Teachers discuss results of their efforts to evaluate the activity they implemented the past week. Discussion follows on the purposes of evaluating an alcohol education program and how it can be best evaluated.	30 mins.	approaches	• chapter 10

(26)	Teachers in small groups identify ways in which the teacher training program they are just completing could be improved and present their conclusions to the other groups. Teachers discuss how students can evaluate alcohol education programs they participate in.	45 mins.	NA	• chapter 9
(27)	Teachers present the results of their independent curriculum development projects to the group for review and evaluation.	60 mins.	approaches	• chapter 10

10

Developing and Evaluating
an Alcohol Curriculum Unit,
with Sample Lesson Plans

Before we describe how you can develop an alcohol curriculum tailored to your particular needs and those of your students, it is well to review what we mean by the word "curriculum." A curriculum is a method for helping students learn a specific body of information, attitudes, or behaviors in an organized fashion. A curriculum normally consists of four components: *objectives*—what the instructor hopes to achieve; *content material*—the specific facts, feelings, or skills students must learn or develop if they are to achieve these objectives; *learning activities*—the things students must do that will enable them to learn or develop these facts, feelings, and skills; and *evaluation methods*—how the instructor (and students) can determine whether implementation of the learning activities was successful in conveying the content material in such a way that the teacher's objectives were achieved.

Curriculum can be in an instructor's head, but typically—and for good reasons—it is written down. Putting your curriculum on paper is essential because few of us can organize these four elements—objectives, content material, learning activities, and evaluation—in our heads in a coherent fashion if more than one or two class periods of instruction are involved. However, even though you put your curriculum in writing, you should remain open to revising it in the light of additional objectives, content, learning activities, and evaluation approaches that occur to you and your students during the teaching process.

ADDRESSING PROBLEMS OF TIME AND COURSE INTEGRATION

Before you develop your curriculum, you will need initially to consider the context in which you plan to teach about alcohol, in terms of your classroom schedule and your other course material. While you may revise your initial conclusions regarding these issues, you will at least need to establish some broad guidelines before developing your curriculum.

First, you will want to decide tentatively how many class periods you can devote to teaching about alcohol given your other course responsibilities. While you may have some flexibility in this matter, you will probably have to settle on a minimum and maximum number of periods or parts of periods you will spend on this topic—for example, at least three class periods but no more than six. Second, you will need to determine whether you expect to conduct these classes in immediate succession, spaced throughout the academic year, or with some combination of both approaches. The objectives you seek and the content and learning activities you select to achieve these objectives may be different depending on whether a month goes by between each class devoted to alcohol or whether several consecutive days are devoted to the topic.

For example, you may be able to use a particular teaching method (say, role play) more frequently if your classes devoted to alcohol are spaced over an entire year, whereas if they occur close together you would vary the instructional strategies you use to avoid creating boredom from repeating the same teaching method. In addition, spacing classes over the period of several weeks or months may mean spending additional time reviewing what has been studied earlier, and you cannot expect to create as consistent a sense of progression as may be possible if you devote several class periods in a row to alcohol education.

Third, you will need to consider whether to teach about alcohol by integrating the topic with other topics you cover in your course or by maintaining it as a separate unit of study by itself. For example, you may wish to teach about alcohol in conjunction with a study of other drugs in order to compare and contrast them, in which case the learning activities you implement may be those that best enable you to relate these two topic areas. If you believe that alcohol use and abuse should be singled out for separate attention, unrelated to your other course topics, not having to mesh your study of alcohol with the rest of your teaching plans may give you more flexibility in selecting which activities on drinking to use.

Finally, you will need to learn whether you alone, or a group of teachers, will be providing

instruction about alcohol both during the course of a single academic year and over a period of two or more years. Making these determinations may involve you in working with your department head or curriculum coordinator to develop a consistent plan that all members of your department or your school implement. Or it may simply require an informal understanding between you and other teachers about when and how alcohol will be taught during the elementary, secondary, and postsecondary years.

To help you make these four decisions which should precede your curriculum efforts, the following considerations can be kept in mind:

• Avoid "one-shot" approaches in which alcohol education is the subject of attention for only a single class period. Little is learned in this approach, and students tend to conclude that drinking can't be a very important subject if it is treated so quickly. Further, more learning about alcohol use and abuse is likely to take place not only if several class periods are devoted to its study but also if pupils study it several times during their school years. In addition to providing reinforcement of learning, such multi-year spacing can capitalize on the fact that students are intellectually capable of absorbing different concepts and forming different attitudes during distinct periods in their lives. Teaching alcohol over the years also provides an opportunity for students to investigate alcohol-related topics that are appropriate to the various behavioral stages they pass through from the elementary through the college years.

While some redundancy of learning may occur in this extended process of alcohol education, it is not difficult to teach different concepts about alcohol each year given both the massive amount of information and plethora of attitudes related to drinking and not drinking which students can examine (see chapter 3) and also the large number of different learning approaches which can be implemented for this educational purpose (see, for example, chapter 5). At the end of this book there are enough Instructional Activities on enough different drinking issues to make it easy to teach about alcohol during a number of academic years. The sample lesson plans at the end of the present chapter illustrate how such progressive learning might be accomplished.

- *Be flexible* in deciding whether to treat alcohol in consecutive class periods or periodically throughout the year and whether to integrate your learning activities on alcohol with your other course material or treat it as a separate topic. At times, you may want to have your students study about drinking for two or three days in a row and then wait a month before resuming their study of alcohol. You may also find it best to integrate some aspects of alcohol education with your other course material while you treat other features by themselves. Resolve these programming issues tentatively before developing your curriculum, and be prepared to change your plans based on new ideas you or your students develop as you prepare your curriculum and as you teach it. For example, you may have planned to teach about alcohol the first Monday of every month throughout the year. However, the third Monday your students become particularly engrossed in a drinking issue and no sense of "closure" or resolution is reached by the end of the period. In such a case, continue to teach about alcohol the following class period if you can postpone or cancel the other topic you had planned to address that day.

In terms of integrating alcohol education with your other course material, if you are teaching about alcohol in relation to other drugs and find that your students are confusing the two, consider focusing exclusively on alcohol for a time. More often, you may find that while you are teaching about alcohol separately from a study of other health concerns, you or your students identify a significant relationship between drinking and another topic covered in your course—for example, alcohol and heart disease, alcohol and calories, or alcohol and relaxation. In such cases, you can combine the study of alcohol with, respectively, a study of chronic illness, weight control, and mental health by either adding these other topics to your alcohol classes or postponing your discussion of drinking issues until you come to these other issues later in the year.

Above all, try to remain flexible in the amount of time you set aside for studying about alcohol in response to the concerns and interests your students have in the topic.

While it is never easy to juggle the amount of time devoted to each topic in a course—there is always too much to cover in the allotted time—remain open to the notion that since alcohol abuse is a problem of staggering proportions and the moderate use of alcohol provides a significant amount of enjoyment to millions of people, you should try to devote an amount of classroom time to alcohol studies commensurate with the major negative and positive role drinking plays in our society.

- *Remember that anything done well is better than nothing*, and that something done in haste and superficially is probably best left undone. If you are prepared to develop even a three-day curriculum devoted to alcohol that meets real student needs in a constructive manner, by all means do so. Often, this simply involves reducing our expectations of what can be accomplished in a limited amount of time but still doing our best to achieve these narrowed objectives we have singled out as having a high priority in our course. (There is always the chance that while you intended to devote only two or three class periods to alcohol, you will change your mind when you have seen how vitally concerned most youngsters are with drinking issues and will decide you ought to spend more time on the topic than you had originally planned.) If you have a limited amount of time to teach about alcohol, focus primarily on helping your students to understand their own current attitudes toward alcohol and drinking experiences rather than on introducing new concepts and information to the class. This way you can help some students at least begin to clarify and explore their present thoughts and immediate concerns about alcohol.

At the end of this chapter you will find four curriculum units, one each for grades 4-6, 7-9, and 10-12, and one for the postsecondary level. No sample lesson plans for the lower elementary level have been developed, because at this age level the "teachable moments" approach to alcohol education, which has been described in detail in chapter 6, is the most appropriate instructional strategy. The sample upper elementary unit consists of five half-periods and five full class periods. These Instructional Activities, selected from those provided in the back of the book, are intended to be spaced through-out the academic year. While no indication of breakdown by years is provided, they could also be spread over the course of the three-year period. The junior high unit entails three half-periods and eight full periods—about two weeks of time. The senior high unit involves four half-periods and nine full periods—again, a total of about two weeks of study. Finally, the post-secondary unit provides five half-periods and ten full periods. The secondary and postsecondary units have been designed with the expectation that they would be taught in a single year, in consecutive class periods, and unrelated to other course subject matter. It is important to stress that *these curriculum units have been provided for illustrative purposes only*. The units do not represent an ideal length of time, grade break-down, or subject matter approach. They only suggest what your curriculum may look like if you adhere to the curriculum development steps that follow.

DEVELOPING AN ALCOHOL EDUCATION CURRICULUM

There are three major steps to developing a cur-riculum unit or series of lesson plans on alcohol. These steps include identifying your students' concerns about alcohol and what resources they bring to the classroom for exploring those con-cerns, selecting activities that will address those concerns and ordering them into a logical learn-ing sequence, and developing methods by which to evaluate whether the activities indeed met your students' concerns. Each of these three steps is discussed briefly below.

1. Determine Your Students' Concerns and Resources

A concern is a feeling of uneasiness about some unresolved aspect of life. Concerns involve *feel-ings* and some sort of *personal tie* with the object of one's concern. They differ in this respect from interests. A person may be inter-ested in the problem of alcoholism in the Soviet Union but concerned about his or her spouse who is an alcoholic. Students may be interested in hearing their friends describe what it felt like to get drunk, but what may really concern them is that they felt "chicken" for not having gotten drunk themselves. An interest is a surface in-volvement, a concern goes deeper. It involves a feeling of apprehension and some sort of per-sonal relationship with the objective of the concern.*

Your students' concerns *provide the most effective stimulus for learning*. People learn best when the topic of study is one that is of concern to them, for personal feelings are involved rather than simply a detached intellectual interest. Many teachers (and parents) are familiar with how quickly and profoundly students learn skills and behaviors when the learning is related to their personal lives, whether it is automobile operation in driver education or play strategies in football. There is no better incentive for learning skills, information, and behavior than the intense motivation that a concern produces.

Therefore, to implement an effective alcohol curriculum, you must first determine your stu-dents' concerns and then select those Instruc-tional Activities from the large collection provided (supplemented by others you and your students may wish to develop) that meet these needs. This approach enables you to create a unique curriculum tailored to the specific con-cerns of your own classes. Furthermore, a cur-riculum that is developed on the basis of present student concerns is not necessarily limited to them. In the process of exploring present con-cerns, students will often develop new ones which should be treated within the context of your unit.

You should devote at least one class period to concern-discovery activities prior to selecting the activities you plan to use. This discovery process requires you to be understanding, respectful, and flexible since alcohol areas that may con-cern your students may not be of concern to you.

There are several Activities that are especially useful for learning what concerns your students have about drinking. These Activities are #2, #3, #7 #17, and #24. In addition, you can directly ask your students to indicate their ex-periences, attitudes, and concerns about alcohol. Finally, you can learn your students' concerns by encouraging them to select activities that they would like to study. Your students can also develop learning activities of their own.

*It is perfectly appropriate, time permitting, to deal with students' interests. (Furthermore, concerns are sometimes masked as interests.) However, where priori-ties must be established, dealing with student concerns comes first.

Figure 10.1 is a chart that provides the progression of common student concerns about alcohol from grades 1–12. However, you will normally find that many students in each of your classes may have different concerns from each other, so you must decide which ones to focus on. Where possible, arrange the unit you plan to teach so that different students can explore their own particular concerns individually or in small groups in independent study activities. This type of independent study has been further explained in chapter 5.

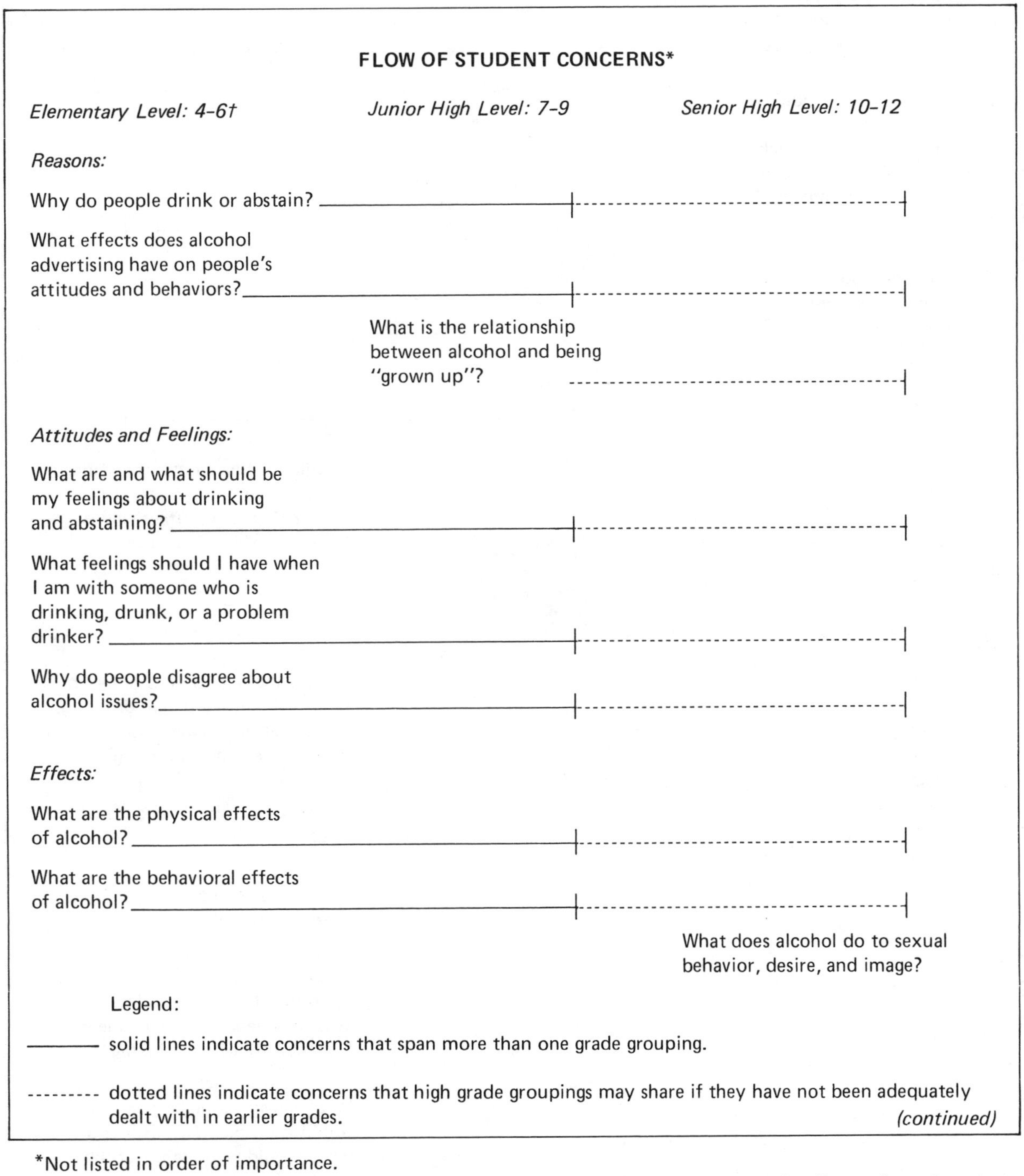

FLOW OF STUDENT CONCERNS*

Elementary Level: 4–6†   *Junior High Level: 7–9*   *Senior High Level: 10–12*

Reasons:

Why do people drink or abstain?

What effects does alcohol advertising have on people's attitudes and behaviors?

What is the relationship between alcohol and being "grown up"?

Attitudes and Feelings:

What are and what should be my feelings about drinking and abstaining?

What feelings should I have when I am with someone who is drinking, drunk, or a problem drinker?

Why do people disagree about alcohol issues?

Effects:

What are the physical effects of alcohol?

What are the behavioral effects of alcohol?

What does alcohol do to sexual behavior, desire, and image?

Legend:

——— solid lines indicate concerns that span more than one grade grouping.

- - - - - dotted lines indicate concerns that high grade groupings may share if they have not been adequately dealt with in earlier grades.   *(continued)*

*Not listed in order of importance.

†Elementary concerns about alcohol in grades 1–3 are either infrequent or sporadic. For a discussion about potential lower elementary level concerns, see chapter 6.

FIGURE 10.1

Elementary Level: 4–6   *Junior High Level: 7–9*   *Senior High Level: 10–12*

Interpersonal:

What should I do about other
people who drink, don't drink,
or drink too much? _____|

What are and what should be
the rules parents make about
drinking? Why do they make
these rules? What are and what
should be the punishments for
breaking them?_____|

How do I and how should I
handle pressures from my
friends to drink or abstain? _____|

                              How much and what do
                              people drink?_____|----------------------------|

                                                              Should I influence the government
                                                              and other institutions on alcohol
                                                              issues? How can I effectively do
                                                              this?

Problem Drinking:

                                                              What is the relationship between
                                                              social drinking, problem drinking,
                                                              and abstention? When does
                                                              drinking become a problem?

                                                              How should I and others feel about
                                                              alcoholics?

                                                              Why do some people lose control
                                                              over their use of alcohol?

                                                              What does it feel like not to be able
                                                              to control one's use of alcohol?
                                                              What can happen to someone who
                                                              loses control of his drinking?

                                                              What can someone do about his
                                                              drinking problem? What is and
                                                              what should be done for problem
                                                              drinkers?

                                                              (continued)

Elementary Level: 4–6	Junior High Level: 7–9	Senior High Level: 10–12

Drinking and Driving:

What effects can drinking have on driving, riding as a passenger, and being a pedestrian? _____|

What should I do about people who drive after drinking too much and people who ride with drivers who have drunk too much?_____|

What should and what will my parents do if I drive after drinking too much or ride with a driver who has drunk too much?_____|

Who is, and who should be responsible for alcohol-traffic safety problems? What can be done about these problems?

What are and what should be the laws about drinking and driving? What are and what should be the penalties for illegal drinking and driving?

Safety:

How can alcohol hurt me besides in traffic accidents? _____|

Alcohol Industry:

What is alcohol? What is it used for?_____|

How is alcohol made? ------------------------------------|

What rules are there and should there be about alcohol advertising? --------------------------|

What rules should there be about alcohol sales?

Law and Custom:

What are the possible alternate drinking behaviors that societies can practice and promote?

What are and what should be the non-traffic alcohol laws? What actions are and what actions should be taken against people who break these laws? What should be the legal drinking age?

In addition to identifying your students' concerns, there may still be other issues about which you or the local community feels students should address. For example,

- You or your school administration may be concerned that your students learn not only about what has relevance to them at the moment but also that students study and prepare for what *will* be important to them *in the future*, such as drinking and driving.
- The community may be concerned that students come to terms with specific, local alcohol issues, such as local option, public drunkenness, public disturbances, vandalism, littering, or drinking by minors.

When you or your community has concerns about alcohol issues that are not already student concerns, you may be able to stimulate student concern about them by relating them to present student concerns and by clarifying their future relevance to your students' lives. For example, you may be concerned about drinking and driving problems, but your eighth grade students may not yet be concerned about this topic. It may be possible for you to stimulate student concern in this issue by using drinking and driving activities that make the issue relevant to eighth graders, for example:

- role plays of girls dating older boys who are drunk yet want to drive them home
- discussions of what to do with drunken parents or other relatives who want to drive
- discussion of the number of pedestrians who are injured and killed by drunken drivers
- discussion of airline regulations on alcohol for pilots and other airline personnel

In selecting your own, the community's, and even national concerns for attention in your curriculum, make a sincere attempt to generate student concern in these other areas, but do not persist in that attempt when it is clear students are unable to become concerned.

Before you select activities to teach, you will also need to determine your students' resources. People accept and reject new learning differently, depending on their background, personality, skills, and experiences. By examining these factors for each of your classes, you can de-termine which teaching methods will be most effective.

Some potential sources of information for assessing these resources include guidance records, quizzes, direct questioning of your students, consultation with your students' present and former teachers, talking with community spokespersons, and reading the local press.

Four pieces of information in particular will help you select activities that your students can profitably engage in:

- Age and "grade level." How old are the students and what is their level of academic achievement?
- Ways in which students learn effectively. How do these students usually learn best? (memorizing? being challenged? exploring? participating? watching? reading? from parents, TV, friends, books, teachers?)
- Previous learning and experience. What have these students learned about alcohol from prior courses or personal experience?
- Community characteristics. What elements of the students' community background have the most influence on them? (language? prejudice? problem solving? nationality? socio-economic status? religion? independence? defensiveness? residence?)

2. Select and Order Learning Activities

Once your students' concerns and resources have been identified, you are ready to select activities that address these concerns and are appropriate to these resources. In choosing activities, pick ones that mix teaching methods to avoid boredom and one-track learning techniques, and leave enough spare time in your unit to deal with new concerns your students may develop as they engage in the initial activities you select.

Once you have selected the activities you would like to use (and hopefully have involved your students in the selection process), you must decide what order to teach them in. In sequencing them, you will want to make sure:

- opening activities ensure high student motivation
- information, skills, and attitudes needed for each activity have been previously learned

- teaching methods are mixed to avoid boredom

Finally, you will need to adapt your activities and curriculum unit to fit the maximum amount of time you have available.

A sample curriculum unit for each grade level has been provided at the end of this chapter as illustrations of what a unit you develop might look like. All the exercises in the sample units are taken from the Instructional Activities provided at the end of the book.

3. Develop Methods for Evaluating Your Unit

Evaluation is essential for you and your students to discover what they are learning and whether they are successfully addressing their concerns (and perhaps yours) about alcohol. In particular, evaluation should seek to determine whether youngsters can *make decisions* that demonstrate the ability to *apply* knowledge and skills, not just retain or develop them, and can channel attitudes and feelings into constructive behaviors.

The normal evaluation technique is a written or oral test that measures what information students have learned. But youngsters often memorize materials and parrot attitudes only for the test and then forget them. Furthermore, retention of information is not the major goal of an alcohol curriculum: exploring concerns to develop desirable feelings and behaviors is. Therefore, the evaluation methods you should consider using are role play, collages and mobiles, and story completion exercises. Such methods require students to make choices and decisions that are the prerequisites for performing desired long-term behaviors. Assess the choices your students make, and require them to do the same.

Evaluation of actual learning is also more likely to be more accurate when several different kinds of education techniques are used to supplement each other—for example, a role play and a story completion. (These methods are more productive because they involve the students' new learnings in the very process of evaluating old ones.)

Several of the Instructional Activities can be used for evaluation purposes, including activities #6, #8, #14, #18, #19, #21, #22, #23, #24, #28, #29, and #30.

ADDITIONAL READING

Abrams, L. Annette; Garfield, Emily F.; and Swisher, John D., eds. *Accountability in Drug Education: A Model for Evaluation*. Washington, D.C.: The Drug Abuse Council, 1973.

Bailey, J. P., Jr., and Wakely, J. T. *Analysis of Educational Programs for Primary Alcoholism Prevention*. Research Triangle Park, North Carolina: Research Triangle Institute, 1973.

Criteria for Assessing Alcohol Education Programs. Sacramento, Calif.: California State Department of Education, 1976.

Finn, Peter. "Should Alcohol Education Be Taught with Drug Education?" *Journal of School Health* 47 (1977):466-469.

———. "Alcohol Education in the School Curriculum: The Single Discipline vs. the Interdisciplinary Approach." *Journal of Alcohol and Drug Education* 24 (1979):41-57.

———, and Platt, Judith. *Alcohol and Alcohol Safety*. Six volumes. Washington, D.C.: U.S. Government Printing Office, 1972.

Globetti, Gerald. "Attitudes of High School Students toward Alcohol Education." *Journal of School Health* 40 (1970):36-39.

———. "A Conceptual Analysis of the Effectiveness of Alcohol Education Program." In *Research on Methods and Programs of Drug Education*, edited by Michael Goodstadt. Toronto: Addiction Research Foundation, 1974.

McCarthy, Raymond G., ed. *Alcohol Education for Classroom and Community*. New York: McGraw-Hill, 1964.

Milgram, Gail G. "Alcohol Education in the Schools Perceived by Educators and Students." *Journal of Alcohol and Drug Education* 20 (1974):4-12.

———. *Alcohol Education Materials 1973-1978: An annotated Bibliography*. New Brunswick, N.J.: Rutgers Center of Alcohol Studies, 1979.

——— and Page, Penny Booth. "Alcohol Education Materials, 1978-1979: An Annotated Bibliography." *Journal of Alcohol and Drug Education* 24 (1979): 1-107.

U.S. Department of Health, Education, and Welfare. *In Focus: Alcohol and Alcoholism Media*. Washington, D.C.: U.S. Government Printing Office, 1977.

Sample Curriculum Unit: Grades 4–6

Activity #	Activity	Focus	Method	Class periods
1	*Drinking Experience Polls*: Students design, take, and administer to others one or more questionnaires regarding drinking experience and attitudes toward drinking.	Prevalence Attitudes Reasons	Poll/ Discussion	1/2
2a	*Surfacing and Exploring Attitudes about Alcohol*: Students engage in one or more activities designed to surface attitudes about alcohol, and discuss their feelings about drinking and not drinking.	Attitudes	Discussion	1/2
6	*The Pleasures of Drinking*: Students explore the enjoyment of drinking and examine the reasons most people drink but many do not.	Reasons Attitudes	Discussion Independent Study Interviews	1
27	*Experimenting with Drinking*: Students discuss experimenting with drinking.	Curiosity Fear	Discussion	1/2
10	*Alcohol's Passage through the Body*: Students trace the passage of alcohol through the body on a specially prepared body diagram.	Effects	Diagram	1/2
31	*Peer Pressure to Drink*: Students engage in one or more activities revolving around peer pressure to abstain, drink, or drink abusively.	Peer Pressure	Story Completion Discussion Role Play	1
36	*Defining Excessive or Problem Drinking*: Students discuss what they think constitutes excessive and problem drinking.	Problem Drinking	Discussion	1
35	*Information about Alcoholism*: Students are presented with information about the nature, causes, and treatment of alcoholism.	Alcoholism	Lecture	1/2
28	*Parental Attitudes toward Children's Drinking*: Students role play and react to scenarios in which parents find their children drinking, drunk, or high, or driving after drinking.	Parents and Children	Role Play	1
41	*Coping with Problem Drinking and Alcoholism in the Family*: Students describe how they might respond to a problem drinker in the family and discuss constructive approaches.	Attitudes toward Alcoholism	Writing Story Completion Discussion	1

Sample Curriculum Unit: Grades 7–9

Activity #	Activity	Focus	Method	Class periods
1	*Drinking Experience Polls*: Students design, take, and administer to others one or more questionnaires regarding drinking experience and attitudes toward drinking.	Prevalence Attitudes Reasons	Poll/ Discussion	1/2
2d	*Surfacing and Exploring Attitudes about Alcohol*: Students engage in one or more activities designed to surface attitudes about alcohol, and discuss their feelings about drinking and not drinking.	Attitudes	Discussion	1/2

(continued)

Sample Curriculum Unit: Grades 7–9 (continued)

28	*Parental Attitudes toward Children's Drinking*: Students role play and react to scenarios in which parents find their children drinking, drunk, or high, or driving after drinking.	Parents and Children	Role Play	1
6	*The Pleasures of Drinking*: Students explore the enjoyment of drinking and examine the reasons most people drink but many do not.	Reasons Attitudes	Discussion Independent Study Interviews	1
11	*Alcohol's Physical and Behavioral Effects*: Students discuss alcohol's effects on the mind and body.	Effects	Discussion	1
18	*Interviewing Parents*: Students interview their parents regarding the effects of alcohol they experience when they drink.	Effects	Interview	1
31c	*Peer Pressure to Drink*: Students engage in one or more activities revolving around peer pressure to abstain, drink, or drink abusively.	Peer Pressure	Story Completion Discussion Role Play	1
35	*Information about Alcoholism*: Students are presented with information about the nature, causes, and treatment of alcoholism.	Alcoholism	Lecture	1/2
36	*Defining Excessive or Problem Drinking*: Students discuss what they think constitutes excessive and problem drinking.	Problem Drinking	Discussion	1
41	*Coping with Problem Drinking and Alcoholism in the Family*: Students describe how they might respond to a problem drinker in the family and discuss constructive approaches.	Attitudes toward Alcoholism	Writing Story Completion Discussion	1
42	*Treatment for Alcoholism*: Students engage in various activities designed to help them learn about and evaluate different treatment approaches for alcoholics.	Treatment	Interviews Reading Research Discussion	1

Sample Curriculum Unit: Grades 10–12

Activity #	*Activity*	*Focus*	*Method*	*Class periods*
1	*Drinking Experience Polls*: Students design, take, and administer to others one or more questionnaires regarding drinking experience and attitudes toward drinking.	Prevalence Attitudes Reasons	Poll/ Discussion	1
6	*The Pleasures of Drinking*: Students explore the enjoyment of drinking and examine the reasons most people drink but many do not.	Reasons Attitudes	Discussion Independent Study Interviews	1
31	*Peer Pressure to Drink*: Students engage in one or more activities revolving around peer pressure to abstain, drink, or drink abusively.	Peer Pressure	Story Completion Discussion Role Play	1
8	*Level of Information Questionnaire*: Students answer an alcohol questionnaire to determine their level of knowledge.	Effects	Question- naire	1/2

(continued)

Sample Curriculum Unit: Grades 10–12 (continued)

11	*Alcohol's Physical and Behavioral Effects*: Students discuss alcohol's effects on the mind and body.	Effects	Discussion	1/2
5	*Is Getting Drunk OK?*: Students discuss whether and when it may be appropriate to get drunk.	Reason for Drinking	Discussion	1
36	*Defining Excessive or Problem Drinking*: Students discuss what they think constitutes excessive and problem drinking.	Problem Drinking	Discussion	1
20	*Misconceptions about Drinking and Driving*: Students answer questions about drinking and driving and discuss the answers.	Drinking and Driving	Questionnaire/ Discussion	1/2
33	*Drinking and Driving Dilemmas*: Students engage in one or more activities in which their personal safety in a drunk driving situation is explored.	Personal Safety	Story Completion Discussion Role Play	1
34	*Information about Alcoholism*: Students express their perceptions about alcoholics and any misconceptions they may have are corrected.	Nature of Alcoholism	Questionnaire/ Discussion	1/2
37	*Simulating "Craving" and "Withdrawal"*: Students deprive themselves of a highly desirable activity in order to experience some of the feelings alcoholics may have with regard to alcohol.	Nature of Alcoholism	Simulation Discussion	1
41	*Coping with Problem Drinking and Alcoholism in the Family*: Students describe how they might respond to a problem drinker in the family and discuss constructive approaches.	Attitudes toward Alcoholism	Writing Story Completion Discussion	1
42	*Treatment for Alcoholism*: Students engage in various activities designed to help them learn about and evaluate different treatment approaches for alcoholics.	Treatment	Interviews Reading Research Discussion	1

Sample Curriculum Unit: College

Activity #	Activity	Focus	Method	Class periods
1	*Drinking Experience Polls*: Students design, take, and administer to others one or more questionnaires regarding drinking experience and attitudes toward drinking.	Prevalence Attitudes Reasons	Poll/ Discussion	1/2
25	*Evaluating Drinking Experiences*: Students evaluate "great" and "dumb" things they have done after getting high or drunk or have observed others do after drinking.	Effects	Discussion	1/2
5	*Is Getting Drunk OK?*: Students discuss whether and when it may be appropriate to get drunk.	Reason for Drinking	Discussion	1
6	*The Pleasures of Drinking*: Students explore the enjoyment of drinking and examine the reasons most people drink but many do not.	Reasons Attitudes	Discussison Independent Study Interviews	1

(continued)

Sample Curriculum Unit: College (continued)

8	*Level of Information Questionnaire*: Students answer an alcohol questionnaire to determine their level of knowledge.	Effects	Question- naire	1/2
11	*Alcohol's Physical and Behavioral Effects*: Students discuss alcohol's effects on the mind and body.	Effects	Discussion	1/2
44	*Legal Solutions to Drinking Problems*: Students evaluate what action to take with a convicted drunk driver and dis- cuss other legal aspects of alcohol use and abuse.	Law Treatment Drinking and Driving	Discussion	1
30	*Rules for Drinking by Youngsters*: Students discuss what restrictions they would set for their children on drinking and why.	Parents and Children	Discussion	1
31	*Peer Pressure to Drink*: Students engage in one or more activities revolving around peer pressure to abstain, drink, or drink abusively.	Peer Pressure	Story Completion Discussion Role Play	1
32	*Responsibility for Others' Drinking Behavior*: Students engage in one or more activities revolving around issues of responsibility for other people's drinking behavior.	Inter- personal Responsi- bilities	Discussion Role Play	1
34	*Information about Alcoholism*: Students express their perceptions about alcoholics and any misconceptions they may have are corrected.	Nature of Alcoholism	Question- naire Discussion	1/2
36	*Defining Excessive or Problem Drinking*: Students discuss what they think constitutes excessive and problem drinking.	Problem Drinking	Discussion	1
41	*Coping with Problem Drinking and Alcoholism in the Family*: Students describe how they might respond to a problem drinker in the family and discuss constructive approaches.	Attitudes toward Alcoholism	Writing Story Completion Discussion	1
42	*Treatment for Alcoholism*: Students engage in various activities designed to help them learn about and evaluate different treatment approaches for alcoholics.	Treatment	Interviews Reading Research Discussion	1

Instructional Activities

INTRODUCTION

Thirty-three activities are provided in this chapter from which you can choose those that are appropriate to your students and that you can accommodate in the time you have available to focus on alcohol education. Over half of these activities have been field tested in the classroom, while the rest have grown out of the authors' personal experiences in teaching alcohol education in the classroom and training teachers to provide alcohol education. You will find it helpful before turning to the activities themselves to become familiar with how they are arranged, the format in which they are presented, and how they have been designed.

Arrangement of the Activities

The activities that follow are numbered consecutively and organized into four general topic areas:

Topic	Activity Numbers
1. Drinking Attitudes and Prevalence	#1-5
2. Alcohol's Physical and Behavioral Effects	#6-16
3. Interpersonal Drinking Issues	#17-23
4. Problem Drinking and Alcoholism	#24-33

Matrix of activities by

- *teaching method*
- *focus or topic*
- *grade level*

Teaching Method	Grade Level				
	*Lower Elementary**	*Upper Elementary**	*Junior high/middle school*	*Senior high*	*College*
game		10,11	10		
interview/poll		1,4,13	1,4,13,31	1,4,13,31	1,4,13,31
lecture		9,24	9,24	9,24	9,24
questionnaire		6,24	6,14,24	6,14,24	6,14,24
role play/simulation		12,18,21, 22,23,26	5,12,18, 21,22,23, 26,28	5,18,21,22, 23,26,28, 29,32	5,18,21,22, 23,26,28, 29,32
small group discussion		2,3,17,20,21 22,23,24,25, 26,27,30	2,3,16,17,20, 21,22,23,24, 25,26,27,28, 30,31,33	2,3,16,17, 20,21,22, 23,24,25, 26,27,28, 29,30,31,33	2,3,16,17, 20,21,22, 23,24,25, 26,27,28, 29,30,31,33
story completion/writing	19	19,21,30	15,19,21, 23,30	15,19,21, 23,29,30	15,19,21, 23,29,30

Focus/Topic

alcoholism (see also problem drinking)		24,26	24,26, 30,31, 33	24,26,29, 30,31,32, 33	24,26,29,30 31,32,33
attitudes toward alcohol		1,2,4,17, 27,30	1,2,4,17, 27,28,30	1,2,4,17, 27,28,29, 30	1,2,4,17, 27,28,29, 30
drinking and driving			14,15,23, 33	14,15,23, 33	14,15,23, 33
effects		6,8,9,10, 11,12,13	6,8,9,10, 12,13,16	6,8,9,13, 16	6,8,9,13, 16
laws/local option			5,33	5,33	5,33
parents and children	19	18,19,20	18,19,20	18,19,20	18,19,20
peer relations		21,22	21,22,23	21,22,23	21,22,23
problem drinking (see also alcoholism)		25,30	25,30,33	25,30,32, 33	25,30,32, 33
reasons for drinking		1,3,4	1,3,4	1,3,4	1,3,4

*See also chapter 6, "Alcohol Education at the Elementary Level."

You can select activities by these general topic areas. You can also select them by specific focus, teaching method, or grade level by using the cross reference.

Format of the Activities

For each activity we have indicated its principal *focus*, the *teaching method*(s) involved, the grade levels it can be used with, and the time it will take to implement based on a calculation of 40-60 minutes in a typical class period. Many activities can be easily adapted for use with a wide range of grades and with considerable variation in implementation time.*

Nature of the Activities

Three principal concepts have guided our development of the activities.

1. Detailed teaching instructions with flexibility. The activities provide you with as much information as possible on how to implement alcohol-specific exercises. Despite the thorough instructions, each activity is flexible enough to allow you to adapt it easily to your particular students, syllabus, school, and community.

2. Active instructional strategies. Most of the activities involve students in action-oriented exercises, such as role play, games, simulations, interviews, polls, and small group discussion. Few involve lectures or reading assignments on "the facts" about alcohol because we believe that most students will learn more about alcohol if they are actively involved in exploring the many issues related to drinking and not drinking. Most students will learn a great deal of information about alcohol in the course of engaging in these student centered activities, while many pupils will be stimulated by them to seek out more information on their own. Nonetheless, you may see the need to provide your students with additional content information

about alcohol. You can do this in one of three ways:

- lecture, using Activities #9 and #24, that outline much of the information about alcohol and drinking provided in chapter 3
- assign readings from the items suggested in the bibliography in chapter 12
- assign research projects as suggested in the section on "Independent Study" in chapter 5

3. Affect in educational approaches. Feelings and attitudes play a tremendous role in people's views about drinking and in their personal drinking behavior. The activities have been designed to help students to surface, identify, explore, compare, and evaluate their feelings, attitudes, and behaviors concerned with alcohol so that they may develop or continue healthful drinking or abstinence habits. The activities will also enable students to explore their feelings about drinking so that they can respond constructively to the use, abuse, and nonuse of alcohol by family members, friends, and society at large.

It is important to remember that some of these activities may occasionally elicit responses—or a marked lack of response—from a few students which may indicate that these youngsters may be coping with an alcohol problem within themselves or within their families. Sensitive handling of this situation is necessary when you suspect that this may be the case and possible referral of the students at an opportune time to appropriate sources of help within the school may be warranted.

A list of all the activities and the grade levels for which they are appropriate follows.

Index of Learning Activities

Grade levels	Activity	Drinking attitudes and prevalence
3–College	#1	DRINKING EXPERIENCE POLLS. Students design, take, and administer to others one or more questionnaires regarding drinking experience and attitudes toward drinking.
3–College	#2	SURFACING AND EXPLORING ATTITUDES ABOUT ALCOHOL. Students engage in one or more activities designed to surface attitudes about alcohol and discuss their feelings about drinking and not drinking.
4–College	#3	IS GETTING DRUNK OK? Students discuss whether and when it may be appropriate to get drunk.

*Chapter 6 provides complete instructions for teaching about alcohol to very young students.

Grade levels	Activity	
4–College	#4	THE PLEASURES OF DRINKING. Students explore the enjoyment of drinking and examine the reasons most people drink but many do not.
4–College	#5	REGULATING DRINKING IN THE LOCAL COMMUNITY. Students role play a town council meeting discussing local option.

Grade levels	Activity	Alcohol's physical and behavioral effects
4–College	#6	LEVEL OF INFORMATION QUESTIONNAIRE. Students answer an alcohol questionnaire to determine their level of knowledge.
1–3	#7	STUDENT KNOWLEDGE ABOUT ALCOHOL. Students discuss drinking, drunkenness, and alcohol to reveal their level of knowledge about these subjects.
4–College	#8	ALCOHOL'S PASSAGE THROUGH THE BODY. Students trace the passage of alcohol through the body on a specially prepared body diagram.
5–College	#9	ALCOHOL'S PHYSICAL AND BEHAVIORAL EFFECTS. Students discuss alcohol's effects on the mind and body.
5–10	#10	ALCOHOL WORD GAMES. Students develop word games in which alcohol related terms are used and defined.
4–7	#11	ALCOHOL DRINKING GAME. Students play game called THINK/DRINK, in which they simulate drinking.
3–9	#12	SIMULATION OF WOOZINESS. Students spin around and "experience" drunkenness.
3–College	#13	INTERVIEWING PARENTS. Students interview their parents regarding the effects of alcohol they experience when they drink.
7–College	#14	MISCONCEPTIONS ABOUT DRINKING AND DRIVING. Students answer questions about drinking and driving and discuss the answers.
8–College	#15	ASSESSING DRIVING IMPAIRMENT. Students complete a story involving drinking and driving and discuss whether and how they can tell if someone is too impaired to drive safely.
7–College	#16	EVALUATING DRINKING EXPERIENCES. Students evaluate "great" and "dumb" things they have done after getting high or drunk or have observed others do after drinking.

Grade levels	Activity	Interpersonal issues
4–College	#17	EXPERIMENTING WITH DRINKING. Students discuss experimenting with drinking.
4–College	#18	PARENTAL ATTITUDES TOWARD CHILDREN'S DRINKING. Students role play and react to scenarios in which parents find their children drinking, drunk, or high.

Grade levels	*Activity*	
2–College	#19	**RESOLVING CONFLICTS ABOUT DRINKING BETWEEN YOUNGSTERS AND PARENTS.** Students complete stories about drinking conflicts between youngsters and their parents and discuss the completions.
4–12	#20	**RULES FOR DRINKING BY YOUNGSTERS.** Students discuss what restrictions they would set for their children on drinking and why.
4–College	#21	**PEER PRESSURE TO DRINK.** Students engage in one or more activities revolving around peer pressure to abstain, drink, or drink abusively.
3–College	#22	**RESPONSIBILITY FOR OTHERS' DRINKING BEHAVIOR.** Students engage in one or more activities revolving around issues of responsibility for other people's drinking behavior.
6–College	#23	**DRINKING AND DRIVING DILEMMAS.** Students engage in one or more activities in which their personal safety in a drunk driving situation is explored.

Grade levels	*Activity*	*Problem drinking and alcoholism*
4–College	#24	**MISCONCEPTIONS ABOUT ALCOHOLISM.** Students express their perceptions about alcoholics and any misconceptions they may have are corrected.
4–College	#25	**DEFINING EXCESSIVE OR PROBLEM DRINKING.** Students discuss what they think constitutes excessive and problem drinking.
3–College	#26	**SIMULATING "CRAVING" AND "WITHDRAWAL."** Students deprive themselves of a highly desirable activity in order to experience some of the feelings alcoholics may have with regard to alcohol.
4–College	#27	**SURFACING AND EXAMINING ATTITUDES TOWARD ALCOHOLISM.** Students discuss giving money to panhandlers who are drinking and examine the attitudes toward alcoholics which surface during their discussion.
9–College	#28	**EXPLORING ATTITUDES TOWARD ALCOHOLICS.** Students role play scenes in which a parent is concerned about his or her child's friendship with the child of an alcoholic and then discuss the attitudes toward alcoholics revealed in the simulation.
9–College	#29	**SIMULATING ENCOUNTERS WITH ALCOHOLICS.** Students role play scenes in which nonalcoholics and alcoholics must interact; pupils then discuss their feelings about alcoholics and how best to help alcoholics.
3–College	#30	**COPING WITH PROBLEM DRINKING AND ALCOHOLISM IN THE FAMILY.** Students describe how they might respond to a problem drinker in the family and discuss constructive approaches.
6–College	#31	**TREATMENT FOR ALCOHOLISM.** Students engage in various activities designed to help them learn about and evaluate different treatment approaches for alcoholics.
9–College	#32	**EVALUATING ALCOHOL ABUSE PREVENTION AND TREATMENT APPROACHES.** Students decide how money should be allocated for alcohol problems in their state.
6–College	#33	**LEGAL SOLUTIONS TO DRINKING PROBLEMS.** Students evaluate what action to take with a convicted drunk driver and discuss other legal aspects of alcohol use and abuse.

Activity 1
DRINKING EXPERIENCE POLLS

Focus:	Prevalence	*Capsule Description:*
	Attitudes	Students design, take, and administer to others
	Reasons	one or more questionnaires regarding drinking
Method:	Poll/Discussion	experience and attitudes toward drinking.
Grade Levels:	3–College	
Time:	1/2–3 Periods	

ACTIVITY

Three sample polls are provided at the end of this activity:

1. Poll one: How much and how often people drink and in what situations they drink (one poll each for upper elementary level and secondary/college level).
2. Poll Two: Why people drink or abstain.
3. Poll Three: What attitudes people have about drinking and not drinking.

One approach to using these polls would be as follows:

1. Have your students in small groups develop their own questions and then compare them with the samples provided at the end of this activity. The class can then develop a single master questionnaire incorporating the best questions from each group's poll and the sample poll.
2. Administer the questionnaire anonymously to the class. Also stress that no student need answer any question he or she would rather leave blank. Break the class into three groups and pass out one blank copy of the poll to each group. One group tallies the polls completed by the boys in the class, while another group tallies the girls' responses. The other group fills out the questionnaires with how it *thinks* the majority of the class answered each question by putting down the expected percentages of boys' and girls' responses to each question. Discuss *actual* results and compare them with what students *thought* the poll would reveal.
3. Have the class revise and improve the poll. Students should develop standardized instructions for administering the poll such as:

My class is doing a project to determine how and why people drink and abstain. Would you answer the following questions based on your experience.

4. In small groups or as a class, students can administer the poll anonymously to other people, such as other students, school faculty, parents, and other members of the community. One group of pupils can be

responsible for administering it to other students, another group to faculty, and so on.

5. Have the students tabulate the results and present them to the class. Discuss what was learned.

Sample follow-up questions you can ask the students after they have taken the questionnaire themselves or administered it to others include the following:

Poll One (Drinking Experience)
Discussion Questions

1. What types of influences may affect people's drinking behavior?
2. Do the poll results show any differences in the drinking behavior of boys and girls? If so, what might account for these differences? Should men and women drink "differently?" Why? How?
3. Since___% of the class drinks at least sometimes, should the legal age of purchase be lowered? Raised? Should the laws be enforced more strictly? More leniently?
4. Do the students think that their drinking behavior or abstention now will have any bearing on their drinking behavior when they are older? For example, if they don't drink now, do they think they won't drink when they are 30? If they drink a lot now, do they think they might be problem drinkers when they are older?

Poll Two (Reasons for Drinking and Abstaining)
Discussion Questions

1. What are the most common reasons people give for drinking and abstaining? Do different groups (for example, teachers vs. other students) give different reasons? If so, what might account for these differences?
2. How honestly do the students believe their questions were answered? Why might some people be reluctant to give truthful answers? What does this say about the role of alcohol in our society?

Poll Three (Attitudes toward Drinking)
Discussion Questions

1. What are the most common attitudes toward alcohol people seem to have who were polled? Do different groups (for example, younger vs. older people) have different attitudes? If so, what might explain these differences?
2. Does the class feel that any of the attitudes expressed on the poll are "inappropriate"? If so, why does the class feel this way?
3. How do people develop attitudes toward alcohol? Can people's attitudes toward drinking and abstaining change? If so, what can influence attitude change?

Your Age: _____   Your sex: _____

Circle your answers.

1. Have you ever drunk alcohol (at least one glass)? (circle one)

   Yes   No   If not, skip to question 8.

2. If so, how many times? (circle one)

   1   2-4   5-10   11-20   over 20

3. When you drank, was it usually (circle one)

   alone?   with others?

4. When you drank, what kind of drink was it? (circle one *or more*)

   beer   wine   whiskey   other: _____

5. How old were you when you had your first drink (that is, one full glass of wine, one can or bottle of beer, one shot of hard liquor, or one mixed drink)? (circle one)

   under 8   9   10   11   12   13   don't remember

6. Where and with whom did you have your first drink? (circle one *or more*)

with parents	with relatives	with friends	alone
at home	at a friend's home	at a relative's home	other: _____
in a car	in a restaurant	in school	

7. If you drink now, where and with whom do you drink? (circle one *or more*)

with parents	with relatives	with friends	alone
at home	at a friend's home	at a relative's home	other: _____
in a car	in a restaurant	in school	

8. Do you think you can or could handle alcohol as well as or better than someone who is:

40 years old	yes	no
21 years old	yes	no
9 years old	yes	no

9. Do you think there should be a legal drinking age? (circle one)

   yes   no

10. If you do, what should it be? (circle one)

    under age 10   11-15   16   17   18   19

    20   21   over 21

Your age: _____   Your sex: _____

1. Have you ever had a *drink* of wine, beer, or liquor—not just a sip or taste?
    _Yes   _No   If you answered NO, skip to question 7.

2. How old were you when you had your first drink?
    _ Can't remember   _ 12–14 years old
    _ Under 9 years old   _ 15–17 years old
    _ 9–11 years old   _ 18 years old or older

3. What do you usually drink when you do drink?
    _ Beer
    _ Wine
    _ Liquor (whiskey, vodka, gin, mixed drinks, etc.)

4. How often do you usually drink?
    _ Every day   _ Three or four times a year
    _ Three or four times a week   _ Once a year
    _ Once a week

5. Think of all the times you have had alcohol recently. *When you drink,* how much do you usually have *at one time,* on the average?
    _ 6 or more cans or glasses of beer, wine or mixed drinks
    _ 4–5 cans or glasses of beer, wine or mixed drinks
    _ 2–3 cans or glasses of beer, wine or mixed drinks
    _ One can or glass of beer, wine or mixed drink
    _ Less than one can or glass of beer, wine or mixed drink

6. Where do you drink alcohol? (Check *all* that apply.)
    _ At parties where others are drinking and your parents or other adults are not present.
    _ At home on special occasions such as birthdays, or holidays such as Thanksgiving, etc.
    _ Driving around or sitting in a car at night.
    _ At dinner at home with the family.
    _ At places where friends hang around when their parents or other adults are *not* present.
    _ During or after a school activity such as a dance or football game when your parents are *not* present or can't see you.
    _ Alone — when no one else is around.

7. Have any of your friends suggested to you that you should try drinking?
    _ Yes   _ No

8. Have you ever felt that other kids were "putting pressure" on you to drink?
    _ Yes   _ No

9. How do most of the kids you hang around with feel about kids your age drinking?
    _ Approve   _ Disapprove
    _ Neither approve nor disapprove   _ I don't know what they think

2. POLL ON REASONS FOR DRINKING AND NOT DRINKING

Your age: _____   Your sex: _____

1. Do you ever drink alcohol?
    __Yes   __ No   If not, skip to question 7.

2. For which of the following reasons do you *usually* drink:
    __ to relax   __ to be sociable
    __ to have fun   __ to enjoy the taste
    __ to get high   __ to quench my thirst
    __ to get drunk   __ to see what might happen
    __ to act grown up   __ to forget about worries
    __ to do what my friends are doing   __ to celebrate
    __ to be different   __ for religious reasons
    __ for kicks   __ to calm down
    __ to communicate better   __ to enjoy sex more
    __ other (specify) _____

3. For which of the reasons listed above do you *sometimes* drink?

4. When you drink, do you usually have only one reason or are there more than one?
    __ usually one reason only   __ usually two or more reasons

5. Has the reason or have the reasons you drink changed over the past several years? If so, how have they changed?
    __ Yes: They changed as follows: _____
    __ No

6. Do you feel your reasons for drinking are generally:
    __ good reasons   __ bad reasons   __ some good, some bad

7. For which of the following reasons do you not drink?
    __ don't like taste   __ just aren't interested
    __ against my religion   __ alcohol makes me sick
    __ don't like to lose control   __ drinking looks bad
    __ too expensive   __ my friends don't drink
    __ believe it's wrong   __ like to be different
    __ other: (specify) _____

8. Did you used to drink and then stopped?
    __ Yes   __ No

9. Do you think that some day you might try drinking?
    __ Yes: If so, why? _____
    __ No

1. Which, if any, of the following are good reasons for drinking alcohol *in moderation*? You may circle as many as you want.

escape problems	feel mature
relieve nervousness	pressure from friends
tradition	to relax
get "high"	to be sociable
taste	religious ceremonies
celebration	to be different
kicks	
other (specify) _____	

2. Which, if any, of the above are good reasons for getting *drunk*?

3. Which, if any, of the following are good reasons for never drinking alcohol? You may circle as many as you want.

dislike taste	expense
fear of dangers	just not interested
religion	friends don't drink
other (specify) _____	

4. Which of the following, if any, are legitimate reasons for drinking *for the first time*? You may circle as many as you want.

curiosity	to feel mature
kicks	to be different
to be sociable	pressure from friends
relieve nervousness	religious ceremony
to relax	get "high"

5. Do you agree or disagree with each of the following statements?

	Agree	Disagree
a. There are no good reasons for drinking at all.	___	___
b. There are no good reasons for getting drunk.	___	___
c. There are no good reasons for never drinking alcohol.	___	___
d. There's something wrong with people who never drink.	___	___
e. People who don't drink and say it's because they don't like the taste are really just afraid to drink.	___	___
f. It's really difficult to have a good party unless people have a few drinks in them.	___	___
g. There are no good reasons for teenagers to drink.	___	___
h. Alcohol companies shouldn't be allowed to advertise their products at all.	___	___

		Agree	Disagree
i.	Alcohol companies should not be allowed to advertise hard liquor on TV.	___	___
j.	Alcohol has no good effects on people.	___	___
k.	Alcohol has no bad effects on most people.	___	___
l.	Alcohol has some good and some bad effects on people.	___	___
m.	It is always wrong to get drunk.	___	___
n.	There are times when it's all right to get drunk.	___	___
o.	Alcohol should be taxed so high that most people can't afford to drink it.	___	___
p.	There are several good reasons for drinking in moderation.	___	___
q.	It's wrong to drink alcohol.	___	___
r.	A drink or two at social occasions can serve a useful purpose.	___	___
s.	This country should give up drinking alcohol once and for all.	___	___
t.	There's something wrong with people who have a drink or two to relax at night.	___	___

6. Which, if any, of the following people are drinking too much? What makes you think so? (be brief)

    a. He goes bowling every Saturday night and ends up drunk but doesn't get into trouble.

    b. He has a cocktail before dinner and a highball before bedtime.

    c. She takes one drink and she has to keep drinking until she's drunk.

    d. Every Friday they go out, get drunk, and look for a fight.

    e. Whenever Sam's mother-in-law visits, he goes out drinking with his friends.

    f. He has two martinis with lunch, a cocktail when he gets home from work, and a drink or two before bedtime.

    g. Mr. and Mrs. Jones have half a bottle of wine with their dinner nearly every night.

    h. Whenever she plays bridge with her friends, about once or twice a week, she has two beers. At parties she has a couple of drinks, too.

    i. He goes out with his friends two or three nights a week, gets pretty drunk and then sleeps it off the next morning.

Activity 2
SURFACING AND EXPLORING ATTITUDES ABOUT ALCOHOL

Focus:	Attitudes	
Method:	Discussion	
Grade Levels:	3-College	
Time:	1/4-2 Periods	

Capsule Description:
Students engage in one or more activities designed to surface attitudes about alcohol and discuss their feelings about drinking and not drinking.

ACTIVITY

Four brief mini-activities follow that you can use singly or in combination to help your students identify their attitudes toward alcohol so that they can compare and discuss their feelings about drinking and not drinking.

1. Interpreting Pictures of drinking

Supply your students with drawings or photographs depicting alcohol use from magazines or newspapers, or pictures that appear to portray drinking behavior. Cut off the explanatory captions before showing the materials to the students, but number the pictures and captions so that captions can later be reunited with the pictures to which they belong.

Give each student two or more pictures and instruct the class to write what they think is occurring in each picture and why drinking is taking place.

You or the students read the explanations written by the class and have the students explain why they interpreted each picture the way they did.

After each picture is discussed, read the corresponding caption and have the class discuss how they were able to decide accurately what was taking place or why they may have misinterpreted the pictures.

Finally, make a list on the blackboard of the reasons the students gave why people drink.

2. Analyzing Humor about Alcohol

Assign your students to collect over a period of several weeks any cartoons, jokes, comic strips, and greeting cards they read and heard that describe alcohol use. Suggest several sources such as daily and Sunday newspapers, magazines, television, and radio.

When the class has collected sufficient materials, break the students into small groups and give them written instructions to:

1. Examine each others' materials.
2. List the reasons stated or implied why the individuals in the cartoons, etc., are drinking.
3. Decide and record what the cartoonist's attitudes seems to be toward drinking.

4. Decide and record what your attitudes are about the drinking behavior.

The groups report their findings to the class and compare and discuss their results.

3. Examining Songs about Drinking

Have your students collect records, lyrics, and tape recordings of songs that describe drinking. Sample songs of the past that touch on alcohol are:

- "Drink to Me Only with Thine Eyes" (English Ballad)
- "One for My Baby and One More for the Road" (Frank Sinatra)
- "Let's Go Get Stoned" (Ray Charles and contemporary revival)
- "Have Some Madeira, My Dear" (Swann and Flanders)
- "Thunder Road" (Robert Mitchum)
- "Copper Kettle" (Joan Baez)
- "Three Jolly Coachmen" (The Kingston Trio)
- Many Irish drinking songs and Negro Blues songs
- Many ballads, such as:
    "There Is a Tavern in the Town"
    "What Shall We Do with the Drunken Sailor"
    "Little Brown Jug"

Play the songs in class and, if possible, pass out or read the lyrics. Have the class identify what attitudes about drinking are expressed in each song and whether these attitudes are "healthy" ones or not and why. Your students can also write additional verses to the songs they heard or read that continue—or shift—the song's attitude toward alcohol. For some "old time" songs that involve drinking, you can consult the *Fireside Book of Folk Songs* (Simon and Schuster), the *Fireside Book of Favorite American Songs* (Simon and Schuster), and *Tom Glazer's Treasury of Folk Songs* (Grosset and Dunlap).

4. Drinking on Special Occasions

Ask your students to brainstorm the "special occasions" when alcohol often is and is not served. As the students offer their suggestions, write them on the board. When major occasions have been identified, discuss the categories of occasions represented—celebrations, religious ceremonies, parties, etc. Point out that for many Americans alcohol will be present at many important social, cultural, and religious events, but that it will not be present at many other events. Select one such event where alcohol is usually served and ask the class if *everyone* who would attend such an event would drink alcohol and why. Then select an event at which drinking would probably not occur and discuss why. Tell the class to look for occasions during the next week—special *and* ordinary events—at which drinking takes place and to think about why alcohol is served at them. The "occasions" can take place in their homes, on television, or among their friends or their parents' friends.

Activity 3
IS GETTING DRUNK OK?

Focus: Reasons for Drinking
Method: Discussion
Grade Levels: 4–College
Time: 1/2–1 Period

Capsule Description:
Students discuss whether and when it may be appropriate to get drunk.

ACTIVITY

Have your students write brief responses to the scenarios provided at the end of the activity. The following class, break the students into small groups and instruct them to discuss whether getting drunk is all right in each situation and why or why not. Have the groups report their conclusions to the class and compare their thoughts. With younger students, you can conduct the activity as a class discussion. Two considerations the students should explore are:

- Is it ineffective in the long run not to face and solve problems?
- Is it all right not to face problems that are temporary or cannot be solved?

You may also want to bring up for consideration variables the class may need to discuss in terms of deciding whether getting drunk is all right or not, such as:

- How many times is the person going to use alcohol as an escape?
- How much is he or she suffering?
- How much will his or her use hurt himself or others?
- Is his or her suffering permanent or temporary?
- Is his or her problem soluble if confronted or insoluble?
- Is the person getting drunk with full awareness of possible consequences?

A useful follow-up exercise would be for students to develop their own scenarios for other members of the class to evaluate in terms of whether they represent situations in which getting drunk is all right or not.

- A person's spouse and two of his or her three children have been killed in an auto accident. Is it OK for him or her to get drunk that night? The next two nights? Why or why not?

- A person is fired from a job and has three children and a spouse to support. He or she will probably have to go on unemployment for at least a few weeks. Is it OK for him or her to get drunk that night? The next two nights? Why or why not?

- A person has been paralyzed by a stroke and is confined to bed for the rest of his or her life. Is it OK for him or her to get drunk once a week? Once a month? Why or why not?

- A father comes home from work, has six cans of beer before dinner, and falls asleep. Is it OK for him to get drunk every night? Once a week? Once in a while?

- A woman drives to a friend's party and has a great deal to drink. She falls asleep on the sofa and wakes up the next morning. Was it OK for her to get drunk that night?

Activity 4
THE PLEASURES OF DRINKING

Focus: Reasons
          Attitudes

Methods: Discussion
          Independent Study
          Interviews

Grade Levels: 4-College

Time: 1/2-2 Periods

Capsule Description:
Students explore the enjoyment of drinking and examine the reasons most people drink but many do not.

ACTIVITY

As we noted in chapter 7, it is extremely important that students explore early in any alcohol education unit the pleasure most people derive from alcohol use so that they will be convinced that you will be teaching about alcohol objectively. A number of exercises your students can engage in which will help them to examine and discuss the enjoyment of drinking follow.

1. Interview wine stewards in restaurants on how wine can enhance a meal.
2. Attend and observe events at which responsible drinking takes place.
3. Eat dinner with a family that serves wine with its meals and discuss what they like about drinking wine.
4. Interview people who cook with alcohol, including chefs in restaurants and neighbors.
5. Interview relatives, neighbors, and strangers in terms of the pleasures they derive from drinking.
6. Research the use of alcoholic beverages by different ethnic groups.

Follow up all of these exercises with a discussion of the reasons people drink—many of which, of course, will have been identified in the course of these exercises. Then consider why a third of American adults never drink and another 15 percent drink less than once a month.

Conclude the activity by having your students discuss what they think "responsible" drinking for enjoyment consists of.

Activity 5
REGULATING DRINKING IN THE LOCAL COMMUNITY

Focus: Local Option
Method: Role Play
Grade Levels: 6–College
Time: 1–2 Periods

Capsule Description:
Students role play a town council meeting discussing local option.

ACTIVITY

Have six of your students role play members of a town council that has assembled to discuss whether to ban bars in its community. Appoint one student as chairperson for the meeting and request volunteers for the following six roles:

- A police officer who is upset by the serious drunk driving problem in the town.
- A bar owner who will go out of business if the sale of alcohol is banned.
- A middle-aged parent who doesn't want a teenage son or daughter to drink.
- An office worker who enjoys having a couple of beers with friends after work at the local bar.
- A taxpayer who is upset about the type of people who come from other towns to drink in the bars.
- A college student who would have to drive to the next town to do his or her drinking—and then drive home.

Have the rest of the class observing the role play think about who is presenting the most cogent arguments and why. Have the observing students try to guess what each role player's role profile is based on the player's statements during the simulation. Afterwards, ask observers what positions they thought the role players were supposed to represent and have the role players read their actual role profiles aloud. If some of the observers incorrectly identified the role player's intended positions, have the class consider what might account for this discrepancy.

At the conclusion of the role play, ask the council and the rest of the class to vote separately on whether or not bars should be prohibited. Discuss what the various arguments were that were presented for and against the proposition.

As a follow-up activity, students can interview their parents and other members of the community to learn their feelings about the issue. Students can ask adults or other students who have lived in communities that had different drinking laws from those of the local community what the differences were, whether they approved or disapproved of them and why, and what effects, if any, the different laws had on drinking or other behavior of the other community.

Activity 6
LEVEL OF INFORMATION QUESTIONNAIRE

Focus: Effects
Method: Questionnaire
Grade Level: 4–College
Time: 1/2–1 Period

Capsule Description:
Students answer an alcohol questionnaire to determine their level of knowledge.

ACTIVITY

A useful opening activity for a unit on alcohol is to distribute a short questionnaire designed to help them and you learn how much they know and don't know about alcohol. (For younger students, you may wish to read the questions out loud or use activity #7, which follows.) This exercise may be particularly useful in cases where students feel "we already know all the answers," since normally the results will reveal widespread ignorance about alcohol's effects.

Pass out and have each of your students answer two copies of the questionnaire provided on the following page. If you are reading the questions aloud, have your students record their answers on two separate pieces of paper. Tell them not to put their names on their papers, explaining that this is not a test but a method for them and you to find out how much they know about alcohol so you can decide what aspects of drinking to focus on in the rest of your unit.

When the questionnaires have been completed, collect one set and have a student tabulate the totals on the blackboard. Compute what percentage of the class answered each question

incorrectly. Discuss the correct answer to each question, keeping in mind that many students may have answered some of the questions correctly for the wrong reasons. The correct answers are provided below. More complete explanations for each answer may be found throughout the text in chapter 3.

Be sure to point out to your students that many adults who have answered these same questions give the wrong answers. For example, 40 percent of adults in one study thought that drinking black coffee would sober them up quickly and another 22 percent weren't sure. Studies of adults have also shown that heavy and problem drinkers know less about the effects of alcohol than do abstainers, light drinkers, and nonproblem drinkers. These findings make it possible for you to stress with your students that you are not studying alcohol because *they* are expecially ignorant about drinking; many adults are just as misinformed.

Consider passing out this questionnaire to your students again after your unit is over. Tabulate the results to see if your class improved its performance. Students who kept copies of their first questionnaire can see whether their answers improved.

118

		True	False
1.	Alcohol is a drug.	T	F
2.	Most of the alcohol people drink enters the bloodstream through the stomach.	T	F
3.	The caffeine in a couple cups of strong coffee will help sober a person up.	T	F
4.	A 12-ounce can of beer has more calories than a shot of whiskey.	T	F
5.	A mixed drink made with one shot (1½ ounces) of hard liquor has more alcohol in it than a 12-ounce can of beer or a 5-ounce glass of wine.	T	F
6.	If a bottle of whiskey says 86 proof on the label, that means it is 43% alcohol.	T	F

7. What percentage of fatal traffic accidents involve someone who was drinking?

   (a) 1%   (b) 10%   (c) 50%   (d) 80%   (e) no one knows

8. On the average, how many people in the United States are killed each day in car accidents in which one or more drivers were drinking?

   (a) 3   (b) 10   (c) 50   (d) 100   (e) no one knows

		True	False
9.	Fifty percent of all American adults do not drink more than once a month.	T	F
10.	One in eight seventh graders (approx. 12 years old) reports having been drunk at least once last year.	T	F
11.	Mixing different kinds of drinks can increase the effects of alcohol.	T	F
12.	Moderate amounts of alcohol (1-2 drinks) impair most people's ability to engage in ordinary manual or intellectual tasks.	T	F
13.	Alcohol chills the body.	T	F
14.	Some cures for hangovers are better than others.	T	F

Correct Answers:

1. T

2. F   Most enters by way of the small intestine.

3. F   Nothing can speed the passage of alcohol through the body.

4. F

5. F

6. T

7. (d) 50%

8. (c) 50

9. T   About 30 percent don't drink at all; another 20 percent drink no more than once a month.

10. F   One in four seventh graders reports having got drunk last year.

11. F   Alcohol is alcohol, although mixing drinks may make one sicker because of the nonalcoholic ingredients.

12. F

13. T   People feel warmer after drinking, but body temperature goes down.

14. F   Only time cures a hangover; aspirin may help.

Activity 7
STUDENT KNOWLEDGE ABOUT ALCOHOL

		Capsule Description:
Focus:	Effects	Students discuss drinking, intoxication, and
Method:	Discussion	alcohol to reveal their level of knowledge about
Grade Level:	1-3	these subjects.
Time:	1/2-1 Period	

ACTIVITY

In teaching younger students it is often difficult to learn not only their level of knowledge but also their feelings and attitudes about alcohol. This is important in order to help you plan an alcohol unit and also to give you some idea of just how emotionally charged this subject will be.

A useful method is to hold up pictures depicting the following words and have them discuss each concept:

* Alcohol
* Drink
* Drunk

When speaking to younger children about alcohol clear direction must be given so that a child will not reveal in front of perhaps less than understanding classmates any family problems that involve alcohol. If, as a result of this or other activities, a child is suspected as coming from an alcoholic or problem-drinking home, see chapter 2 for techniques of management and appropriate sources of referral.

Directing the children to discuss rather than

role play is important before the activity is started.

Role play should only be allowed in specific situations when the youngsters clearly understand their characters.

Another method for revealing the attitudes and level of knowledge of younger students about alcohol is to line up on a table in clear view of each student an empty soda can, juice can, beer can and milk container.

Ask students to identify each and discuss who might drink the contents of each container. Ask also the situations in which they would be drinking and the effects.

The same precaution applies to role playing and discussing this activity as the previous one. Younger students are quick to fantasize and to act out. Care by way of specific direction on your part must be taken to avoid any potential disclosure which would be embarrassing to the child. This is not to dissuade you from attempting this type of activity with your class but merely to point out the potential directions it may take.

Again children suspected as coming from homes where drinking may be a problem can be assisted privately by the pupil personnel staff of your school. See chapter 2 for details.

Activity 8
ALCOHOL'S PASSAGE THROUGH THE BODY

Focus:	Effects	
Method:	Diagram	
Grade Levels:	4–College	
Time:	1/4–1/2 Period	

Capsule Description:
Students trace the passage of alcohol through the body on a specially prepared body diagram.

ACTIVITY

Pass out copies of the blank body chart provided on the following page and have your students try to identify what the body organs are that are displayed. Review what the organs are and what major functions they perform. Then have your students draw, to the best of their knowledge, a line indicating how alcohol passes through the body and indicate what happens when it reaches each of these body organs.

If you use this activity early in your unit on alcohol, it is useful for helping students to realize that most people are really unaware of what happens to the alcohol they drink and how it is "processed" by the body in different ways

from other food. If you use the activity later in your course or at the end, it can serve to review or reinforce what your students have already learned about alcohol's passage through the body and its effects on body organs. It may be particularly instructive for both purposes to break your class into small groups of three or four students each and have the groups fill in the chart and then compare results.

After the class has had a chance to indicate how it thinks alcohol passes through the body, pass out copies of the filled in body diagram that follows the blank diagram or display the filled in diagram on an overhead projector. Review the steps in alcohol's passage through the body as illustrated on the diagram.

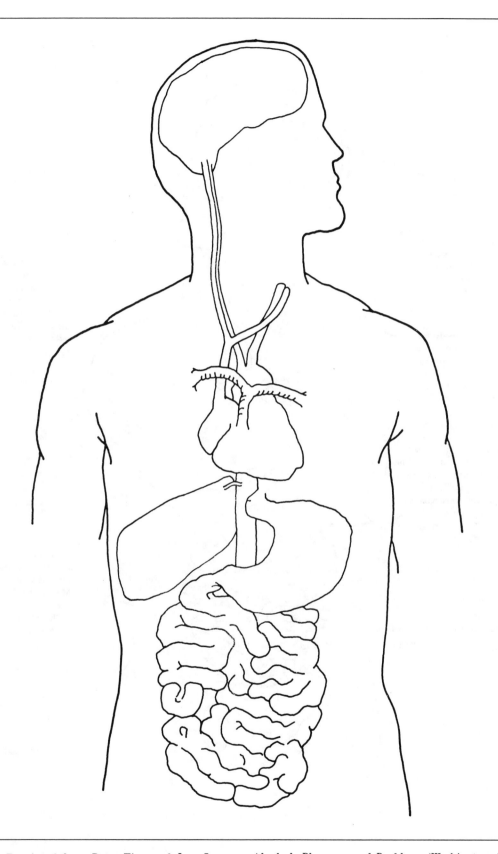

Source: Reprinted from Peter Finn and Jane Lawson, *Alcohol: Pleasures and Problems* (Washington, D.C.: U.S. Government Printing Office, 1976), pp. 6–7. Illustration by Linda Clement.

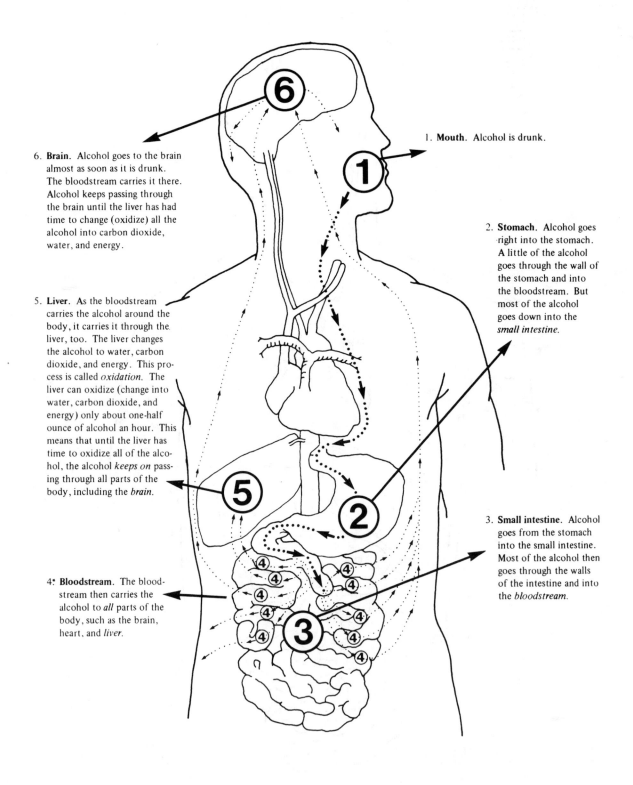

1. **Mouth**. Alcohol is drunk.

2. **Stomach**. Alcohol goes right into the stomach. A little of the alcohol goes through the wall of the stomach and into the bloodstream. But most of the alcohol goes down into the *small intestine*.

3. **Small intestine**. Alcohol goes from the stomach into the small intestine. Most of the alcohol then goes through the walls of the intestine and into the *bloodstream*.

6. **Brain**. Alcohol goes to the brain almost as soon as it is drunk. The bloodstream carries it there. Alcohol keeps passing through the brain until the liver has had time to change (oxidize) all the alcohol into carbon dioxide, water, and energy.

5. **Liver**. As the bloodstream carries the alcohol around the body, it carries it through the liver, too. The liver changes the alcohol to water, carbon dioxide, and energy. This process is called *oxidation*. The liver can oxidize (change into water, carbon dioxide, and energy) only about one-half ounce of alcohol an hour. This means that until the liver has time to oxidize all of the alcohol, the alcohol *keeps on* passing through all parts of the body, including the *brain*.

4. **Bloodstream**. The bloodstream then carries the alcohol to *all* parts of the body, such as the brain, heart, and *liver*.

Source: Reprinted from Peter Finn and Jane Lawson, *Alcohol: Pleasures and Problems* (Washington, D.C.: U.S. Government Printing Office, 1976), pp. 6–7. Illustration by Linda Clement.

Activity 9
ALCOHOL'S PHYSICAL AND BEHAVIORAL EFFECTS

Focus: Effects
Method: Discussion
Grade Level: 5–College
Time: 1/4–2 Periods

Capsule Description:
Students discuss alcohol's effects on the mind and body.

ACTIVITY

In this activity, you can present for discussion as much of the information from chapter 3 as you feel is appropriate for your students. In general, as we have stressed earlier, your students will learn more about alcohol and remember it longer if they study it in the context of other activities—role play, small group discussion, independent study, surveys, peer teaching—than if they are lectured about it.

You can enliven your presentation by using audiovisual materials, such as those suggested in the Resources. Of particular value for grades 5–12 are the two film series JACKSON JUNIOR HIGH and DIAL A-L-C-O-H-O-L, both available on a free loan basis from the National Audiovisual Center, Washington, D.C. 20409. There are four films in each series (15 minutes each for the junior high level series, and 30 minutes each for the senior high level series), each with its own story line. Factual information is woven into the plot in an interesting manner, and important issues about alcohol are raised and left for the viewer to resolve. Free teacher manuals and student booklets are also available to accompany the films. (See the Resources section on audiovisual materials for further information.)

Below are the major topics you might want to cover in a lecture on alcohol.

1. manufacture of alcohol and history of its use.
2. alcohol's passage through the body—mouth to stomach to small intestine to blood stream to brain to liver; the process of oxidation.
3. alcohol's physical effects on the body:
    *   body temperature; hangovers
    *   physical tolerance; delirium tremens
    *   liver, brain, stomach, and other body organ damage
    *   fetal alcohol syndrome
    *   death
4. alcohol's behavioral effects on:
    *   pleasure
    *   inhibitions
    *   thinking
    *   performance
5. why alcohol affects different people differently—and the same person differently on different occasions—depending on:
    *   amount of alcohol consumed
    *   speed of drinking
    *   type of beverage consumed
    *   body weight
    *   food eaten prior to drinking
    *   thoughts and feelings about drinking: psychological tolerance; expectations, mood while drinking
    *   social context in which alcohol is used

Activity 10
ALCOHOL WORD GAMES

		Capsule Description:
Focus:	Effects	Students develop word games in which alcohol
Method:	Games	related terms are used and defined.
Grade Level:	5-10	
Time:	1/4-1 period	

ACTIVITY

Present a list of word games to your class that can be adapted to require the use of primarily or entirely words related to alcohol and drinking. If possible, build in mechanisms to the games which require players to indicate that they understand what the words mean. Sample games include:

- crossword puzzles
- Scrabble
- unscrambling words
- twenty questions

One or two illustrations of each of these games are provided on the following pages. Students can play or read them to get a better idea of how to develop their own. Students can play the games individually, in small groups, or as a class.

More learning and evaluation opportunities take place in creating crossword puzzles than in filling them in. Students begin them by first listing alcohol terms they want to include and then fitting them into a puzzle, adding other words as needed.

Across

(1) Some people get _____ after drinking alcohol.

(6) Alcohol doesn't have such a strong effect when people have some _____ in their stomach.

(8) An alcoholic drink made from grapes.

(9) A boy's name. The first 3 letters are a conjunction.

(11) If someone who is drunk wants to drive you someplace, you can agree or _____ (rhymes with agree).

(14) Physical education (abbreviation).

(15) Most wines have either a red or yellow _____.

(16) Some people think drinking is dull; others think it's _____.

(18) A type of hard liquor.

(19) If you played hockey while you were drunk, you would probably _____ on the ice many times.

(21) Another word for "I."

(22) As far as we know, one or two drinks a day has _____ bad effects on a healthy person.

(24) You may eat it for breakfast, but it is also what whiskey is made from.

(25) He sang "Hound Dog," "Love Me Tender," and "Jailhouse Rock."

(26) If someone drinks too much, he or she may pass _____.

(27) When someone drinks alcohol, it travels by the bloodstream from the small intestine _____ the liver.

(28) A huge company that makes telephones and sends telegrams.

(30) The word "salty," but change the "y" to another vowel.

(32) Beer is often sold in a _____ pack.

(33) An urgent request; a type of begging.

(34) Abbreviation for the word "year."

Down

(1) "I'll _____ a bottle of French wine for three bottles of German beer. Is it a deal?"

(2) Some people, after they've had a few drinks, start to feed you a _____ about all the great things they say they've done.

(3) Player (or position) on a football team.

(4) The word "ever" spelled with one of its letters missing.

(5) A type of evergreen tree. (Rhymes with "you.")

(6) Drunk drivers cause about half of the _____ thousand auto deaths which take place every year.

(7) People who are on a _____ shouldn't drink too much alcohol because it has many calories.

(10) The word "even" with one letter missing.

(12) Alcoholics often have to _____ about why they took a drink.

(13) The 5th and 14th letters of the alphabet.

(16) If your mother or father found you drunk, would she or he have a _____ ?

(17) Drinking too much alcohol may _____ your stomach.

(18) Alcohol helps many people rest and _____ after a nervous day. (Synonym for sleep.)

(19) There are ice cream _____ and Scotch and _____.

(20) Sixth note of the musical scale.

(21) Name for a player on a New York baseball team.

(22) Some people who drink too much behave silly and _____, as if they were crazy.

(23) Relative of a beaver.

(26) A liquid that helps a car run smoothly.

(31) A group that helps alcoholics. (Initials)

A student who makes a word must be able to define it to get credit.

```
              W H I S K E Y
              A           E
              N           A G E
          H I G H         S
              O           T
              V
          B   E
        B E E R
          N   D
          D I S T I L L
          E   S   I C E
    S H E R R Y   Q
        O         S U G A R
        P         O
        S         D R U N K
                  R
                  Y
```

One student thinks of an alcohol term and writes it down with the letters scrambled. The others unscramble it, but must define it when they've figured it out.

litsidl = distill   yelpes = sleepy

temfrne = ferment   quirol = liquor

krund = drunk   accitolk = cocktail

zydiz = dizzy   xlear = relax

eber = beer

A student thinks of an alcohol term. The other students take turns trying to guess it but are limited to twenty (or fifteen or ten) questions. If unable to guess it within that number, they lose and originator wins. Questions are not random guesses but attempts to narrow down the topic the word describes. They can be answered only by yes or no. Wrong guessers are eliminated from the game.

Originator: "OK, I've got a word."
Rachel: "Does it have anything to do with safety?"
O: "What kind of safety?"
R: "Traffic safety."
O: "No. That's one question."
Bob: "Personal health?"
O: "No. That's two."
Sybill: "Is it something alcohol can do to people?"
O: "Yes. Three questions."
Sue: "I know! It's 'hangover'."
O: "No! You're out of the game. That's four questions."
Frank: "Do you have to drink a lot for it to happen?"
O: "No. Five questions."
Raymond: "Is it something good?"
O: "Yes. Six questions."
Karen: "Is it 'relax'?"
O: "Yes! In seven questions."

Activity 11
ALCOHOL DRINKING GAME

Focus: Effects
Method: Game
Grade Levels: 4-7
Time: 1/2-1 Period

Capsule Description:
Students play game called THINK/DRINK, in which they simulate drinking.

ACTIVITY

Break your class into small groups and have them play the game provided on the following pages. Players pretend to drink alcohol for the first time and determine what effects drinking might have on them by computing their blood alcohol concentration. For several small groups to play simultaneously, you will need to duplicate copies of the BAC Wheel and Drinking Consequence Cards which follow the game instructions.

Think/Drink Game Teacher Instructions

Teaching Objectives. This exercise, which can be either a solitary or small group activity for students, is aimed at the sixth and seventh grade in terms of the reading level required and the issues addressed. However, some teachers and

Source: This game was designed by Ray Glazier. The BAC Wheel at the end of the game was prepared by Judith Platt. The activity is reprinted from Peter Finn and Judith Platt, *Alcohol and Alcohol Safety,* vol. 2 Washington, D.C.: U.S. Government Printing Office, 1972.

some classes may find it usable and appropriate as early as the fourth grade and as late as grades eight and nine. Research has shown that sixth and seventh graders are interested in the physical sensations, the concomitant emotional states and the behavioral effects of alcohol consumption. Before they can learn about alcohol problems, students need honest and complete answers to questions like: "Why do people drink alcohol?" "Does alcohol taste good?" "Does alcohol make you feel good?" "How do you know when you're 'high' and what is it like?" "What would happen to me if I drank a certain amount of alcohol?" The major objective of this exercise is to provide answers that are as honest and complete as possible to these questions about the physical, emotional and behavioral effects of alcohol consumption without bringing a bottle into the classroom.

A secondary objective is to demonstrate the mechanism of peer group pressure as it applies to individual decisions and judgments in a drinking situation. Even at the sixth and seventh grade level, students are strongly influenced by pressure from their friends. The earlier this pressure is dealt with in the classroom, the better the chance of fostering student independence against such pressure.

Game Materials. There are six decks of feedback cards:

Number	Suggested Colors	Blood Level
8	WHITE	.01%-.04%
8	BLUE	.05%-.09%
8	GREEN	.10%-.14%
8	YELLOW	.15%-.22%
8	ORANGE	.23%-.29%
8	RED	.30% and up

You or your students will need to duplicate the cards and paste them, *according to blood level*, on different color poster paper, for example, all .01%-.04% cards on white paper, .05%-.09% on blue, etc. After pasting, cards can be cut out.

The only other required equipment, except for scrap paper for individual scorekeeping, is the circular device that calculates the blood alcohol content. The BAC Wheel can be duplicated and copies easily put together from the circles and instructions on the pages following this Activity. Paste them on poster paper for durability and then assemble (or have your students assemble) as many wheels as there will be small groups, or, if desired, assemble enough for each student to have his or her own.

Preliminary Comments. A student with a well-developed interest in this topic or a particular nonsocial student might be encouraged to experiment with the calculator and the six decks of feedback cards alone, but additional excitement and peer pressure involvement are provided by a small group approach to the materials. Whether used alone or in groups, the same procedure given below is used.

A group of no more than six is recommended; larger groups will mean longer waits between "turns" and greater restlessness. We suggest small groups with a mix of sexes, body weights, races, ethnic backgrounds and learning abilities ("slow learners" will benefit from nonsegregation). One of each group is chosen to start. Others follow suit clockwise from the starter, one at a time.

Each color-coded deck of "feedback" cards

covers a certain range of alcohol percentage levels in the blood (see color-percentage listing above under Games Materials). These six percentage ranges have been chosen on the basis of research, showing major affective and/or behavioral changes. Since the individual reaction to a certain blood alcohol content varies according to personality and situational factors (body weight and time span have already been compensated for by the BAC Wheel), there are eight different cards for each color-coded BAC range. The cards contain positive, negative and mixed effects described in graphic, though sometimes humorous, terms. The designers have deliberately used humor as a tension-reducing antidote to anxiety which may be aroused by some of the more frightening results on the cards.

Be sure to encourage players to talk back and forth, as they will undoubtedly "egg on" each other, which is part of this learning experience. Informal circles on the floor or with desks turned into small circles are more conducive to this interaction than normal classroom arrangement. Each round of turns is the equivalent of 1/2 hour of "partying." This must be announced to players, because it will enter into their alcohol blood level calculations in terms of 2 rounds = 1 hour. You should also announce that a player may "pass" on his turn, i.e., decline to drink, or may drop out at any point and become an observer. (Group social pressures will militate against dropouts, but this is realistic.) You can expect that, as the game proceeds, players will dare and challenge each other to experiment by "drinking" more and more.

Game Procedure*. Step 1: Cut out and set up BAC Wheels and the six card decks by color as indicated (shuffle each deck).

Step 2: Pass out one set of cards for each group and one BAC wheel per group or per student.

Step 3: Explain that players are to pretend they are at a party where drinks are being served, and they are each free to decide for

---

*Although the BAC Wheel and the card decks deal with decimals and percentages, a working knowledge of these two math concepts is not absolutely necessary, as long as players are able to recognize corresponding numbers. In certain groups you may find it necessary to manipulate the BAC Wheel yourself and refer each player to the correct card color.

themselves (in turn) when and how much they want to "drink."

Step 4: Explain the BAC Wheel and the six decks of cards in terms of what a player does when it is his or her turn—namely he or she

a. decides whether or not to "drink" in that 30-minute period and how much—from 1 to 4 mixed drinks.
b. operates the BAC Wheel according to his or her consumption decision, the game "time" and the player's real body weight.
c. takes the top card from the color-coded, pre-shuffled deck that contains the alcohol blood level range indicated for him or her by the BAC Wheel in step (b).
d. reads the information card aloud to his or her group and then records on a notepad how much he or she drank and a brief summary of this result. (With poor readers, you may have to read the results aloud for them.)
e. turns the card drawn face down beside the deck of yet unused cards of that color.
f. allows the next player to follow suit, beginning with step (a), by passing the BAC Wheel on to the next player (if each player does not have his or her own wheel).

NOTE: When players are told that they have "passed out," they retire to the sidelines to observe.

Step 5: When a deck of cards is used up, students shuffle it again and replace the deck right side up.

Step 6: Use your discretion as to when to end the game, e.g., when two players have "passed out" or when one player has "passed out" and the others have decided to stop "drinking."

Step 7: Tell players that there are no scores in this game; they should be able to tell by their scrap paper record of events whether they "won" or "lost."

Step 8: Players may want to repeat the exercise to find out more.

Step 9: If players do not express a desire to replay the exercise exactly as in steps 4–8, have them replay it in the same fashion using *teen-age* or *adult* body weights to see what difference this makes. (Students may choose and record at the top of their scrap sheets the body weight of some older person they know, or you may simply have boys add 50 lbs. to their body weights and girls add 35 lbs.).

Step 10: After all students in the class have had *direct* experience playing *THINK/DRINK*, move on to a class discussion focused on the questions below.

Follow-Up Discussion. Based on their individual notes, players answer for the teacher and for the group the following questions:

a. What good things seemed to happen to you? Why were these "good"?
b. What bad things happened? Why were these "bad"?
c. At what alcohol blood level, if any, did things seem to "go wrong"?
d. Why do you suppose there were different cards within each range of alcohol blood levels?
e. What happened with different body weights?
f. What happened with the passage of time?
g. Why did you drink as much as you did in the game?
h. Do you think this experience will affect your drinking behavior when you grow up? If so, how? If not, why not?

If there is no time during the class period for this follow-up discussion, you may want these questions to be answered in the form of a homework writing assignment or a verbal report to the rest of the class on the following day.

It is crucial, however, that somehow students think about most of these questions if complete learning is to take place.

Teacher: Please cut cards out on paper cutter, discard scrap edges.

.01%–.04%   #1

You feel a little happier than you did already, but—other than that—you can't notice any real difference. You keep thinking to yourself, "I must really hold my liquor well!" If you had a driver's license, you might be tempted to drive a little faster than usual. So far reactions still seem to be good. You wish this stuff didn't taste so awful!

.01%–.04%   #2

You were already feeling sad when you came to the party; now you feel just a little more "down." You do not really feel much different, and no one would know you had been drinking, unless they smelled your breath. If you were older, you'd be sure that you could do what you always do, even drive.

.01%–.04%   #3

Now you feel a bit better than you did before the party started. It seems as if the only thing that happened was that you relaxed and "loosened up" a little. You were always careful about what you do, so you think to yourself that some more alcohol won't hurt you a bit! But you wonder, if you had a car, would you drive it?

.01%–.04%   #4

Wow! Maybe you shouldn't have had anything to drink on an empty stomach. Your ears feel hot, as if you were blushing about something. But, all in all, you don't feel any different in the way you act, just a little happier, more confident you will meet someone exciting, that's all. What's wrong with that?

.01%–.04%   #5

You just came from a big dinner at home. This little bit of alcohol doesn't seem to have done a thing for you! Should you try some more, to see if you feel anything? No one else would know you had been drinking; you hardly feel it yourself! But you wish this stuff settled better in your stomach.

.01%–.04%   #6

For the first time, you really feel like one of the "in crowd." You can't tell whether it's that little bit of alcohol or the "new you," but you really feel pretty good! You are thinking about having more, but you don't want to get drunk and make a fool of yourself. What is the "right" thing for you to do?

.01%–.04%   #7

That really burned on the way down! It didn't taste very good either. You sort of wonder what people see in this stuff. Maybe you'll try a different drink. The only difference you feel is that you are sleepy now, and you don't really know why.

.01%–.04%   #8

You had a fight with your parents about whether or not you could come at all tonight. You were worried about this fight, but now your worries seem to have flown out the window. That little bit of drink really seems to be helping you enjoy yourself at this party!

.05%–.09%   #9

Wow, do you feel good! You've never been able to get up the nerve to dance before, but tonight you're the "life of the party." If someone dared you to take all your clothes off, you'd probably do it! Who cares? Whee!

.05%–.09%   #10

Your forehead feels numb inside, but you don't care. For some reason, you feel like a good fight, so you're going around teasing everyone—even your friends. If you had your car, you might just race anyone down the road, and you know you'd win! You hope the next drink will go down smoother than the others.

.05%–.09%   #11

You have a tingling feeling all over and a buzzing in your ears. One minute you feel on top of the world, the next minute you're "blue" and want to crawl off into a corner by yourself. You realize that you're in no shape to drive, and you'd probably drive the way you feel— first you'd speed and then you'd crawl.

.05%–.09%   #12

You wouldn't have believed it! Here you are, talking to everyone and making jokes. And you were always so shy before! You think it is really wonderful what a little booze can do. Who cares if you can't walk in another hour or two? Maybe you'll just stay here all night.

.05%–.09%   #13

For some reason, you keep bumping into everyone. But you just feel too good to keep saying you're sorry, so you don't bother. When people ask you how you're going to get home, the mature you says, "A few drinks make me the best driver on the road!" and you laugh.

.05%–.09%   #14

For some reason, people seem to be picking on you. You feel strong enough to knock a few of them out on the floor cold. It's a good thing you're in such a good mood, or you might just do that! You feel a little numb all over; no one could hurt you! This stuff tastes funny, but you *like* it.

.05%–.09%   #15

You really feel great! What a fun party this is! Everyone here seems to be friendly and talkative. You are thinking to yourself that maybe you should do this more often. You haven't had such a good time in ages! Who cares what it tastes like; it's what it does that counts.

.05%–.09%   #16

Maybe it was those greasy french fries you had on the way here, but you feel a little wobbly in your stomach. Or maybe it's because this stuff tastes like lighter fluid! Why did you come to this stupid party anyway? You might just get up and go home.

.10%–.14%   #17

IN EVERY STATE YOU ARE LEGALLY DRUNK
When you walk around, you feel like you are floating, but furniture and doorways keep getting in your way! You know enough that if you got into a car, you would probably have trouble finding the keyhole to start the engine. But you don't care—you're not driving tonight—so there!

.10%–.14%   #18

IN EVERY STATE YOU ARE LEGALLY DRUNK
But you feel just fine, and you don't have any trouble walking a straight line—well, hardly any! After all, your arm made it around that cute friend in the slow dance. You don't realize that if you decided to drive home and did something like go through a STOP sign, you could be arrested for drunk driving and convicted.

.10%-.14%   #19

IN EVERY STATE YOU ARE LEGALLY
DRUNK
And you believe it! You never felt so clumsy
in your life; you just knocked over someone
else's drink. Even so, you are sure you could
make it home safely in your car, if you were
old enough to drive. But you don't care what
the law says. Let someone try to stop you!

.10%-.14%   #20

IN EVERY STATE YOU ARE LEGALLY
DRUNK
You feel dizzy, and you are sure you are
making a fool of yourself. You can't even
get your zipper up after going to the bathroom, but somehow you don't care. You just
want to get home as fast as you can, any way
you can.

.10%-.14%   #21

IN EVERY STATE YOU ARE LEGALLY
DRUNK
You feel a little dizzy, but you don't feel
drunk. You *never* get drunk! But your friend
over there is drunk and you wish you could
take him home and keep him out of trouble.
Even if you had trouble finding the car door
handle, and even if you got in the wrong car
the first time, you know you could drive
home safely if you went very slowly.

.10%-.14%   #22

IN EVERY STATE YOU ARE LEGALLY
DRUNK
You did feel pretty awful for a while, but
now that you've thrown up your dinner, you
feel almost human again! You figure that if
you could make it all the way down the hall
to the bathroom, you can certainly get home
safely. If you were an adult, you'd just drive
your car home; you wouldn't care about the
"little accidents," just as your "old man"
doesn't.

.10%-.14%   #23

IN EVERY STATE YOU ARE LEGALLY
DRUNK
You were the "life of the party," and getting
in a car makes you feel like the "king of the
road." But you have to admit that you talk
like you have marbles in your mouth, and
you feel a little bit like going to sleep right
here.

.10%-.14%   #24

IN EVERY STATE YOU ARE LEGALLY
DRUNK
Every time you try to get up for another
drink you trip over someone! But you are
determined to have another, because you
like this weird, new dizzy feeling. You feel
you can do whatever you want, because
everyone *knows* you're drunk!

.15%–.22%   #25

BY ANY DEFINITION, YOU ARE DRUNK!
Your head is spinning in circles! One minute
you feel like laughing, the next minute you
feel like crying. You can't seem to do anything right, including walking and talking.
You're thankful you're not old enough to
drive for you know you couldn't do it.
Maybe you should call a taxi.

.15%–.22%   #26

BY ANY DEFINITION, YOU ARE DRUNK!
You feel very dizzy, tingly all over, and
somewhat sick to your stomach. It seems like
you've been doing only two things all
evening: getting another drink and going to
the bathroom. You know you're doing fine
for look how your body is handling the
booze. You can't wait to get in the car with
your friends and *fly* all the way home! You
still feel really good.

.15%–.22%   #27

BY ANY DEFINITION, YOU ARE DRUNK!
You didn't really mean to get so terribly
drunk and sick to your stomach. You feel
clumsy, ugly and stupid. You just barely
remember spilling a drink down someone's
neck and getting sick on the way to the
bathroom. How are you going to be able to
face these friends ever again?

.15%–.22%   #28

BY ANY DEFINITION, YOU ARE DRUNK!
If you don't stop yelling and throwing things,
you may get arrested for drunken, disorderly
conduct! But this is the best party you've
been to in years! You feel great! A "friend"
keeps telling you not to try to go home
yourself, but you know enough that you
might have an accident or get arrested, or
both, so you keep yelling.

.15%–.22%   #29

BY ANY DEFINITION, YOU ARE
DRUNK!!
You feel wonderfully silly! You never
realized before what a beautiful voice you
have. Why do people keep telling you to stop
singing? Dumbbells! Maybe you'll just get in
your car and roar out of here! The sirens behind you can join in the chorus.

.15%–.22%   #30

BY ANY DEFINITION, YOU ARE
DRUNK!!
Well, you wanted to know what this felt like,
but you don't like it at all! You feel very
dizzy and somewhat sick; you just know
you're going to feel awful in the morning.
You just decided to go straight home and
sleep it off. (Will you make it home safely?
or will that square but sober friend you
came with take you?)

.15%–.22%   #31

BY ANY DEFINITION, YOU ARE
DRUNK!!
Your friends are becoming invisible. You
keep putting your arms around the wrong
person. You try to explain this to her (his)
boyfriend(girlfriend), but the words don't
come out right. You keep thinking that if
only you could find your car, you'd drive
home, But all the cars look alike to you now.

.15%–.22%   #32

BY ANY DEFINITION, YOU ARE
DRUNK!!
You feel so dizzy and confused that you
couldn't possibly drive home all in one
piece, even if you knew how. You asked a
friend, who is just as drunk as you are, to
drive you home, because the friend was always a good driver. (Was this a good idea?
Only time will tell.) What a sore head
you're going to have in the morning. You're
sleepy too.

.23%–.29%   #33

You're just sitting here quietly on the floor,
not moving any part of your body. Every
now and then, someone comes by and tries
to talk or get you to dance, but the only
thing in the world you want to do is just sit
here, not moving. You feel so strange, you
can't imagine doing anything else; you sit
still to keep your head from breaking.

.23%–.29%   #34

You lost your dinner in the bathroom sink a
while ago. Now you get sick to your stomach,
but there's nothing left to come up. For some
reason, all you want to do is just sit here in
the bathtub. Why don't people stop banging
on the bathroom door?

.23%–.29%   #35

Now that you've finished being sick to your
stomach for the third time in an hour, you'd
like to go home. But, you can't remember
where you put your car keys, or your car—
for that matter! (Maybe you shouldn't drive
anyway.)

.23%–.29%   #36

You feel as if there is nothing inside your
head at all—no thoughts, no feelings. All
around you people are talking and dancing,
but you can't think of anything to talk about.
For the last five minutes you've been sitting
here, trying to remember something, anything, but . . . you're so sleepy!

.23%–.29%   #37

The last time you got up to go for another
drink, you only fell down. So you decided
just to sit here on the floor and watch.
You're not having fun any more, but you
can't figure out how to get home. One of
your good friends just walked by. (Now,
what *is* his name?)

.23%–.29%   #38

Someone just told you to stop staring at
them; you don't really know how long
you've been sitting here, staring without
really noticing anything that was going on.
This party turned out to be no fun at all
for you after all those drinks, Go to the
bathroom again, if you can!

.23%–.29%   #39

A while ago you felt just awful, but now you
just can't feel anything at all. In fact, you
can't seem to keep your thoughts on anything that is going on. You wish you were
home safe in bed, but you have no idea how
to get there! You're so sleepy, you might
just curl up right here.

.23%–.29%   #40

What interesting wallpaper! You have no
idea how long you've been sitting here,
staring into the corner. It must have been
a long time, because no one else seems to be
here. If only you could get up, you could
find someone and get a ride. (You couldn't
drive a car, even if you knew how.) You
don't know if you can get up or not.

.30% and up   #41

YOU HAVE JUST PASSED OUT!
No one noticed you slide down behind the
sofa. When you wake up (some time
tomorrow), you will probably not remember anything that happened at the party.
You know you will be sore where you were
lying on the floor, and your head will feel
like it is going to burst!

.30% and up   #42

YOU HAVE JUST PASSED OUT!
No one noticed you passed out in the shower
stall in the bathroom. You probably will not
be found till the next morning, when you
know you will not remember a thing. You
will be very lucky to be alive, because the
amount of alcohol you drank can kill, and
you couldn't break your fall in the shower.
Does your head *hurt*!

.30% and up   #43

YOU HAVE JUST PASSED OUT!
You fell onto a bed in an empty room and blacked out completely. Unless you are lucky enough to be found by a friend sober enough to call an ambulance or get you to a hospital himself, you may very well die from how much alcohol you drank. The party's over!

.30% and up   #44

YOU HAVE JUST PASSED OUT!
Not only did you black out, you went into a coma. Several other people at the party thought you had died, which might have happened to you after drinking so very much. When you were brought around, you were sore all over. You didn't remember the evening at all and were embarrassed to find out you had wet your pants!

.30% and up   #45

YOU HAVE JUST PASSED OUT!
Luckily for you, you blacked out behind the wheel of your car before you could start it up. (You had drunk enough that it might have killed you anyway!) In the morning you know you won't remember any of what happened at the party, where you made a complete fool of yourself.

.30% and up   #46

YOU HAVE JUST PASSED OUT!
After drinking an amount of alcohol which might kill, you made the mistake of trying to leave the party in a car with a friend who was driving drunk. You hit a parked car on the way. You are in the hospital with a concussion and a broken arm; you don't know yet how your friend is.

.30% and up   #47

YOU HAVE JUST PASSED OUT!
You had just decided to leave the party when you blacked out on the stairs on the way out and fell down one whole flight. A neighbor called an ambulance, and you are now lying in bed out cold with a sprained ankle. The doctor doesn't know how you even lived, because of all you drank.

.30% and up   #48

YOU HAVE JUST PASSED OUT!
You not only blacked out alone in the bathroom, you went into a coma. Your friend who found you thought it was funny, but your weak breathing and weak heartbeat told your friend it was serious. You might very well have died if your friend hadn't been sober enough to have taken you to the hospital right away.

To learn to use the wheel which follows, let's take an example. Suppose you've had three *average* drinks. That could be beers, glasses of wine, or mixed drinks.

1. Line up the 3 in the Number of Drinks row with the outer ring which shows your weight.

2. Read the figure which appears in the upper window. This is your BAC if you've taken the three drinks within a quarter hour.

3. By looking at the bottom window, you can determine what your BAC would be with the passage of time.

Experiment with other combinations. What would your BAC be if you weighed fifty pounds more? What would it be if you had two drinks or ten drinks in two hours?

Of course, your BAC would be a little lower if you took your drinks after or during a big meal.

1. Paste each page onto cardboard or manila paper.
2. Trim around each circle.
3. Use a razor to cut the two sections marked "CUT OUT."
4. Put the smaller circle on top of the larger one, carefully fastening them together at the stars (centers) with a paper fastener.

Source: Reprinted from Peter Finn and Judith Platt, *Alcohol and Alcohol Safety,* volume 2. Washington, D.C.: U.S. Government Printing Office, 1972.

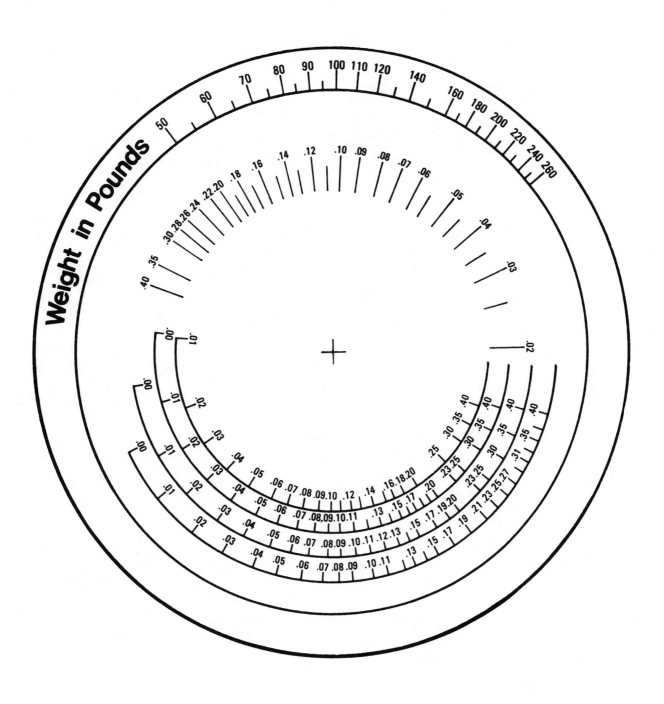

Source: Reprinted from Peter Finn and Judith Platt, *Alcohol and Alcohol Safety*, volume 2. Washington, D.C.: U.S. Government Printing Office, 1972.

Activity 12
SIMULATION OF WOOZINESS

Focus: Effects
Method: Simulation
Grade Levels: 3–9
Time: 1 period

Capsule Description:
Students spin around and "experience" drunkenness.

ACTIVITY

Take your class to a large, hazard-free area, such as a gym. Put your students into pairs. Each pair conducts a series of experiments in which one member of the pair at a time spins around until he or she is fairly dizzy. He or she then tries to perform several tasks, such as:

- catching a ball
- walking a straight line
- standing on one leg
- reading a sentence.

Each member of the pair should be tested before spinning around to see if he or she can perform these tasks when not dizzy. Instruct the pairs to keep a record of the results.

When every student has spun around, have the pairs discuss

1. the activities they would refuse or not want to do while feeling dizzy;
2. whether they would drive a car while dizzy. If they wouldn't, then:
3. why they think people *do* drive after they have become "woozy" after drinking.

Pairs report test results to the class and discuss their answers to the three questions. You may need to explain that many people drive after becoming "woozy" because alcohol can increase their confidence in their abilities while at the same time decrease their ability to make judgments (a loss of judgment not experienced in the simulation). In addition, the impaired reflexes and coordination resulting from intoxication are not always as obvious to the drinker as is the dizziness caused by spinning.

Activity 13
INTERVIEWING PARENTS

Focus:	Effects
Method:	Interview
Grade Level:	3–College
Time:	2–4 Periods

Capsule Description:
Students interview their parents regarding the effects of alcohol they experience when they drink.

ACTIVITY

Break your class into small groups and instruct each group to develop a list of questions to ask the members' parents, other family members, friends, or relatives about how alcohol affects them. Have each group report its questions to the class and develop a master set of questions. Sample questions might include:

1. Which, if any, of the following usually happens to you after two cans of beer, two mixed drinks, or two glasses of wine (check all answers given):

get sleepy	get warmer
get silly	get colder
feel happier	get angry
nothing	talk more
feel more relaxed	other (specify):

2. Have these effects changed over the years—that is, have two drinks always had this (these) effect(s) on you?
3. Which of these effects, if any, do you like? Which don't you like?
4. If drinking has none of these effects for you, why do you drink?

5. Does drinking have different effects on you depending on
    - whether and how much you've eaten?
    - time of day?
    - whom you're with?
    - how tired you are?
    - how happy or sad you feel before drinking?
    - where you are drinking?
    - whom you are drinking with?

Students can also develop a list of questions to ask parents who are abstainers, such as:

1. Did you used to drink alcohol? (If so, students can ask questions 1–3 and 5 above with reference to the person's prior drinking experience.)
2. If so, why did you stop?
3. Do you miss not drinking?
4. If you've never drunk alcohol, have you ever been tempted to do so? Have you ever been pressured to do so?
5. Why did you decide to stop drinking? (Or: Why did you never start drinking?)

Students may also want to record the respondents' sex, age, ethnicity, and other demographic data to see later if fathers gave different answers from mothers, younger parents from older parents, and so on.

Before having your students ask their parents the questions they develop, read the section on polls in chapter 5. In addition, consider that this activity might anger some parents who may feel their personal habits are being investigated. You might want to precede the student interviews with a letter to parents explaining the purpose of the study (to learn about the various effects alcohol has on different people) and assuring anonymity (students alone will analyze the answers and no names will appear on the questionnaires). In addition, emphasize that the parents are, of course, perfectly free to refuse to take the poll. As an alternative to polling parents, you can have your students ask their questions of other teachers in the school, whom you can inform in advance of the poll and its purpose.

After the students have conducted their polls, have the class tally the results. Different small groups can tabulate them by sex, age, ethnic group, and so on. Have the class or groups present their findings and then discuss whether they feel the effects mentioned are typical for most people, are "good" ones or "bad" ones, and are ones that they have observed in people they have seen drinking.

As a follow up to this activity or as a substitute, students can describe the effects of drinking on people they know, including themselves, and consider whether some effects can be observed by others which the drinker does not feel or is not aware of and whether a drinker may experience some effects that an observer may not see.

Note: Children who come from homes where one or both parents have difficulties as a result of their drinking may become anxious when this activity is suggested. It is important to be sensitive to this, and for this reason the alternative of interviewing a family friend instead of a family member is suggested.

Being sensitive to the response from your students to this activity will enable you to identify which ones may be having problems with their parents' use of alcohol and may therefore be in need of support.

Activity 14
MISCONCEPTIONS ABOUT
DRINKING AND DRIVING

Focus: Drinking and Driving
Method: Questionnaire/Discussion
Grade Levels: 7–College
Time: 1/2–1 Period

Capsule Description:
Students answer questions about drinking and driving and discuss the answers.

ACTIVITY

Have your students complete the questionnaire provided at the end of the activity. Tell them not to write their names on their papers. Tabulate the results on the blackboard and then provide the correct answers, with explanations of each based on the information provided in chapter 3. Conclude the activity by asking the class to discuss ways in which drinking too much may impair driving ability, such as the following:

- performing normal driving tasks more slowly, including braking, turning, signalling, stopping
- passing on curves and hills
- weaving
- driving excessively slowly or fast
- running through stop lights and stop signs
- responding tardily or overreacting to un-

expected occurrences, like children running out, or to unexpected happenings, like curves
- failing to see pedestrians and cars that suddenly appear soon enough, clearly enough or at all
- driving the wrong way down one-way streets
- crossing the double lines and driving out of lane

Activity #15 also treats drinking and driving and is a useful follow-up activity to this one.

Answers to Questionnaire

1. (a)
2. (c)
3. (c)
4. (c)
5. (d)

1. In most states a 150-lb. person is presumed to be under the influence of alcohol when he or she has had how many beers, glasses of wine, or average mixed drinks with hard liquor in two hours?

    (a) 1–2   (b) 3   (c) 4   (d) 5   (e) 6   (f) over 6

2. How much more likely is it that the average drinker who has four average drinks an hour before driving will get into a car accident than someone who has had nothing to drink?

    (a) no more likely   (c) twenty-five times more likely

    (b) six times more likely   (d) no one knows

3. What percentage of fatal traffic accidents involve someone who was drinking?

    (a) 1%   (b) 10%   (c) 50%   (d) nearly all   (e) no one knows

4. On the average how many people in the United States are killed each day in car accidents in which alcohol is involved?

    (a) 3   (b) 10   (c) 70   (d) 200   (e) no one knows

5. Which one of the following *most* affects the amount of alcohol in the blood?

    (a) stomach content   (c) drinking experience

    (b) weight   (d) time passed

Activity 15
ASSESSING DRIVING IMPAIRMENT

Focus:	Drinking and Driving
Method:	Story Completion/Discussion
Grade Levels:	8–College
Time:	1/2–2 Periods

Capsule Description:
Students complete a story involving drinking and driving and discuss whether and how they can tell if someone is too impaired to drive safely.

ACTIVITY

Have your students write endings to the story provided at the end of the activity. Then break the class into small groups and instruct the groups to read the completions written by the other members of the group. Tell the groups to try to agree on how people can tell if someone has had too much to drink to drive safely.

When the groups have completed their work, have a reporter from each group explain its conclusions to the class and list its signs of impairment on the blackboard—for example:

- sleepiness (yawning, drooping eyelids)
- slurred speech
- unstable walk
- unusual clumsiness
- excessive talking or silence
- silly behavior
- unusual energy
- more sexual aggressiveness
- boasting
- lack of concentration on the topic of conversation
- violence, more aggressiveness than normal

- any behavior that person does not usually engage in
- has been observed drinking the equivalent of two or more ounces of alcohol (not drinks) within an hour.

Conclude the activity by pointing out three major problems involved in identifying people who are too impaired to drive:

- Many drinkers who are impaired *seem* relatively sober to others in terms of how they talk, walk, and even drive. Many of us claim to know someone who can drink heavily and still drive "better than I can sober." However, while such drinkers may have learned how to compensate for some of alcohol's effects, if an *emergency* arises when they drive—such as skidding, a flat tire, a pedestrian or car seen only at the last moment, or momentary blinding at night by another car's high beams—heavily drinking drivers will be unable to react quickly to such a crisis. The best way to learn if such people who seem to be able to "hold their liquor" have drunk too much to drive safely is to keep track of how many ounces (not drinks) of alcohol they've consumed.

- The more alcohol people drink, the less capable they are of *judging* whether they themselves are too drunk to drive. Many people who have several drinks really believe and *feel* they are perfectly capable of driving safely: the alcohol itself impairs their mental ability to judge their driving ability. Mention to students that the solution here may be to

accept the opinion of a trusted friend on whether they are too drunk to drive and to keep track or have someone else keep track of how many ounces of alcohol (not drinks) they've had.

- A driver's underlying (and often hidden) attitudes toward driving can become unexpectedly more pronounced after drinking too much. Some drivers become more reckless, others more cautious.

This is the beginning of a story. WRITE HOW IT ENDS. There is no "right" answer. There are lots of ways it could end. Be as creative as you like.

The party had been going full blast for over four hours. Everyone had been talking, joking, and living it up. A lot of people had been drinking the fantastic rum punch, but there was also beer and hard liquor. Richard and his girlfriend, Susan, and Darroll and his girlfriend, Paula, had come together to the party in Richard's car and spent most of the evening talking with each other.

Richard was having an especially good time. He was drinking beer all night, almost one right after the other. In fact, Susan was getting a little nervous because after the last party they went to, Richard had had a little too much to drink. When he drove her home he wandered over the center line, went through a red light, and kept jamming on his brakes very suddenly. So Susan had decided to check on Richard during this party to see if he was in condition to drive. But it's difficult at a party to have a good time and also keep track of how much your boyfriend has been drinking and if he has drunk too much to drive safely. But Susan *had* spotted several clear signs that Richard was *not* sober enough to drive, and she had talked to Paula in the ladies' room about Richard. Paula, in fact, agreed to stick up for her if she needed help persuading Richard not to drive because Paula, too, had noticed some signs that Richard shouldn't be driving.

About an hour later, Darroll suggested they all go home. But as Richard pulled out the keys to his car, Susan took him aside and said,

WRITE HOW THE STORY ENDS

Activity 16
EVALUATING DRINKING EXPERIENCES

Focus:	Effects	*Capsule Description:*
Methods:	Discussion	Students evaluate "great" and "dumb" things
Grade Levels:	7–College	they have done after getting high or drunk or
Time:	1 Period	have observed others do after drinking.

ACTIVITY

Have your students who have been drunk or high write brief descriptions of the "dumbest" and the "greatest" thing they have done after drinking excessively. Have students who have not gotten high or drunk write brief descriptions of someone high or drunk whom they have observed in real life or in the movies who engaged in something they feel was "dumb" or "great" while high or drunk. Then break the class into small groups, being sure to mix students who have not been high or drunk with ones who have, and give them written instructions to:

1. Read each others' papers.
2. Place yourselves in the situations that resulted in the "dumb" behavior and discuss and record answers to the following:
   a. Did you (or did the person who was observed) feel the action was "dumb" at the time?
   b. Would you (or would the person observed) drink again in a similar situation?
   c. Why or why not?
3. Repeat the discussion in point 2 for the "great" behavior, and then discuss:
   a. What risks were involved in getting drunk and doing something "great."
   b. Whether the "great" results were worth those risks.
   c. Whether the "great" results could have happened while sober.
   d. Whether they had control when drunk over whether the results of their drinking would be "great" or "dumb" and whether they would have such control in the future.

Each group reports its results to the class for comment and comparison. You may want to comment in particular on the subjectivity of the terms "dumb" and "great"—that what seems "dumb" or "great" to one person may not to another.

Activity 17
EXPERIMENTING WITH DRINKING

Focus:	Curiosity; Fear	*Capsule Description:*	
Method:	Discussion	Students discuss experimenting with drinking.	
Grade Levels:	4–College		
Time:	1/2–1 Period		

ACTIVITY

Two major and interrelated aspects of teenage drinking that are often neglected but are extremely important are *teenage experimentation with drinking* and *teenage fear of drinking*. The question for many youngsters is not whether or not to drink, but how much and where. Most kids are going to experiment with alcohol. What they need to discuss is under what conditions they can experiment safely—for example, in protective circumstances with friends or adults present to watch how they react and change. Students can also discuss how much to drink when they experiment. In terms of quantity, students need to realize that there are 1,000 deaths a year due to alcohol overdoses. The combination of alcohol and other drugs can be particularly hazardous.

Related to this curiosity about alcohol is the fear that many youngsters have about what alcohol can do to them. Students need frequent opportunities to express their concerns in a nonjudgmental atmosphere in which their fears can be confirmed or allayed, as appropriate.

To provide one opportunity for your students to explore their curiosity and fear regarding alcohol, break the class into small groups and have each group address the following questions:

1. Many youngsters appear to want to experiment with drinking because they are curious about how it will affect them. (Many youngsters, of course, are not curious about alcohol.) Discuss whether youngsters who are curious about alcohol should experiment with drinking. Decide why or why not. Write down your conclusions.

2. If you decide that some or all youngsters who are curious about drinking should experiment with alcohol, at what *age* and in what *situations* should they experiment? For example, is it all right for them to try drinking at 14 years of age if their parents are with them? At 12 years of age in a park with several friends? Discuss also *how much alcohol* and what *kind of drinks* they should or should not experiment with and why.

3. Write down what you decide.

4. Do some youngsters have fears about what alcohol might do to them? If so, what are some of these fears?

5. If some youngsters are afraid, what, if anything, should they, their parents, their

friends, the school, or others do about these fears?

Have the groups report their discussion results to the rest of the class and follow up the reports with a general discussion designed to try to iron out disagreements which may have arisen between the groups. Ask the class to consider what activities they can engage in during the rest of your unit on alcohol that might help address any fears about alcohol that class members may feel.

Activity 18
PARENTAL ATTITUDES
TOWARD CHILDREN'S DRINKING

Focus:	Parents and Children	*Capsule Description:*
Method:	Role Play	Students role play and react to scenarios in
Grade Levels:	4–College	which parents find their children drinking,
Time:	1–3 Periods	drunk, or high.

ACTIVITY

This activity has two parts which may be conducted together (in either order) or separately. In the first part, students role play parents who find a son or daughter drinking. In the second part, the class discusses scenarios in which a parent discovers a child high or drunk.

Part One. Describe the activity briefly to your students and then ask for volunteers to play the parts. Sample role profiles are provided at the end of the activity. Make sure that the players do not see their counterparts' role profile until the end of the role play. However, preface the role plays with a "scene-setting" introduction that describes how the role players have encountered each other.*

*Note: If you have difficulty initiating role plays or your students have not engaged in them before, you may want to: (1) take one of the role play parts yourself in the first role play; (2) duplicate and pass out the role profiles to the students so they can have them in front of them to refer to; or (3) have students engage in a written story completion exercise as a "practice." Also, see chapter 5.

After each role play, students who took the parts can discuss how they felt about themselves and about the other role player during the role play. The students then discuss what they would have done or said had they been in similar positions. You might also ask the class to respond to some of the following questions in light of the role plays.

- If you were a parent, would you set rules for your children on drinking? If so, what rules?
- How would you react if you found a twelve-year-old brother, sister, or cousin drinking a can of beer? What, if anything, would you do or say?
- What do you think about this statement: "Youngsters (anyone under the legal drinking age) are unable to handle alcohol unless an adult is present."
- Do you think kids who don't drink just don't want to, don't because their parents disapprove, or have still other reasons for abstaining?
- What motives do parents have when they seek to persuade their children to do or not to do something? What are valid motives for

attempting to persuade children to do something?

Part Two. Students write responses to one or more of the scenarios provided after the role profiles. The scenarios require them to take the role of a parent who has found his or her son or daughter drunk or high. Break the class into small groups in which students who gave different responses to the scenarios are represented. Have the groups discuss the best course of action the parent could take in each scenario and why. Have the groups report their conclusions to the rest of the class and attempt to resolve differences in approach that they may have developed.

ROLE PLAY #1

Parent. You have just spotted your 13-year-old son (daughter) in the park drinking beer. When your neighbor called to say he had seen him (her) with some friends racing through the park carrying a six-pack of beer, you just couldn't believe it. You were also pretty embarrassed. Now you're just plain mad. You have been riding around in the car for well over an hour looking for him (her) and getting more upset with each passing minute. You thought he (she) knew better than to do something foolish like this.

You stop the car and get out, and start to walk over to your son (daughter) and his (her) friends. What, if anything, do you say or do?

Son or Daughter. For a long time now, you and your friends have wanted to find out what it's like to "really" drink. Your parents sometimes serve wine with a meal if it's a special occasion, but that's not what you call drinking. Finally, today Jeff's older brother gave him a six-pack of beer—first you all had to promise not to tell anybody where you got it. You and your friends went to the park to drink it. The beer doesn't taste very good, but it sure is making you feel pretty good. Maybe there's something to this "booze" after all. Just as you turn to get another beer, you notice your father (mother) walking toward you. What, if anything, do you say or do?

ROLE PLAY #2

Parent. You have just received a call from the police requesting you to come to the station to pick up your son (daughter). You were told he (she) was found at a party that had gotten out of hand—there had obviously been a lot of drinking taking place. You know your son (daughter) has been drinking at parties, but he (she) always told you everything was always under control. You better get down to the station and find out for yourself just what is going on. You finally get to the police station and see your son (daughter) standing with a bunch of other kids on the other side of the room. What do you say or do?

Son or Daughter. You can't believe the party got busted. Why couldn't you have gone out with Pat or Jimmy, as you usually do. Instead you had to go to some dumb party with a bunch of people you hardly know. Nothing like putting a little excitement in your life . . . . Now you're down at the police station, feeling scared and drunk. Your father (mother) is never going to believe this one. In fact, there he (she) is walking over to you. What do you say or do?

You are the parent of a 16-year-old son. He has just come home from a party at the house of a friend whose parents were gone for the weekend. The "host" supplied all the kids with drinks from his parents' liquor cabinet. Your son had 2 or 3 beers and is a little tipsy. What, if anything, do you do? Why?

You are the parent of a 15-year-old daughter. She has just returned from what you had thought was a movie with her girlfriend, but you smell beer on her breath and finally she tells you she and her friends stopped in the park on the way home and had some beer with three older boys from school. She says she only had a few sips. What, if anything, do you do? Why?

A neighbor has tipped you off that your 14-year-old son is drinking in the park with a couple of friends. You drive down and find him drinking beer with his friends. What, if anything, do you do? Why?

Your 17-year-old son has been a dinner guest at his friend's home. He tells you that they served wine at dinner and cocktails before, and their children always participate, so he did too. What, if anything, will you tell him?

Activity 19
RESOLVING CONFLICTS ABOUT DRINKING BETWEEN YOUNGSTERS AND PARENTS

Focus: Parents and Children
Method: Writing/Discussion
Grade Levels: 2–College
Time: 1/2–2 Periods

Capsule Description:
Students complete stories about drinking conflicts between youngsters and their parents and discuss the completions.

ACTIVITY

Pass out copies of the unfinished stories provided at the end of this activity and have your students write the missing part—end, beginning, or middle. For younger students you can read the stories aloud.

Tell your students that there are no "right" or "wrong" beginnings, middle, or ends. They should fill in the missing parts as they wish, making sure only to be as realistic as possible. This does not mean always writing (or telling) what *would* most likely have happened but what certainly *could* have happened in real life.

After the students have completed the stories, break them into groups of two to four students each and give them written instructions to:

1. Read each others' stories.
2. Compare your endings, beginnings or middles and explain to each other why you wrote what you did.
3. Discuss and record what each ending, middle, or beginning *should* have been *if* your only reason in writing it were to show the *best* way to handle the problem.

Have the groups report their conclusions to the rest of the class and discuss any different conclusions they may have come to.

Tom and Jim were sitting in Tom's bedroom. It was Saturday night, past mid-night, and Jim was sleeping over. Both were 15 years old and in the tenth grade.

Since Tom's parents were out to a movie with friends, and Tom's older sister was at a party with her boyfriend, Tom and Jim decided to take advantage of being alone and try something they had both been wanting to do.

They had raided the refrigerator for snacks and brought two cans of beer with them back to Tom's room. The first taste was really not very good—but neither boy wished to "cop out" on the other. So each had forced another swallow until the taste didn't seem so bad anymore and they had finished the cans.

They were on their way upstairs from the kitchen with two more cans of beer when Tom's 19-year-old sister Lucy returned home. Tom knew she saw what they were up to, but he casually said "Hi" and hoped she would leave it at that.

WRITE WHAT HAPPENED IN BETWEEN THIS PART OF THE STORY AND THE PART DESCRIBED BELOW

It was a cold Sunday morning when Jim's father, Mr. Jones, came to pick him up. But the weather wasn't nearly as bleak as the look on Mr. Jones' face. He barely looked at Jim, thanked Tom's parents for having Jim and for calling him, and ushered Jim to the car with as cold a look as Jim had ever seen. Jim knew what was coming—he had just watched Tom go through it.

(After completing the middle, students can exchange stories and write what happened next.)

"But, Mom, I have nothing to be ashamed of—nothing to be sorry for." Jane couldn't understand her mother's anger. She was 16 years old, had always been treated with respect and shown she could handle responsibility, especially in her numerous calls for babysitting jobs.

"You were planning to drink, Jane," said Mrs. Finplat, "and that's only a hair better than having done it!"

"Mother, I can *talk* about anything at all—and that's *not* the same as doing it! Besides, why do you take Mrs. Green's side—not mine? She's just an old gossip anyway."

"You will speak respectfully of Mrs. Green, my dear. She's been our neighbor from the day you were born. I am not taking Mrs. Green's side—that has nothing to do with this matter. Planning to drink at your age—why it's outrageous. I will have to bring this to your father's attention as soon as he gets home. And I must call Gloria's mother too—I feel she must know about this."

Jane leaned back in her chair in disbelief. Her mother had gotten things all out of proportion. She simply couldn't convince her that she had done nothing wrong. Maybe Gloria would have better luck with her parents. Jane thought, "Maybe we should have drunk after all. She couldn't act any worse if we had."

WRITE HOW THE STORY BEGAN

Billy Stone and Jeff White had been best friends ever since they began Cub Scouts together, back in second grade. They had worked with each other on badges, taken swimming lessons together, and tomorrow were both going to try out for Little League.

Billy asked his folks if Jeff could sleep over, so they could go to tryouts together.

"It's O.K. with us, Billy, if Jeff's parents agree," said Bill's mother. "But Daddy and I are going out to dinner, so be sure to tell Mrs. White that you'll have a sitter here."

The Whites agreed, and Jeff came to Bill's house, with his suitcase and baseball gear. After dinner, they watched TV for a while, but there was nothing good on.

"What do you want to do now, Jeff?" asked Billy.

"I don't know. How about Monopoly or cards?" Jeff answered.

"I hate playing cards, and Monopoly's no good with just two players," said Bill.

"What about your sitter?" Jeff replied. "Maybe she'll play with us, or think of something."

"Oh, she's just going to spend the whole time fixing her nails and talking on the phone," Bill said. "She never wants to do anything."

The boys decided to get a snack and talk in bed.

"It'll be a good idea to get rested before tryouts anyway," they decided.

When they looked in the refrigerator for something to eat, Jeff saw some bottles of beer.

"Ever try any?" he asked.

"Heck, no!" said Bill. "My folks don't let me."

"Let's just open one to see what it's like," Jeff suggested.

"I don't know. I don't think so. We'd better not," Bill said nervously.

"They'll never know. There must be a dozen in there. You're not scared, are you?" Jeff teased.

"No!" Bill cried. "I'm not."

The beer was awful, but neither boy wanted to admit it. They were so tired after each having a whole bottle that they just dumped the empty containers on the floor between their beds and went to sleep.

WRITE HOW THE STORY ENDS

"Aw, he's just chicken. He wouldn't drink milk if someone told him it could make you feel good. I always figured that when the chips were down he'd back out. Pass me another can, will you Jack."

WRITE HOW THE STORY BEGAN

Activity 20
RULES FOR DRINKING BY YOUNGSTERS

Focus: Parents and Children
Method: Discussion
Grade Levels: 4-12
Time: 1/2-1 Period

Capsule Description:
Students discuss what restrictions they would set for their children on drinking and why.

ACTIVITY

Prior to this class, give your students a sheet on which they fill in rules they believe should be enforced for a teenage son and daughter regarding alcohol use. A sample form appears below.

You are the parent of a son and daughter your age. What rules, if any, regarding their use of alcohol will you set? You may want to consider:

	Son	Daughter	When	Amount	Type	Penalty for disobeying
• drink at home?						
• outside home?						
• drive after drinking?						
• buy liquor?						
• serve liquor to friends?						

Divide the class into small groups so that students with different viewpoints, as expressed on their complete forms, are included in each group. Have the groups attempt to resolve their disagreements and then have each group present its conclusions to the class. Record the different groups' rules on the blackboard and see if the class can develop a consensus on what each rule should be. Make sure the rationale for each rule is fully explored (several students may agree on a particular rule for very different reasons).

As a follow-up exercise to this activity, you and your students can invite parents to class to discuss the rules the class has developed and to explain and discuss the rules the parents have established for their own children. Parents of students in the class should be excluded to avoid embarrassment. One approach to structuring the meeting is to have one or two parents meet with small groups of students for informal discussion, and then each group can report its agreements and disagreements to the rest of the class. Before the discussion, the class should write a list of questions it plans to ask the parents and develop several scenarios for the parents to respond to along the lines of those provided in activity #18. The class can also consider role playing the situations in activity #18 with parents taking the roles of sons and daughters and the students playing the parts of the parents.

Another follow-up exercise your students can engage in is to debate what the legal drinking age should be in their state. Once again, a small group discussion approach may be best, in which students with different views about the best age are placed in the same groups to thrash out a consensus.

Activity 21
PEER PRESSURE TO DRINK

Focus: Peer Pressure
Methods: Story Completion
               Discussion
               Role Play
Grade Levels: 4–College
Time: 1/2–3 Periods

Capsule Description:
Students engage in one or more activities revolving around peer pressure to abstain, drink, or drink abusively.

ACTIVITY

This activity has three options, although you may want to use more than one, especially at different times during your unit.

1. Give your students—or read aloud—the stories provided at the end of this activity and instruct them to write in—or describe verbally—the incomplete portions. Tell your students that there are no "right" or "wrong" beginnings, middles, or ends. They should fill in the missing parts as they wish, making sure simply to be as realistic as possible. This does not mean always writing what would most likely have happened but what certainly could have happened.

When students have completed one or more stories, break them into small groups and give them written instructions to:

- Read each other's stories.
- Compare your endings, beginnings, or middles and explain to each other why you wrote what you did.
- Discuss and record what each section *should* have been if your only reason in writing it

were to show the *best* way to handle the problem.

Have the groups report their discussion results to the rest of the class and compare results. Then discuss whether peer pressure exists among youngsters and adults at various age levels and how strong the pressures are to drink, abstain, or drink abusively. Ask the class why people exert pressure on each other to drink, abstain, or drink abusively and how people who are being pressured can resist, if they would like to. Also discuss whether peer pressure can be beneficial and what might distinguish "good" peer pressure from "bad" peer pressure.

2. Have your students explore ways to cope with peer pressure to drink or abstain by responding to hypothetical letters from various age students in situations of conflict about alcohol use. Sample letters are provided at the end of the activity. Students can write or present verbally answers to the letters either as a class or, still better, in small groups. If you break the class into small groups, tell the groups to act as a "consultant bureau." Each "bureau" must

177

answer each letter with a letter of advice. If the students in a particular group disagree among themselves about what their responses should contain, they may develop more than one letter. The entire class can then compare all the letters and list on the blackboard the different approaches suggested for resisting peer pressure. Follow-up discussion can center on discussing how different approaches may be most useful for different people on different occasions.

3. Your students can also role play scenes in which someone is being pressured to drink,

drink excessively, or abstain. Sample role profiles which you can use are provided at the end of the activity. Follow-up discussion can focus on what techniques seemed to be effective in resisting pressure, how people feel about using them, and why people try to exert pressure on others to drink, abstain, or drink abusively.

With all three options, you can have your students individually or in small groups develop their own incomplete stories, "Dear Abby" letters, or role profiles for other students or groups in the class to respond to or act out.

1. This is the beginning to a story. How will it end?

Penny Smith hung up.

"Wouldn't you know it?" she muttered. "Every time I take a babysitting job, the kids plan a get-together. I miss all the fun."

She called everyone she could think of to find a substitute, even Goony Grace. No dice. They were all busy. And the Masons had asked her to sit weeks ago. She just couldn't back out at the last minute.

She tried and tried to forget about missing the fun, but the more she tried, the more she thought about it.

Then she wondered . . . did she dare . . . no, she couldn't. She couldn't have them all come to the Masons' after she got the little kids in bed. Could she? Maybe they could all stop by, just for a few minutes. That wouldn't be so bad.

Ignoring her conscience, she called back. Well, said the kids, they'd see. Maybe.

That night, at the Masons', she was nervous.

"What time do you think you'll be home?" she asked Mrs. Mason.

"Well, dear, it's quite a special outing for us, so I imagine fairly late. Around one. Is that all right? You don't have a curfew tonight, do you?" Mrs. Mason smiled.

"No, no, it's O.K.," gulped Penny.

FINISH THE STORY

2. Write the middle to the following story.

Sally Prince hated the big family picnic every summer. She was just the wrong age. The grownups sat around after eating and gossiped and drank beer or high-balls. Her teenage cousins and their friends always went off by themselves with a record player. The little boys played some noisy game, and she was expected to stay with the little girls. There was just nobody her age.

"Sally is so sweet to the younger ones," everyone complimented her parents.

Well, Sally didn't feel sweet, and she promised herself that now that she was 12-1/2 she wasn't going to be a free babysitter anymore.

Worst of all, her folks wouldn't let her stay home when she begged them. There were relatives who saw her only once a year, and her parents were so proud of her, they said; they just loved having her come. They even promised her a new, more grown-up outfit.

"You're growing up, dear," said Mrs. Prince. "You'll probably be spending this picnic mostly with the older children."

"Children!" thought Sally. "That's what's wrong with parents. They don't understand!"

To her, the older cousins were glamorous creatures from another world, with their music, fancy clothes, makeup, jangling jewelry.

WRITE THE MIDDLE

"I have never been so humiliated in my life," wept Mrs. Prince. "Everyone must have noticed that you were DRUNK!"

"I was not!" stormed Sally. "And anyway, you made me go, and said I could be with the older CHILDREN."

3. This is the beginning of a story. How will it end?

Lou Moffat was one of the 23 members of his junior high school football team. After a grueling season, the team had just won its division in a close contest with the school's arch rivals. Lou and the other players were ecstatic as they paraded into the locker room right after the game, yelling and cheering and rough housing. The coaches, too, were happy, and congratulated the boys in the locker room and then quickly showered and left, while most of the boys, savoring their victory, fooled around, took their time in the showers and had a massive water fight. Then all but a few of the kids went home.

Just after Lou got out of the shower, however, Sam Lockwood quietly, but loudly enough to be heard by the few kids remaining, announced, "Hey, you guys. I snuck in a bottle of champagne. Now that the coaches are gone let's open it and *really* celebrate!" Sam popped the cork amid cries of "Alright" and "Right on" and the kids started passing the bottle around.

Lou had never drunk alcohol before, except for a little wine with his parents at Christmas or on other holidays. He knew that the coaches or some other teacher might come back into the locker room at any moment, and he was nervous not only of what they might do but also what would happen if the coaches or whoever else caught them told his parents. He also knew that when the bottle reached him all the kids would expect him to drink. There were only five kids left in the locker room and the kid next to him was wiping off the bottle with his tee shirt before taking a swig; it would only be a matter of seconds before it was passed to him.

WRITE THE ENDING

4. This is the beginning of a story. How will it end?

The 8:15 bell rang. At the same moment, Rick Brown slid through the door and fell into his homeroom seat. As attendance was being taken and notices passed out, he turned with an exaggerated sigh.

"Boy! Did I tie one on last night," he exclaimed.

"Big deal!" retorted Ken Smith, behind him.

"Man, that was some party. You should have come. They had beer, all kinds of booze, and some really groovy chicks," grinned Rick.

"Yeah, sure. And flunk the math final," grunted Ken. "I could really afford that."

"Well, little old Bob, here, is gonna help me out, aren't you, Bob?" asked Rick. "I really didn't have time to look the stuff over," he continued, "and I need a decent grade to stay on the basketball team."

Bob Wells looked at Rick. He really did look rotten. His eyes were pink and watery and his face was flushed. Rick had been pretty nice to him when he came to Hayworth High this fall. Bob was quiet and shy, being new to town, and Rick had taken him under his wing. A nice thing for a big man in school to do, a star basketball player, popular with everyone. He had introduced Bob to a lot of kids, included him at his lunchroom table, and even got him a job in charge of basketball equipment.

"Well," faltered Bob, "if it would be any help, you can have all my notes to look over until the test."

"Great!" exclaimed Rick. "That should help a lot. I knew I could count on you."

Bob gave Rick the notes, relieved that he could be of help to someone who had befriended him.

At 3rd period, Rick sat in the seat next to Bob. He looked worried.

"Those notes did help some," he said, returning them. "I'll be O.K. if old man Gray doesn't throw the whole course at us."

Exam papers were passed out and the room fell silent. Bob looked at the test and his heart sank. This was a killer, and although he could handle it, he doubted that Rick could. He started to write.

Ten minutes went by. There was no sound but the scratching of pencil on paper and an occasional sigh. Mr. Gray stood alertly in front of the room.

A small note landed on Bob's desk. Bob cupped his hand over it and transferred it to his lap. Glancing down, he read:

SLIDE YOUR PAPER TO THE EDGE.

I'M DEAD IF YOU DON'T.

Bob was sweating. Mr. Gray might see if he wrote an answer, or completed his test in an unnatural position, inches from Rick.

WRITE THE ENDING

Dear Abby,

I'm 13 years old and sometimes when I go out with my three best friends they get an older brother to buy us some beer. Usually someone's parents are out and we go over to his house and drink. My friends get pretty high and sometimes drunk. I try to drink as little as possible, but they keep pressing me to drink more. If my parents catch me, I'll be grounded for weeks, and I'm not really that interested in drinking anyway. But these are my closest friends. What can I do?

Pressured

HOW WILL YOU RESPOND?

Dear Abby,

Last week I went to the movies with three friends. On the way home we ran into one of their older brothers who had a case of beer in his car. He gave us a six pack saying, "It's about time you found out what life's all about." My friends thought this was a great chance and we all went to the river to drink. I refused to drink because I think I'm too young (I'm 12 years old) and because it's not worth getting caught by my parents and upsetting them and being punished. But my friends have now passed the word around the school that I'm chicken and a fink. The kids who believe them are the ones I want for friends because they're my type of friend, but I'm sick of getting picked on and being given the "cold shoulder." What can I do?

Bothered

HOW WILL YOU RESPOND?

Dear Abby,

We live in a "dry" town where everyone pretends not to drink. Of course, all the people who like their liquor just drive to the next town to get alcohol. My family has wine with meals at home, which isn't against the law. But the kids I go around with call my family "a bunch of drunks" behind my back. Just last night a very good friend told me that I shouldn't start by having wine with meals, or I'll end up an alcoholic. That's never happened to anyone in my family that I know of. But could my friends be right?

I don't want to be picked on by my friends, but I want to fit in at home, too. Whom do I listen to?

Befuddled

HOW WILL YOU RESPOND?

Nondrinker or Social Drinker. You are 15 years old and sometimes go out with your three best friends, Sam, John, and Bob, when they've had an older brother buy you all some beer. Usually someone's parents are out and you go over to his house and drink. Your friends get pretty high and sometimes drunk. You try to drink as little as possible but they keep pressing you to drink more. If your parents catch you, you'll be grounded for weeks, and anyway you don't really like alcohol. But these are your closest friends.

You're now at a house drinking, but you've so far had only half a beer. How will you respond to your friends' efforts to get you to drink more?

Peers. You and your three other friends form a close group, and you all like to go drinking sometimes when you can get some beer and a vacant house. But Louis tries to drink as little as possible and acts chicken whenever the rest of you drink (though he's a great kid in every other way). It spoils your fun to have one of you sober.

You're now at a house drinking and he's already hardly drinking at all. What will you say to him to get him to drink with you and have some fun and not spoil it for you?

Nondrinker or Social Drinker. You've been dating this guy you really like, but he not only never drinks (which is OK) but he also objects to your drinking wine with meals and beer at parties. He feels "nice" girls don't drink, except for champagne on New Year's, and he and you keep getting into fights over it. You like to relax with a beer or two at parties.

You're at a party now and he's starting to complain about your drinking. How will you respond?

Peer. You don't like the idea of girls drinking because it presents a lousy image. Your girl, whom you really like in all other respects, is on her second beer already at this party. She doesn't usually have more than two or three and usually stays sober. Still, it looks cheap, especially drinking it right from the can. You want her to stop. What will you say?

Nondrinker or Social Drinker. You have been dating and are seriously interested in a pretty girl. Every time you have dinner with or visit her family, they pester you to have some wine with dinner or a drink. You don't like to drink, but the family feels you've insulted their hospitality. You've just gone over for Sunday dinner, and you don't feel like getting hassled again about drinking. What will you say if offered a drink?

Peer. You are dating this boy whom you like, but whenever he visits your house or has dinner he refused to accept your hospitality by sharing wine at dinner or a drink. What kind of man is he, anyway? He always drinks Coke. He's just come in for Sunday dinner, and you want to make him feel at home so you offer him a drink.

Nondrinker or Social Drinker. You, Bob, have gone to the movies on this Saturday afternoon with three friends, Sam, Fred, and Richard. On the way home, you run into one of their older brothers who has a case of beer in his car. He gives his younger brother (your friend) a six pack and tells you all to "have a blast—it's about time you found out what life's all about." Your friends think this is a great chance and you all go off to the river, behind the trees, to drink. You don't want to drink, however, but your friends are all starting to open the beer. What do you do now?

Peer(s). You have gone to the movies on this Saturday afternoon with three friends, Fred, Richard, and Bob. On the way home you run into one of their older brothers who has a case of beer in his car. He gives his younger brother (your friend) a six pack and tells you all to "have a blast—it's about time you found out what life's all about." You think this is a great idea, but Bob doesn't seem to. In fact, now that you're all by the river opening the cans, he hasn't picked up one. You don't want him to miss the fun or spoil it for the rest of you. How will you try to persuade him to drink?

Drinker. You are at a friend's house, but nobody is home. Your friend's parents have gone out for the evening. About nine o'clock, you both look in the refrigerator for a snack. You see not only Coke and fruit, but also about ten cans of beer. You say to your friend, "Let's open a can and try some!" You've been wanting to try some beer for a while, but your parents say you're too young. How will you be able to persuade your friend to have some beer with you?

Friend. You have invited a friend over to your house for the evening because your parents have gone out for the night. About nine o'clock, you both look in the refrigerator for a snack. You see not only Coke and fruit, but also about ten cans of beer. Your parents let you take a sip now and then at dinner, but you really don't like the taste of it. Besides, you are afraid to drink too much. You don't know what will happen if you do. Your friend says to you, "Let's open a can and try some!" What do you say?

Activity 22
RESPONSIBILITY FOR OTHERS'
DRINKING BEHAVIOR

Focus: Interpersonal Responsibilities
Methods: Discussion
Role Play
Grade Levels: 3-College
Time: 1/2-3 Periods

Capsule Description:
Students engage in one or more activities revolving around issues of responsibility for other people's drinking behavior.

ACTIVITY

At the end of this activity are scenarios, role profiles, and a story completion exercise that you can use as take-off points for discussing what a person's responsibilities are or should be toward other people who may be drinking abusively. Situations that can be discussed or role played include the following:

- two friends together, one of whom is about to drink
- a host at a party confronted with a guest who is getting drunk and plans to drive home
- two friends, one of whom is drunk and about to drive
- relatives of a pregnant woman who may be drinking in a manner that presents risks to her unborn child
- two friends, one of whom is about to ride with a drunk driver
- two older youths, one of whom is about to buy alcohol for an underage youngster

The discussions can focus on such issues as:

1. In each of the role plays or discussion scenarios, does the individual have a responsibility to the person who is drinking abusively? Why or why not? If so, what is his or her responsibility to the abusive drinker?

2. In each of the role plays or scenarios, what alternative actions could the person exercising responsibility take with regard to the abusive drinker? Where does the responsible person's responsibility stop or end—how many attempts and what kinds of attempts to help the abusive drinker should he or she engage in before deciding to stop trying? Should he or she ever stop trying? Why or why not?

3. What makes some people reluctant to exercise responsibility for other people who abuse alcohol? Can anything be done to encourage greater responsibility? Should something be done? Why or why not?

4. Are there instances in which if we don't take responsibility for someone else who is abusing alcohol and something bad happens (for example, he or she drives home drunk

and gets into an accident), we are to blame for what happens?

5. Should bartenders be legally responsible if a customer is allowed to drink too much and gets into an accident and kills or injures another driver or a pedestrian? In California, over 400 such lawsuits have been brought by victims of drunk drivers against bartenders or bar owners, and several have been successful. Should the bartender or bar owner be responsible? Why or why not?

6. Should a host be legally responsible if he or she allows a guest to drink too much and the guest injures someone driving home? (See suggestions for hosts after last role profile.)

You will probably find that what begins as a discussion or role play around a very specific and even trivial issue of responsibility for some-one else's drinking behavior mushrooms into a more global debate on whether we have a responsibility in general to other people who engage in self-destructive behavior or behavior which may endanger other people (for example, drunk driving). Such a branching out into larger issues is very useful. However, you can improve the quality of the discussion if you require your students to return to specific situations in which a person must choose to exercise or not exercise responsibility for someone else's behavior so that the debate does not dwell too long on simple generalities. It may be helpful in this regard to have your students develop scenarios and role profiles of their own for each other to address or act out. Where possible, have your students develop them in small groups and have other small groups be responsible for addressing them or acting them out.

You are 18 years old. Your best friend is 17 and wants you to buy a case of beer for his 15-year-old younger brother who plans to go drinking in the park with some friends. Will you buy it? Why or why not?

You are 19 and your younger sister (16) has asked you to buy a bottle of champagne for her so she can celebrate her boyfriend's birthday. Will you buy it? Why or why not?

A 22-year-old man is accused of having illegally bought a six-pack of beer for a 13-year-old boy who had asked him to do it as a favor. The boy got drunk and went swimming at midnight and drowned. The man was a friend of the boy's father and felt he was just doing the kid a favor. You are the judge in the case. What do you decide?

A 17-year-old girl asked her older sister to buy a bottle of champagne for her to celebrate her boyfriend's birthday. The sister complied. The girl and her boyfriend drank the bottle in the local park. They began to get silly and loud and neighbors called the police complaining about the noise. They were arrested on a charge of disturbing the peace. You are the judge in the case. What do you decide?

Your father has been drinking heavily and is about to drive your mother to do some grocery shopping. It is 9:00 P.M. and the roads are still icy from the previous day's snowstorm. She has no license and there is no food in the refrigerator. What, if anything, *would* you do? Why? What, if anything *should* you do? (Or: what would you *want* to do?) Why?

Your 17-year-old sister has a date with her boyfriend. You just let him in the door, and he's obviously drunk since he knocked over a lamp trying to sit down and has talked only nonsense. You go upstairs and tell your sister he's drunk, and she tells you to mind your own business. You know they are going in his car to a party way on the other side of town. Your parents are next door with friends. What, if anything, *would* you do? Why? What, if anything, *should* you do? Why?

You are hitchhiking to school because you are already late for first period. A nice-looking, middle-aged lady in a station wagon offers you a ride, so you get in. You are sitting next to her in the front seat, and you can smell whiskey on her breath. In the back are her two small children and a dog. What *would* you do? Why? What *should* you do? Why?

Date. You are 16 years old and at a party with 25 friends. You've been going with your present date for 5 months. She has a habit of drinking too much at parties and then going around flirting with other boys. She's already had two beers and has just opened a third. What, if anything, do you do? (You've had two beers, too, but you can hold your liquor.)

Excessive Drinker. You are 16 years old and at a party with 25 friends. You have been dating this boy for about four months. You like to get "high" at these parties because you feel less shy with other people and it just makes you happy—and you don't mind making your boyfriend a little jealous by flirting with another boy or two. You're on your third beer now.

Date. You are 16 years old and at a party with 14 friends. You've been dating this boy for 3 months and he's never had more than two drinks. But tonight he's already on his fourth and starting to get loud and pushy. What, if anything, do you do?

Excessive Drinker. You are 17 years old and at a party with 14 friends. You've been dating this girl for 2-1/2 months. Tonight you feel especially good and you're on your third beer. Usually you have only two and hardly ever get drunk. You're sure you can hold your liquor.

Minor. You are a 15-year-old girl or boy and you want to celebrate your boyfriend's (girl-friend's) birthday by sharing a bottle of champagne. You have just been refused service in a package store. As you walk out, a kindly looking man who watched as you were refused holds the door for you. He had been buying, too. You figure, as you both step out the door, that he might buy for you. You'd even offer him a $1.00 to do it for you if you had to.

Adult. You are a 22-year-old married man buying some beer for a party you're having tonight. You've been watching a young boy (girl) being refused service because he (she) is too young. You hold the door open for him (her) as you both walk out.

Minor. You are 15 years old and you've promised your two friends you'll get a case of beer so you can go drinking in the park on Friday night (tonight). You've gone drinking before but you've never been the one to supply the beer. Your older brother is away for the weekend or you'd ask him (you really aren't sure he'd get it for you). So you figure his best friend might buy for you, especially if you offer him a few free cans.

Adult. Your best friend's 15-year-old brother is walking over to you. You don't know him too well but you do know that his parents are pretty strict about things. You are lounging around bored and broke in front of the ice cream shop because your best friend has gone away for the weekend. You yourself like drinking beer and getting drunk once in awhile.

Friend. Your best friend is pretty drunk and is ready to drive his girl home. You feel he's in no condition to drive and even if he doesn't hurt himself, his girl, or someone else, he's liable to get arrested and lose his license. But you know you're going to have a tough time convincing him not to drive when he's with his girl. She'd like him not to drive but is afraid to say so. In addition, he has no money to take a taxi and there are no buses around this neighborhood.

Girlfriend. Your boyfriend at this party has been drinking quite a bit, something he usually doesn't do. You've kidded him about it, trying to get him to slow down, but he won't take the hint. Now he's ready to drive you home and you'd rather he didn't drive but you're afraid to tell him not to.

Drinking Driver. You are with your girlfriend at a party and have had quite a bit to drink, but you're not about to admit to her that you're too drunk to drive her home—that you can't hold your liquor. Besides, she lives only four miles away and the roads should be pretty empty at 2:00 A.M.

Friend. You and four friends have been drinking in the park. Three of them start walking home, but the one who owns the car and is really drunk stays to drink a little longer with you. He's going to insist on driving you home because he won't admit he can't hold his liquor and, anyway, seems to get his kicks out of doing risky things. You know that if you refuse to go with him he will still try to drive home. Now that it's 2:00 A.M. he starts to stagger up to leave.

Drinking Driver. You've been drinking in the park with four friends. Three have started walking home and now you're almost ready to give the fourth one a ride home. You've had quite a bit to drink, but it's fun, you feel, to try to drive when you're drunk. You start to get up to go home, and you'll insist on giving your friend a lift—it's more fun driving with someone when you're drunk. Your friend is usually a "sissy" and you want to help him (her) get over that.

Host. You (Lou) and your wife are the hosts at a party of six couples. You have served beer and whiskey. It is the end of the evening and John and Lucy are about to drive home. You don't know how much they've had to drink, but John seems a little unsteady. They live about 4 miles away. Lucy says, "Lou, I don't think my husband can drive safely. What should we do? I don't have a license." What do you say? What, if anything, should you say? Why?

Guest. You (John) and your wife have been having a good time at Lou's party. You've had about four or five beers since nine (it's now 11) and your wife has had a couple. You're ready to drive home now. You live 3 miles away.

Host. You (Sam) are the 18-year-old host at a party for several friends after a football game. Susan is getting drunk on beer and you know that whenever this happens she gets sick, vomits, and has an awful hangover the next day. She came without a boyfriend and has been flirting with several different people. She goes up to you, while you're at the refrigerator, and says, "Grab me another beer, will you!" What, if anything, will you do? What, if anything, should you do? Why?

Guest. You (Susan) are having a great time at Sam's party after the football game. You've had a few beers, but you aren't drunk, you feel, and you won't let yourself get drunk because you throw up when you do. Your boyfriend is not with you this evening, so you've been moving around talking to other people.

Host. You (Peter) and your wife are the adult hosts at a party of six couples. You have been serving mixed drinks. It is the middle of the evening and you can tell that Frank and Susan are both starting to get drunk. They drove over from their home 37 miles away and, because they couldn't find a babysitter, put their baby in one of your bedrooms to sleep until they are ready to drive home. Frank comes over to you and says, "Make a couple Tom Collins for me and my wife." What will you do? What should you do? Why?

Guest. You (Frank) and your wife are having a great time at Peter's party. You were unable to get a babysitter so your drove over (37 miles) with your baby who's now sleeping upstairs. You've both had a few cocktails and feel fine, a little "high" perhaps, but not drunk. It's time to go home, but you decide to have one last drink with your wife. You ask Peter to make two Tom Collins.

Host. You (Bob) are the 18-year-old host at a party for several friends after the football game. Sam, one of your friends, is just getting over mono and is under strict doctor's orders not to drink. Sam's girlfriend has asked you not to serve him anything. Sam is coming over to you right now and you know he's going to ask you for just one beer. What, if anything, will you do? What, if anything, should you do? Why?

Guest. You (Sam) are at Bob's party, but you feel left out because you're not supposed to drink any alcohol because you just got over mono. Your girlfriend is keeping an eye out on you because she doesn't want you getting sick on her. But she's in the ladies room right now so you go over to Bob to ask him to get you just one beer.

Mary has always looked up to her older sister, and so when she learned Peg was pregnant she was thrilled. Mary began to be concerned after her class covered the Fetal Alcohol Syndrome, and she realized that Peg was a fairly regular drinker. She decided to speak to Peg about this and accepted the next dinner invitation her "big sister" offered. Peg greeted her at the door with her nightly cocktail in hand and said, "Tonight we're going to celebrate the fact that you're going to become an aunt—and I'm going to get good and high!" Mary took off her coat and joined her sister and brother-in-law in the living room. When Peg asked her husband to make her another martini, Mary began to get nervous. Finally, she said,

FINISH THE STORY

The bartender: Choose a bartender of know discretion. The eager volunteer may turn out to be a pusher who uses the role to give every glass an extra "shot."

Pace the drinks: Serve drinks at regular, reasonable intervals. The length of the interval will depend on whether the guests are enjoying the company or the drinks more. A drink-an-hour schedule means good company prevails.

Don't double up: Many people count and pace their drinks. If you serve doubles, they'll be drinking twice as much as they planned. Doubling up isn't hospitality; it's rude.

Don't push drinks: Let the glass be empty before you offer a refill. And then don't rush, especially if someone comes up empty too fast. When a guest says "No thanks" to an alcohol drink—don't insist.

Push the snacks: Do this while your guests are drinking, not after. This is important because food slows down the rate at which alcohol is absorbed into the bloodstream. It also slows the rate at which people drink.

Serve nonalcoholic drinks, too: One out of three adults chooses not to drink at all. Occasional drinkers sometimes prefer not to. Offer a choice of drinks besides alcohol—fruit and vegetable juices, tea, coffee, and soft drinks.

Offer more than drinks: When guests focus on the drinks, the party is slipping. Stir up conversation. Share a laugh. Draw out the guest talent. A good host or hostess has more to give than just food and drinks.

Serving dinner: If it's a dinner party, serve before it's too late. A cocktail hour is supposed to enhance a fine dinner, not compete with it. After too many drinks, guests may not know what they ate or how it tasted.

Set drinking limits: When a guest has had too much to drink, you can politely express your concern for him by offering a substitute drink—coffee, perhaps. This is a gentle way of telling a guest that he has reached the limits you have set for your home.

Closing the bar: Decide in advance when you want your party to end. Then give appropriate cues by word and action that it's time to leave. A considerate way to close the drinking phase is to serve a substantial snack. It also provides some nondrinking time before your guests start to drive home.

Activity 23
DRINKING AND DRIVING DILEMMAS

Focus: Drinking and Driving; Peer
          Relations
Methods: Story Completion
            Discussion
            Role Play
Grade Levels: 6–College
Time: 1/2–2 Periods

Capsule Description:
Students engage in one or more activities in
which their personal safety in a drunk driving
situation is explored.

ACTIVITY

At the end of this activity are stories for students to complete, scenarios for them to respond to, and role profiles for them to act out.
Choose—or have your students choose—which
materials to address, and follow up each story
completion, scenario response, or role play with
a discussion on the following issues:

1. What are the alternatives available to the
person in danger in each situation? (List
them on the blackboard.)
2. Which option or options are best? Why?
How does one decide?
3. What are some of the obstacles that make it
difficult for people in these situations to act
in their own best interest—that is, do what
would be safest for themselves? Peer pressure? Inconvenience (having to walk home,
etc.)? Expense (having to take a taxi, etc.)?
Concern for protecting the drunk driver?

This is the beginning of a story. Write how it ends.

Susan didn't particularly like to babysit, but her family didn't have that much money so if she wanted to have any money to buy the things she wanted—records, clothing, etc.—she had to work for it. At least while she was babysitting she could talk to her friends on the phone, watch TV or get her homework out of the way.

Sue had been babysitting for a number of people, but mostly for the Smiths, who had been very nice to her. They mentioned one night that they had friends who wanted a babysitter and would she like to sit for their kids too, if Sue wouldn't mind going to Littleton which was five miles away. Susan was glad to have the opportunity to make some more money, especially since Friday night, the night this other couple needed her, her boyfriend was going to be busy playing night baseball anyway. She could get a lift over from her mother and the Smiths said the other couple would take her home.

So Sue babysat on Friday for this new couple—Ralston was their name—and all went well with their two quiet boys. The Ralstons came home at midnight, and while Mrs. Ralston went straight upstairs to go to bed, Mr. Ralston said, as had been agreed earlier, he would take Susan home. But Susan noticed that when he came in the door he was making silly comments to his wife about, "Too wild for you, was it? Not for me!" and he then tripped over the dinner table leg and yelled, "When are you gonna get rid of this old hunk of furniture your mother crammed down our throats, huh?" His eyes were bleary and, all in all, he seemed pretty drunk.

"Soon as I pay a quick visit to the Ralston Rest Room, I'll drive you home. Be right back."

WRITE HOW THE STORY ENDS

You are just finishing up Little League practice and your brother has come to pick you up. He hates to do this and you know it, but the ballpark is several miles from home and a taxi would be expensive. Your father is working, and your mother is taking care of your brothers and sisters. This time your brother is roaring drunk but insists he's able to drive OK. You have about 25 cents on you. Bus fare home is 40 cents. What *will* you do? What *should* you do? Why?

Your friend has given a party. Now it's 9:15 P.M. and his father, who is quite drunk, has offered to drive you home, since you live too far away to walk. Your own parents are out for the evening. You offer to call a cab since you have some money, but he says that is silly. What *will* you do? What *should* you do? Why?

Driver. You're driving home from a party, giving your best friend a lift home first. You simply don't believe you're drunk even though you had a lot to drink at the party. You feel perfectly capable of driving, and it would take a lot to get you to change your mind.

Passenger. You're getting a ride home with your best friend after a party at which he (she) had a lot to drink, and you had very little because you're just getting over mono. Your friend is bombed out of his (her) mind. He (she) keeps driving in the left lane and has already run two red lights. It's another twelve miles to your home along the freeway.

Driver. You're driving your steady date home from a party where you had a lot to drink, and there's another couple talking in the back seat that you're taking home, too. Your date is sitting next to you, and you're not about to let her or the guy in the back seat know you can't hold your liquor, even though you know deep down you're in no shape to be driving, because you've stalled the engine once and run through at least one red light.

Passenger. You are getting a ride home with a friend. His date is with him in the front seat and you're with yours in the back. You'd like to be concentrating on impressing your date, but your friend is pretty drunk. Every few minutes he does something weird like running through two red lights and stopping at one green light. He's stalled the engine once and tried to comb his hair in the rear-view mirror while driving 50 mph. It's eight more miles to your girl's home.

Activity 24
MISCONCEPTIONS
ABOUT ALCOHOLISM

Focus:	Alcoholism	
Methods:	Questionnaire	
	Discussion	
	Lecture	
Grade Levels:	4–College	
Time:	1/2–2 Periods	

Capsule Description:
Students express their perceptions about alcoholics and any misconceptions they may have are corrected.

ACTIVITY

This activity has three parts. You can conduct one, two, or all three of them. However, if you use more than one, it is suggested that you implement them in the sequence provided below.

1. Distribute copies of the Alcoholism Questionnaire provided at the end of this activity or read the questions aloud and have your students record their answers on note paper. Tabulate the results for the class on the blackboard. If you plan to conduct the second part of this activity, present the correct answers later after that exercise. Otherwise, provide the answers now. If several members of the class answered one or more of the questions incorrectly, ask the students to consider why these misconceptions about alcoholics may be so prevalent. See if the class can identify any other misinformation the public may have about alcoholism. As a follow-up activity, the class can administer the questionnaire to parents, other students, faculty, school secretaries and custodians, and other members of the local community. The results can be analyzed in terms of how misinformation about alcoholism may create a climate in which there are few services for those with alcoholism and alcoholics will be less likely to seek treatment, especially in the early stages.

2. Write the word alcoholic on the chalkboard. Ask your students to jot down on a piece of paper (or brainstorm orally) all the words or phrases that come to mind when they hear or see that word. Using their lists, have your students write or narrate a short story or description of an alcoholic, emphasizing the characteristics and the behavior they associate with one. Ask for volunteers to read their descriptions. The class should assess and discuss each one, looking for such things as:

- exaggeration
- realism
- stereotyping
- varying types of behavior

Have your students determine, as best they can, if the class has an accurate conception about the nature of alcoholism. Contribute corrective information yourself, as needed, based on the information provided in chapters 2 and 3 of this book.

3. Present as much information about alcoholism as may be appropriate to the needs of your students that they cannot learn more profoundly and interestingly through other approaches—independent study, interviews, role play, or field trips. Using the outline presented below, you can present some or all of the information discussed in detail in chapter 3.

1. Differences between social drinking, problem drinking, and alcoholism

2. Nature of alcoholism—loss of control; addiction; physical, emotional, or social harm; disease concept of alcoholism

3. Theories of causation: physiological, psychological, sociological

4. Help for the alcoholic: Alcoholics Anonymous, drugs, counseling, and time. Help for the family members and friends of alcoholics: Al-Anon, Alateen, and family therapy.

You can enliven your presentation by using audiovisual materials listed in the Resources.

1. An alcoholic is someone who
   a. drinks too much once in a while.
   b. usually can't stop drinking once he or she has one drink.
   c. has problems because of his or her drinking.
   d. must get drunk every day to be called an alcoholic.
2. It's impossible for someone to become an alcoholic by drinking just beer.
3. Most alcoholics have jobs and live with their families.
4. Almost all alcoholics are men.
5. Alcoholics are usually people who, if they wanted to, could easily "pull themselves together" and stop drinking without outside help.
6. Most alcoholics are skid row bums.
7. There are many more alcoholics in this country than drug addicts.
8. Once people become alcoholics, it's too late to help them.
9. Problem drinkers can sometimes control whether they drink and how they drink; alcoholics usually cannot.
10. Problem drinkers are often alcoholics in an early stage of their disease.

Answers:

1.	a: False	2. False	3. True	6. False	10. True
	b: True	4. False	7. True	8. False	
	c: True	5. False	9. True		
	d: False				

Activity 25
DEFINING EXCESSIVE
OR PROBLEM DRINKING

Focus: Problem drinking
Method: Discussion
Grade Levels: 4–College
Time: 1/2–1 Period

Capsule Description:
Students discuss what they think constitutes
excessive and problem drinking.

ACTIVITY

Break your class into small groups and have
them brainstorm the characteristics and behavior
of someone who drinks too much and his or her
behavior. When the lists have been completed,
try to see if the class can reach a consensus on
what the *major* drinking behaviors and drinking
consequences are that constitute "drinking too
much." Don't expect or even try to get complete agreement, since our society doesn't have
any well recognized consensus about what constitutes excessive drinking. To some extent, each
individual on his or her own must make that
determination. On the other hand, many drink-

ing behaviors are clearly inappropriate and
irresponsible. You can also raise for consideration other drinking behaviors students can evaluate as constituting acceptable drinking or
excessive drinking, such as:

- one cocktail before dinner
- three cocktails before dinner
- a bottle of wine with dinner
- three beers most days after work to help
  relax
- five mixed drinks with 1 ounce of alcohol in
  two hours at a party
- a six-pack of beer watching television for
  three hours on a Sunday afternoon

Activity 26
SIMULATING "CRAVING"
AND "WITHDRAWAL"

Focus: Nature of Alcoholism
Method: Simulation
Discussion
Grade Levels: 3-College
Time: 1/2-1 Periods

Capsule Description:
Students deprive themselves of a highly desirable activity in order to experience some of the feelings alcoholics may have with regard to alcohol.

ACTIVITY

Have each student pick one or two activities he or she does that the pupil would find very difficult—perhaps impossible—to stop doing. Then have each student agree in a written "contract" with the rest of the class to forego the activity for at least a week, but preferably for a month.

It might be more enjoyable and educational for students to experiment along with a friend or small group, with each person renouncing the same activity.

Depending on their "passions," students might:

- use no salt or sugar in their food
- give up cigarettes
- stop seeing or talking with a close friend
- not kiss or touch their girlfriend, boyfriend, husband or wife
- not make or answer any telephone calls

Source: This activity is adapted from Peter Finn, "Empathizing with Addicts," *Health Education,* 9(2), 1978. Copyright the American Alliance for Health, Physical Education, Recreation, and Dance. Reprinted by permission.

- get up at 4:00 A.M. every morning (that is, not sleep late)
- stop watching television or listening to the radio
- give up Coke, coffee, or another favorite beverage
- give up a favorite sport or other form of recreation
- stop chewing gum

It may be helpful for the students to keep a diary of their behavior and feelings during the experiment to jog their memory when they come to relating their experiences to the class. Students can also consider talking into a tape recorder at the end of each day and playing back excerpts to the class at the conclusion of the experiment.

After the students have refrained from their activities for at least a week, have the class review their diaries and then answer the following specific questions:

1. How many of you succeeded in refraining from your activities for the entire period of time stipulated in your "contracts"? How soon did those of you who failed give in? How do those

of you who failed feel about yourselves? Disappointed? Angry? Indifferent? Relieved? How do those of you who succeeded feel about those who failed? Superior? Sympathetic? Resentful? Neutral?

2. What did it feel like not to be doing the activity? Did you miss it badly? Did you get angry? Frightened? Miserable? Grouchy? Bored? Frustrated?

3. Did your relationships with other people change? For example, did you avoid certain people, or people in general, spend more time than usual with certain people, or with people in general, or relate to people differently—for example, argue with them more than normally?

4. Did talking or being with other students who were refraining from the same activity as you (or a different activity) help you to resist the temptation to give in? Did you ask for—and get—help from other people in your attempts to forego the activity? How did they respond? How would you have liked them to respond?

5. Did other people change their behavior, attitudes, or feelings toward you as a result of your experiment? How did you feel about and react to their changed perceptions or actions?

6. Did you start doing things that you don't usually do, like forgetting things, becoming less observant, overeating or developing physical symptoms such as headaches, stomachaches, tics, loss of appetite, insomnia, or unusual fatigue?

7. Did your other activities change at all—for example, did you compensate for the lack of your "forbidden" activity by participating more in some other pursuit? Did the substitute activity help to take your mind off the thing you wanted to do? Did your efforts at compensation affect any of the people around you?

8. Were you confronted with the opportunity to "lapse," and did your will power diminish in the presence of the forbidden activity or object? Were other people considerate in not mentioning the activity or substance, or helpful in suggesting a substitute?

9. Did you go out of your way to avoid the activity or substance, or things that might remind you of it? Did your avoidance behavior help reduce your craving? Did your efforts affect your relations with other people or alter their attitudes toward you?

10. Did you "cheat" at all? If so, did you try to engage in your activity just a little and find you couldn't resist resuming it completely? Did you bother to hide your lapses from other people? If so, did anyone catch you cheating? How did they react? How did you feel about being discovered?

11. When you finally did go back to the activity, how did it feel? Did you try to "make up for lost time"?

After the class has explored the issues related to these questions, students can discuss how their actions and feelings might be similar to those of an alcoholic. The group should also consider how its experiences may have been different from those of compulsive drinkers. For example, the students knew that they could resume their highly prized activity with impunity at the end of the test period, while an alcoholic who has stopped drinking knows that to revert to his former behavior is to court disaster.

Students may also erroneously conclude, based on their own success in resisting temptation, that alcoholics should likewise be able with relative ease to forswear their self-destructive practices, when the students' experiences may have misled them in this regard because their own craving was a comparatively mild one and one made even more bearable by the realization that it was only temporary.

Finally, focus specifically on how the students feel about alcoholics. Do they feel the same way about alcoholics as they felt about themselves during the experiment? Should they? Did they gain any new insights into what it feels like to be an alcoholic and how alcoholics can best be helped to shake off their addiction?

Activity 27
SURFACING AND EXAMINING ATTITUDES
TOWARD ALCOHOLISM

Focus:	Attitudes	*Capsule Description:*
Method:	Discussion	
Grade Levels:	4–College	
Time:	1/2–2 Periods	

Capsule Description:
Students discuss giving money to panhandlers who are drinking and examine the attitudes toward alcoholics which surface during their discussion.

ACTIVITY

This activity has two parts. You can conduct either or both. If you use both, implement them in the order suggested below.

Have the students write how they would respond to the following scenario:

> You are walking down Washington Street, and a panhandler with alcohol on his breath stops you and asks for a quarter. DO YOU GIVE IT TO HIM? Why or why not? Justify your response.*

Then break the class into small groups and instruct them to discuss and agree on the following issues:

*Be sure to point out at the end of the activity that only a minority of people on skid row are alcoholics, and only a small minority of alcoholics (perhaps 3–5 percent) are on skid row.

Source: This activity is adapted from Peter Finn, "Surfacing Attitudes toward Alcoholics," *Journal of Alcohol and Drug Education* 24 (Fall 1978):58–72. Reprinted by permission.

1. Should they give the panhandler the money? Why or why not?
2. How do they feel about the panhandler?
3. Would they give the panhandler the money if he did not have alcohol on his breath? Why or why not?
4. Would they give the panhandler a dollar if he asked for it? Why or why not?

Have each group present its conclusions to the class and record on a blackboard or flip chart the different attitudes and feelings about the panhandler which were expressed. Have the students evaluate the appropriateness of each attitude.

Relate the issue of giving a panhandler a handout to the controversy over what role social institutions—welfare offices, hospitals, law enforcement agencies—should play with regard to alcoholics. Should money be provided to alcoholics with no strings attached? With certain conditions? Which ones? What other actions, if any should society take with regard to alcoholics? What do the students' opinions on these social issues seem to indicate about their attitudes and feelings toward alcoholics as people?

Distribute to the students two or more of the descriptions provided at the end of this activity of different people being importuned for money by panhandlers. Ask the class to consider in small groups:

1. Whether the accosted person would give the money and why or why not?
2. How the accosted person would feel about the panhandler asking him or her for money?
3. Why the students think that is how the accosted person would feel?

Follow-up Discussion

Have each group report its conclusions to the class and then discuss why different people might respond differently to a panhandler. Would these same people respond differently to an alcoholic in the family? What determines how people feel about alcoholics? Are ethnicity, age, social class, occupation, or drinking habits and experience factors? If so, how do they exert their influence? What role, if any, do family background, previous contacts with alcoholics, and peer pressure play in shaping attitudes toward alcoholics?

- A gentleman dressed in a tuxedo has just come out of a supper club and is waiting for a taxi. He has short, dark hair and stands very erect with a calm, confident air. A panhandler with liquor on his breath walks by and says, "Say, buddy, can you spare a quarter?" How does the gentleman *respond*? What does he *feel* toward the panhandler? What is he *thinking*?

- A young woman, dressed in a nurse's uniform, has just stepped off the bus on the way to city hospital. As she walks to the emergency ward entrance, a panhandler with alcohol on his breath goes up to her and says, "Say, lady, can you spare a quarter?" How does she *respond*? What does she *feel* toward the panhandler? What is she *thinking*?

- A young man wearing a construction worker's helmet is having his lunch at an urban renewal site. He is dressed in a T-shirt and has bulging muscles showing below his short sleeves. He is drinking a beer with his liverwurst sandwich. A panhandler with alcohol on his breath walks by and says, "Say, buddy, can you spare a quarter?" How does the worker *respond*? What does he *feel* toward the panhandler? What is he *thinking*?

- An elderly woman living in a project for the aged is walking down to the local grocery store for milk and bread when a panhandler with alcohol on his breath walks up to her and says, ''Say, lady, can you spare a quarter?'' How does the woman *respond*? What does she *feel* toward the panhandler? What is she *thinking*?

- A young man, dressed in designer jeans and wearing beads over a bright blue sports shirt, is walking out of a coffee shop in the early evening. He is with a girlfriend who is wearing a halter, blue jeans, and sandals. They are both a little high on marijuana. As they walk to his secondhand green and orange Volkswagen van, a panhandler with alcohol on his breath approaches them and asks, ''Say, kids, can you spare a quarter?'' How do they *respond*? How do they *feel* toward the panhandler? What are they *thinking*?

- A well dressed man whose clothes are wrinkled and soiled, as if he's been up all night, stops a young couple on their way home from a play. The man smells of liquor, states he's been to a wedding, lost his wallet and now needs a way to get home. He asks them for a couple of dollars. How do they respond? What is happening? How is this different from the other scenarios, or is it?

You or your students can create new scenarios by altering the accosted person's apparent occupation, hairstyle, age, sex clothing, companion(s), place he or she is leaving or entering, and activity he or she was just engaging in.

Activity 28
EXPLORING ATTITUDES TOWARD ALCOHOLICS

Focus: Attitudes
Method: Role Play
               Discussion
Grade Levels: 6–College
Time: 1 Period

Capsule Description:
Students role play scenes in which a parent is concerned about his or her child's friendship with the child of an alcoholic and then discuss the attitudes toward alcoholics revealed in the simulation.

ACTIVITY

Break the students into pairs and give each student in each pair a role profile (child or parent) from among those supplied at the end of the activity or ones developed by you. Have each pair of students role play its scenario by itself. Circulate around the room, listening in on the various conversations. Stimulate discussion where necessary.

Have each pair present its solution or cause for its deadlock to the class. Have one or two pairs volunteer to re-enact their role plays in front of the class.

Conclude the activity by asking the students to discuss:

1. How they feel about the alcoholics they portrayed in their parts?
2. What attitudes toward alcoholics were revealed during their role plays?
3. Why different students might have experienced different feelings and expressed different attitudes toward alcoholics?
4. Which of the attitudes that were expressed are approrpriate and inappropriate and why?

Source: This activity is adapted from Peter Finn, "Surfacing Attitudes toward Alcoholics," *Journal of Alcohol and Drug Education* 24 (Fall 1978):58-72. Reprinted by permission.

Parent. Whenever you pick up your son from Little League practice or games, you see him talking with Richard Smith, another player. The few times you've come early, you've noticed that they sit together on the bench and, during practice, they talk together as they catch fly balls.

Richard's father, old Joe Smith, is, as everyone in the town knows, an alcoholic. Every few months he and his wife have a terrific fight that's heard all over their neighborhood. One of the guys at the office lives next door to the Smiths and fills you in on all the details.

You've never met Richard, but you know that one of his two older brothers has already been arrested twice for drunk driving.

You're afraid your son may get some bad ideas from Richard, and he never tells you what he and Dick talk about, even though you've tried to find out. Above all, you don't want their friendship to grow into something more serious.

It's dinner time now and you and your wife (husband) are at the table with your son. You feel now is the time to raise the subject. WHAT DO YOU SAY?

Son. While playing Little League baseball, you have become friendly with Richard Smith, another outfielder. He's a great kid and an excellent ball player. He tells really funny stories about some of the wild parties he hears about from his older brothers and other exciting things they've done.

You know from gossip that Richard's father is an alcoholic—but Richard has told you, too; it's nothing he tries to hide. But because his father is an alcoholic, it makes Richard seem a little more interesting to you, since your father is a very quiet man. You wonder what it's like having a father who gets drunk and fights with his wife.

Yesterday, during the game, Richard told you his father was going to take him to the Boston Red Sox game on Sunday and invited you to join them. You don't usually get a chance to go to a big league game—especially one between the Sox and the Yankees—and you desperately want to go. Secretly, you're also very curious to meet Richard's father.

It's dinner time now at your home, and you figure you had better tell your parents where you're going on Sunday. You wonder if they'll object. WHAT DO YOU SAY?

Parent. Your sixteen-year-old daughter has started dating Jack Doe (who is seventeen) and seems to be growing quite fond of him. You are terribly concerned about this because Jack's father and older brother are both alcoholics. Mr. Doe has been to the hospital more than once to "dry out"—and the oldest son seems to be following in his footsteps. You feel Jack will probably end up the same way.

You've met Jack a few times when he's come to pick up your daughter, and you haven't particularly liked him. But you really can't say what it is about him you don't like.

Your daughter has just now come in an hour late from a date with Jack. As you are about to scold her for being late (after all, it's nearly one in the morning), you notice her eyes are a little watery and you smell beer on her breath! This looks like just the chance you've been waiting for to tell her she has to stop seeing Jack. WHAT DO YOU SAY?

Daughter. For several weeks now you have been dating Jack Doe, a classmate at school. You know that his father and older brother are alcoholics, but you feel Jack is different. Sure, he drinks, but no more than any other of the kids his age. (He's seventeen and you're sixteen.) Besides, he's really nice and he needs someone like you who will treat him with respect.

Just now you've come home from a late date with him. You went to the movies with some other kids, and after the show you all went over to one guy's house because his parents were away for the weekend.

Whenever you've been with Jack in the past and there's been beer around, you've never drunk very much, just a couple of beers — enough to get a little high. Jack usually has a couple, too.

Now it's nearly 1:00 A.M. as you come into the house and, sure enough, there's your father (mother) waiting up for you. And you promised you'd be home by midnight! He (she) is probably going to notice you've been drinking and cause a scene, when all you've had is two beers all evening.

If he (she) does get angry, WHAT WILL YOU SAY?

Activity 29
SIMULATING ENCOUNTERS
WITH ALCOHOLICS

Focus:	Attitudes	
	Responses to Alcoholism	
Methods:	Role Play	
	Story Completion	
	Discussion	
Grade Levels:	9–College	
Time:	1/2–2 Periods	

Capsule Description:
Students role play scenes in which nonalcoholics and alcoholics must interact; pupils then discuss their feelings about alcoholics and how best to help alcoholics.

ACTIVITY

Have students volunteer to play parts (do *not* assign them) in role plays in which a family member or an employee is an alcoholic and the other player must decide how to respond to him or her. Sample role profiles are provided at the end of the activity.

Do not let the participants see each other's parts until after the role play or allow the rest of the class or group to read them, either.

If you have difficulty initiating role plays or if your students have not engaged in them before, you may want to (1) take one of the role play parts yourself in the first role play or (2) have the students engage in a written story completion exercise as "practice."

Encourage the students after one or two role plays to create their own role profiles for each other to act out.

Source: This activity is adapted from Peter Finn, "Surfacing Attitudes toward Alcoholics," *Journal of Alcohol and Drug Education* 24 (Fall 1978):58–72. Reprinted by permission.

After each role play, have the participants read their parts to the class. Then ask the players to discuss the feelings they had while role playing. To facilitate this discussion, ask the participant who played the nonalcoholic role:

1. What feelings did you have toward the "alcoholic"? Did you try to express these feelings or keep them to yourself? Why? (Do the observers agree that the feelings were voiced or kept suppressed?

2. How did you feel about these emotions? Did you feel they were healthy? Productive? Inappropriate? Uncontrollable? Embarrassing? Did your emotions change at all during the course of the role play? How? Why?

3. What did you feel your responsibility, if any, was toward the alcoholic? Did you feel capable of exercising that responsibility?

Ask the "alcoholic":

1. What feelings did you have about the other role player? Did you think you understood

how he felt about you, or was it difficult to decipher his true feelings?

2. Did you feel his attitudes were helpful or damaging to you? How would you have liked him to feel about you and act toward you?

Conclude each role play by asking the observing students to express how *they* felt toward the two participants and to evaluate whether their own emotions and attitudes are appropriate ones.

As a variation to this activity, you or your students can rewrite the role profiles in this activity, turning them into short stories that have a missing part—ending, middle, or beginning. Then have your students individually or in small groups write what they believe happened in the omitted part of the story or stories.

After the students have supplied the missing section, break the class into small groups. Have each group read the completions written by all its members. Then have each member of each group explain to the other students in his or her group why he or she thought the plot evolved as it did in that member's written completion. Instruct the groups to try to reach a consensus on what they think the most *plausible* ending (middle, beginning) would be for the story. Finally, have a spokesperson from each group present that group's conclusions to the rest of the class.

Follow-up Discussion

Concentrate your follow-up discussion on what attitudes and feelings (such as disgust, fear, concern, indifference, anger, pity) were expressed toward the alcoholic by (a) the writers of the story completions and (b) the person closest to the alcoholic in the already written part of the story. List these attitudes on a blackboard or flip chart and have the class evaluate their appropriateness.

Two other follow-up activities you can conduct are described below.

1. Have the students individually or in small groups write a brief short story of their own and then select a crucial part to omit. Have the students or groups exchange stories and fill in the missing part of the story they were given. Then bring the original authors and "completers" together to compare the inserted ending (middle, beginning) with what the author had written for the missing section. Students then identify, discuss, and evaluate the attitudes toward alcoholics that were expressed in the two different versions and seek to resolve any discrepancies in attitudes revealed in the two completions.

2. You or your students can develop incomplete stories that focus on *other* illnesses or handicaps, such as heart disease, cancer, paralysis, or blindness. Have the students complete these stories and compare the attitudes their completed portions express toward people with these other illnesses and handicaps and their families with the attitudes the class expressed in their previous story completions toward alcoholics. If there are any differences, what might account for them? Should alcoholics be regarded and treated in the same manner as people with other illnesses or handicaps? Should their families receive the same caring as other families?

Wife. Your husband has been drinking heavily for the past four years, but somehow he manages to keep his job and even perform some of the chores around the house.

He usually doesn't start drinking until noon when he has a few beers at lunch, and then he has a couple more during the course of the afternoon—or at least so you've been told by your neighbor whose husband works for the same company. And he usually comes home with alcohol on his breath, poorly masked, sometimes with some mouth wash or candy.

When he gets home, he immediately has a few shots of whiskey before dinner, continues with beer during the meal, and then sips on whiskey all evening until bedtime. By the time you go to bed, he's pretty bleary eyed and slurring some of his words.

You've tended to ignore his drinking, because it seemed like something many men do. Besides, it hasn't seemed to interfere with his job, so how could he really have a drinking problem?

But recently you read a magazine article that pointed out that most alcoholics *do* have jobs—and families. In addition, it's become impossible for the two of you to spend time anymore with your friends, because your husband always gets drunk and usually insists on driving home, too. Some of your friends have stopped inviting you over to their houses and have begun to turn down your invitations.

Last night, when you were driving home from a movie, your husband nearly got into a serious accident by running a red light. He'd been drinking all day, and you'd stopped for a few more drinks at the local tavern on the way home. You were really frightened, and worried for the children (who were at home).

You've decided to confront your husband with his problem—for you now realize he is an alcoholic and cannot stop drinking without help. You certainly can't go on living this way.

It's Saturday morning—before he's had anything to drink. The kids are playing outside. You and he are sitting over coffee planning the day. You decide now is the time to bring up the subject. WHAT DO YOU SAY?

Husband. For the past three or four years, you've been drinking a little more heavily than you used to, because you find that your job makes you tense and alcohol helps you to relax. You're grateful that it's available—no pills for you! Without a few drinks in you at night, you have trouble falling asleep, too.

But even though you have a beer or two at lunch and a couple of shots of whiskey before and after dinner, you've made sure you're not drinking too much. It hasn't interfered with your job at all—in fact, only last month the boss gave you a raise.

Sometimes, though, you think your wife feels you're drinking too much, so you try to keep her from seeing you drink, because she will just get worried over nothing. For example, last night on the way home from the movies and after a quick stop at the tavern for a nightcap, you almost got into an accident because another driver went through a red light. Your wife became very upset, telling *you* to drive more carefully!

You have noticed recently that one or two of your friends have stayed away from you for some reason, but you figure it's because you got a raise at work and they're jealous. You'll just have to make some other friends who earn as much as you do.

It's Saturday morning, now, and the kids are playing outside. You're sitting with your wife over a cup of coffee. It looks as if she has something on her mind. Maybe she's thinking about that close call last night. If she brings it up and complains about your reckless driving, WHAT WILL YOU SAY?

Supervisor. You have a secretary in your company who has been coming in late to work and missing some days completely. This has been going on for over a year, but she's such a good typist you've ignored it—good typists are hard to come by these days.

However, her immediate boss has already complained several times about her tardiness and absenteeism and suspects it's because she's an alcoholic. He says he's seen her slip out during the late afternoon a few times, and twice he saw her going into the bar down the street.

You've called the secretary in for a talk with you, but you're not quite sure how to go about dealing with the situation since she may deny that she has a drinking problem. Besides, she is such a good worker when she's doing her job. But you clearly have to do something, because her boss isn't going to put up with her action much longer.

You've just ushered her into your office, and she's taken a chair opposite you. WHAT DO YOU SAY?

Employee. You have been drinking rather heavily for several years now and can't seem to live without alcohol—lots of it. You feel so unhappy unless you've had a few drinks.

But because of your drinking you have had hangovers that prevent you from going to work some days and make you late on others. Some days you can't last until you get off work, so you slip down to the bar a block away during the afternoon for a drink or two.

Your boss has already complained several times to you about your tardiness and absences, and now you've been asked by *his* supervisor to come in for a talk. You feel you cannot tell your boss or his supervisor why you've been late and absent because you may be fired, and then you'd have no way to support yourself.

You've just been ushered into the supervisor's office and taken a seat opposite him. If he asks if you have a drinking problem or tells you your tardiness and absences have to stop, WHAT WILL YOU SAY?

Activity 30
COPING WITH PROBLEM DRINKING AND
ALCOHOLISM IN THE FAMILY

Focus: Attitudes toward Alcoholism
Methods: Writing
             Story Completion
             Discussion
Grade Levels: 3–College
Time: 1/2–2 Periods

Capsule Description:
Students describe how they might respond to a problem drinker in the family and discuss constructive approaches.

ACTIVITY

Students write or present orally responses to "Dear Abby" letters in which the writer is concerned about a problem drinker in his or her family.

Have your students write responses to one or more of the "Dear Abby" letters provided at the end of the activity. Then break the class into small groups and instruct them to read all the responses of their members, discuss the best response—probably a combination of several of the individual responses—and write down this new, improved response. Have each group present its response to the rest of the class and compare results. Be sure the groups explain *why* they feel their response is a good one—why it will help the person who wrote to "Abby."

For younger students, you can read the "Dear Abby" letters aloud and have them discuss orally what would be good responses.

After the activity, students individually or in small groups can prepare "Dear Abby" letters of their own for other members of the class to respond to. The "writers" can then evaluate how effective the responses were in terms of addressing "their" problem.

Conduct a follow-up discussion that focuses on:

- the various options that family members can choose from to cope with problem drinking
- attitudes (such as stereotyping) and feelings (such as disgust, pity, fear, anger) expressed in the completions (or in the stories themselves) toward problem-drinker families and problem drinking

Dear Abby:

My father frequently goes on drinking sprees, some of which last for several days. When he's not drinking he is kind and generous. But when he drinks too much he is mean, sloppy, and sometimes violent. He sometimes spends so much on liquor that the family has to do without much food. What can I do? I am . . . years old.

Confused

HOW WILL YOU RESPOND?

Dear Abby:

My mother spends all day watching soap operas and nibbling potato chips and neglects my two baby twin brothers and the house. My father has two jobs to support us and isn't home too much. When I get home from school she's already had several drinks and gets mad at the slightest thing I do. What can I do?

Oppressed

HOW WILL YOU RESPOND?

Dear Abby:

My husband spends every Saturday and Sunday afternoon and Monday night watching the football games. While watching he keeps on drinking beer until by the end of the game he is unsteady and angry, so we can't go anyplace or have any friends in. Tuesday he wakes up with a hangover. The rest of the week he's fine. What can I do?

Confined

HOW WILL YOU RESPOND?

Activity 31
TREATMENT FOR ALCOHOLISM

Focus:	Treatment	
Methods:	Interviews	
	Reading	
	Research	
	Discussion	
Grade Levels:	6–College	
Time:	1–3 Periods	

Capsule Description:
Students engage in various activities designed to help them learn about and evaluate different treatment approaches for alcoholics.

ACTIVITY

This activity presents a number of exercises students can pursue for learning about different approaches for treating alcoholics and assessing their effectiveness and feasibility. Different members of your class can engage in different exercises, either individually or in small groups. It is likely that each exercise will provide students with different information about alcoholism and its treatment.

1. Students can attend open Alcoholics Anonymous, Al-Anon, and Alateen meetings. Information regarding times and locations of meetings can usually be secured by calling the number under these listings or under "alcoholism" in the telephone book or contacting the local department of mental or public health. It may be possible for the students to talk with members after or before the meetings. Students should be prepared with a list of questions in mind that they would like to ask.

2. Students can interview a number of "experts" in the local community who can provide information about treatment for alcoholics, including officials in the departments of mental or public health and community mental health centers, hotline supervisors, physicians, staff in local councils on alcoholism, and guidance counselors in the school. Students could interview several of these individuals and compare what each says about treatment.

3. Students can read pamphlets, flyers, and books about treatment for alcoholism, such as those listed in the Resources section of this book.

4. You can briefly present information about treatment of alcoholics using the information provided in chapter 3.

Activity 32
EVALUATING ALCOHOL ABUSE PREVENTION AND TREATMENT APPROACHES

Focus:	Prevention	*Capsule Description:*
Method:	Simulation/Discussion	Students decide how money should be allocated
Grade Levels:	9–College	for alcohol problems in their state.
Time:	1–3 Periods	

ACTIVITY

This activity can be conducted in two ways. In one approach, the students role play the views specific constituencies, such as members of the State Department of Education, officials in the national brewers and distillers association, policy makers in the State Departments of Transportation, Corrections, Mental Health, and Public Health, members of Alcoholics Anonymous, members of Alateen and Al-Anon, police officers, and other groups concerned with problem drinking. In the second approach, students can express their own opinions regarding the topic under consideration. The role-play approach is the more difficult one for most students to conduct, but it has the educational advantage of requiring students to consider the problem from a perspective different from their own.

Divide the class into small groups and have each group respond to the following scenario:

> The federal government is prepared to give your state $100,000 for whatever project(s) you choose that will either prevent alcohol problems, treat existing alcohol problems, or both. The one condition the government has made is that the entire class must

agree on what the money will be spent on—what the projects will be. If the class cannot agree within two class periods, you lose the money. You will be allowed one-half of this period to agree within your separate groups on how the money should be spent and one-half of the period to present your plans to the rest of the class and try to agree as a class on how to spend the money. If agreement is not reached by the end of the first period, a second class period will be available. During this second period, you will meet again in small groups to see if you wish to revise your plans based on what the other groups have recommended. Then you will meet as a class to see if you can come to an agreement by the end of the period—or lose the money.

Follow-up discussion can focus on both the alcohol issues that were raised and also the decision-making process that was used. In terms of prevention and treatment issues, the class can discuss:

1. Should more emphasis be placed on preventing alcohol abuse or treating it?
2. Which prevention approaches are likely to be the most effective and why? Which treatment approaches are likely to help the

greatest number of alcohol abusers and why?

3. What groups and individuals should decide how money for preventing and treating alcohol problems should be spent? In cases of conflict, which groups or individuals should have the final say?

4. How, in reality, are decisions made with regard to funding programs for alcohol abuse prevention and treatment? Can the average citizen have any influence over this process?

Questions that can be discussed with regard to the decision-making process that was used by the class can include the following:

1. Did the groups tend to compete rather than cooperate? Why? Can anything be done about this? Is this what happens in society at large? Who competes for funds devoted to preventing and treating alcohol abuse? Do they cooperate or conflict?

2. Was cooperation high within each group but low between the groups or vice versa? Was it high or low in both settings? What can be done to improve cooperation both within and between groups who have vested or personal interests that conflict when it comes to alcohol issues?

3. Did the groups generate several ideas before selecting one or did they begin with a single idea that went uncontested? Why? Did everyone in each group agree to the decisions made? How were decisions made? Is this what happens in society at large?

Activity 33
LEGAL SOLUTIONS TO
DRINKING PROBLEMS

Focus:	Law	
	Treatment	
	Drinking and Driving	
Method:	Discussion	
Grade Levels:	6–College	
Time:	1–3 Periods	

Capsule Description:
Students evaluate what action to take with a convicted drunk driver and discuss other legal aspects of alcohol use and abuse.

ACTIVITY

This activity consists of one initial exercise and several possible follow-up exercises. While all the exercises focus on alcohol and the law, in the process of discussing and researching the legal ramifications of alcohol use and abuse your students will have to focus on attitudes toward drinking and problem drinking and ways of helping people who abuse alcohol. In some respects, the study of alcohol and the law provides a unique vehicle for helping students to surface and explore their attitudes toward drinking and not drinking and to consider how people with drinking problems can best be helped.

Have your students write brief responses to one or more scenarios in which they are told: "You are the judge in the following drinking and driving case. What action, if any, will you take?" Sample scenarios are provided at the end of the activity. The following class period, break the class into small groups and instruct them to agree on the best course of action and justifications for choosing their solution. Each group then reports its recommended action and ratio-

nale to the rest of the class for comparison and discussion. After the class discussion, students can develop their own scenarios for other students to respond to.

As follow-up to this activity, or as substitutes for it, your students can engage in one or more of the following exercises:

1. Students discuss what legal action, if any, should be taken against people who are drunk in public. Have the students respond to scenarios in which they are once again the judge who must decide what, if anything, to do with different people who have been arrested for public drunkenness. Sample scenarios follow.
   - A middle-aged, skid row derelict, an alcoholic, without a job or home, was staggering across the street. He has been in court 16 times in the last 7 years for the same offense.
   - a 17-year-old cheerleader from a respectable family was drunk in the hot bleachers of the season's first ball game

and passed out. She has never been to court before.

- A young man with a previous record of getting drunk on weekends was drunk on the street and yelling obscenities at 2:00 A.M.

2. Students interview a juvenile court judge, probation officer, social worker, alcoholism counselor, or police officer on the relationship between alcohol abuse and juvenile delinquency. Sample questions the students might ask follow.

   - Does alcohol misuse cause juvenile delinquency, vice versa, or neither?
   - What happens to a juvenile who has been arrested for an alcohol offense?
   - Do juveniles break other laws because they are drunk?
   - What rehabilitation services are available to delinquents who have alcohol problems?
   - What is the recidivism rate for delinquents arrested on alcohol charges? What might explain it, if it is high?

3. Students interview police officers about how they handle public drunkenness offenses and other offenses involving alcohol abuse, such as drunk driving. Sample questions the students might ask follow.

   - Why is public drunkenness (not) considered a crime?
   - In what kinds of situations do you usually find people drunk?
   - How do you handle them?
   - What kinds of alcohol offenses do juveniles commit and how do you handle them?
   - Do you feel alcohol offenders should be handled differently from other offenders? If so, how and why?

4. Students evaluate possible solutions to problem drinkers in their community. Begin the activity by having students write or describe orally their responses to one or more scenarios in which a police officer confronts a drunk person. Sample scenarios follow.

   - You are a police officer on the town force. You are patrolling Main St. at 3:00 A.M. and you run across Marty Wino, drunk again, sitting on the sidewalk. He is usually drunk on the street at least once a month, but this is the first time you've had the night shift and run into Marty. You know nothing else about him. Do you arrest him? Ignore him? Talk with him? Bully him? Something else?

   - You are a police officer on the town force. You are in your patrol car at 11:00 P.M. and get a call to go to 279 Washington St. where there is a family fight. You get there, are let in by the daughter, and see the husband staggering around and his wife with one or two black and blue marks crying on the sofa. The daughter tells you this happens every weekend, and this time she had called the police. He gets drunk and then beats his wife. Do you arrest him? Turn around and walk out? Talk to him? Bully him? Something else?

   - You and your partner are police officers on the town force. You have been told at 1:00 A.M. to go to 7th and D Streets where a teenage boy is drunk, yelling obscenities to the sky. You find him and recognize him as the boy who gets drunk every weekend and creates a public disturbance. Your partner says that the youngster is his nephew. His mother is divorced and seems to have trouble keeping control over him. Do you arrest him? Ignore him? Talk to him? Bully him? Take him home and talk to his parent? Something else?

The convicted person is a 27-year-old single factory worker. He pleads guilty to driving while intoxicated. He has no previous record. He says he "had a little too much to drink" at a party and the police caught him driving on the wrong side of the street at 1:00 A.M.

The convicted person is a 27-year-old married man with four children. He pleads guilty to driving while intoxicated. This is his third arrest in six years for the same offense. He was drinking with friends in a bar, a policeman tells you, and was driving 65 mph in a 20 mph residential area at 11:00 P.M.

The convicted person is a 19-year-old debutante. She claims innocence but has been found guilty by a jury of driving while intoxicated and driving to endanger. She had been drinking at a bridge party and while driving home injured a boy playing in the street. She has no previous record.

The convicted person is a 47-year-old vice-president of a large bank. He is married and has three children. Despite his plea of innocence, you have found him guilty of drunk and disorderly conduct. He had been drinking heavily in a bar after work and while going from the bar to his car caused a serious traffic accident. He failed to watch for traffic as he crossed a busy street from betwen two parked cars. He was uninjured.

Resources

MATERIALS FOR STUDENTS

Below is a list of books and pamphlets for youngsters on alcohol use, nonuse, and abuse.*

Alcohol: Pleasures and Problems by Peter Finn and Jane Lawson. 1976. Objective overview of the enjoyment of drinking, alcohol's effects, drinking and driving, and problem drinking and alcoholism. $.45 from National Council on Alcoholism, 733 Third Avenue, New York, N.Y. 10017. Grades 7-12.

Kids and Alcohol by Peter Finn and Jane Lawson. 1976. Objective, well-illustrated discussion of alcohol's effects, kids and drinking, and drinking problems. Includes alcohol crossword puzzle and glossary. $.45 from National Council on Alcoholism, 733 Third Avenue, New York, N.Y. 10017. Grades 5-9.

*Materials for postsecondary students may be found in the Additional Readings section at the end of each chapter. Prices based on available 1980 figures.

What Is Alcohol? And Why Do People Drink? by Gail G. Milgram. 1974. 25 pages. Presents reasons it is important to learn about alcohol, describes what alcohol is, why people drink it, and what its effects are. Provides several diagrams and photographs. $.75 from Publications Division, Center of Alcohol Studies, Rutgers University, New Brunswick, N.J. 08903. Grades 9-12.

Coping with Alcohol by Gail G. Milgram. 1980. 108 pages. Objective presentation on the history of alcohol use, nature of alcoholic beverages, adult and teenage alcohol use, and alcohol problems. $7.97 from Richards Rosen Press, 28 E. 21st St., New York, N.Y. 10010. Grades 7-12.

The Drinking Question: Honest Answers to Questions Teen Agers Ask about Drinking. 1976. 23 pages. Straightforward answers to such questions as "What's the fastest way to sober up?" and "How can you tell if somebody is alcoholic?" Well illustrated with photographs. $.55 from the Superintendent of Documents, U.S. Government Printing Office, Washington, D.C. 20402. Grades 9–12.

Thinking about Drinking. 1968. 31 pages. Gives information on how many teenagers drink, why they drink, and how much they drink. Also tells about alcohol's effects. $.35 from the U.S. Superintendent of Documents, Government Printing Office, Washington, D.C. 20402. Free from many local alcoholism agencies. Grades 7–12.

Alcohol: Drink or Drug? by Margaret O. Hyde. 150 pages. 1974. Interesting account of alcohol in history and how it is made. Also discusses social drinking and alcoholism. $4.72 from McGraw-Hill, Box 402, Hightstown, N.J. 08520. Grades 9–12.

Drinking Myths. 1975. 22 pages. $1.18 from Products Division, U.S. Jaycees, Box 7, Tulsa, Okla. 74102. Grades 7–12.

A Programmed Unit on Facts about Alcohol. 1969. 38 pages. Mixture of text, questions based on text just read, and answers. $1.16 from Allyn and Bacon, 470 Atlantic Avenue, Boston, Mass. 02210. Grades 9–12.

Alcoholism by Alvin and Virginia Silverstein. 1975. 127 pages. Despite its title, presents a great deal of interesting information about alcohol's effects, teenage drinking, alcohol in history, and how alcoholic beverages are made. $2.25 from J. B. Lippincott Company, 521 Fifth Avenue, New York, N.Y. 10017. Grades 9–12.

Living with a Parent Who Drinks Too Much by Judith S. Seixas. 1979. 197 pages. Written in the second person and large type, this book provides specific instructions on what to do in dealing with an alcoholic parent. $6.95 from Greenwillow Division of William Morrow and Co., 105 Madison Avenue, New York, N.Y. 10016.

If Your Parents Drink Too Much. Comic book about three teenagers with alcoholic parents and how these youngsters cope in different ways with their troubled home life. Al-Anon Family Group Headquarters, P.O. Box 182, Madison Square Station, New York, N.Y. 10010. Grades 7–12.

Pepper by Elainne L. Melquist. 1974. Illustrated account of a puppy whose master becomes an alcoholic and neglects the animal. Told from the point of view of the puppy. $.35 from the National Council on Alcoholism, 733 Third Avenue, New York, N.Y. 10017. Grades 1–4 (can be read orally).

What's "Drunk," Mama? by the Al-Anon Family Group Headquarters. 1977. Illustrated story about a young girl whose father obtains treatment for his alcoholism. Al-Anon Family Group Headquarters, Madison Square Station, New York, N.Y. 10010. Grades 1–4 (Can be read orally).

Troubled Teens by Edwin Bowers. 20 pages. Discussion of how young people with alcoholic parents can handle their own problems. Single copy free from Public Education, the Bureau of Alcoholic Rehabilitation, Post Office Box 1447, Avon Park, Fl. 33825. Grades 9–12.

People Do Drink and Drive by Jerome W. Witherill. 1972. 25 pages. Presents facts and problem situations involving drinking and driving. $1.20 from the American Driver and Traffic Safety Education Association, 1201 16th Street, N.W., Washington, D.C. 20036. Grades 9–12.

The Driver's Guide to Drinking. 10 pages. Single copies free from the National Safety Council, 425 North Michigan Avenue, Chicago, Ill. 60611. Grades 9–12.

A brief list of fictional treatments of alcohol use and abuse follows. Your local school or public librarian may be familiar with other appropriate titles.

The Seventeenth Summer by Maureen Daly. Story of a 17-year-old girl's first experience with love and drinking. Paperback (Pocket Books). Grades 5–12.

You Can't Get There from Here by Earl Hamner, Jr. Novel about a boy who spends a day in New York City trying to find his father who is an alcoholic. Hardbound (Random House, Inc.). Grades 5–12.

Flap by Clair Huffaker. Novel about a group of Indians who get drunk and take over a bulldozer to protect their land. Paperback (Popular Library). Grades 7–12.

The Lost Weekend by Charles Jackson. Autobiographical novel about a weekend in the life of an alcoholic. Paperback (Noonday). Grades 11–12.

Having Been There: The Personal Drama of Alcoholism edited by Alan Luks. Short stories about alcoholics—many apparently written by alcoholics. Hardbound (Charles Scribner's Sons). Grades 9–12.

Jennifer by Zoa Sherburne. Story about a girl whose mother is an alcoholic and how she learns to handle the situation. Hardbound (William Morrow & Co.). Grades 5–12.

The Long Ride Home by James L. Summers. Fifth grade and up. Story that shows the effects an alcoholic father has on his high school son and daughter. Hardbound (Westminster Press). Grades 5–12.

The Adventures of Huckleberry Finn by Mark Twain. Famous story of a young boy and his raft. The beginning of the book describes his father's drunken behavior. (Bantam Books). Grades 5–12.

One Day at a Time by Regina Woody. Story of a 13-year-old girl whose mother is an alcoholic. Hardbound (Westminster Press). Grades 6–12.

My Name is Davy, I'm an Alcoholic by Anne Snyder. Story about a teenage alcoholic. Paperback (Signet). Grades 5–12.

First Step by Anne Snyder. Story about a young girl whose mother is an alcoholic. Paperback (Signet). Grades 5–12.

AUDIOVISUAL MATERIALS

There are a great many films and filmstrips available that focus on alcohol use and abuse. Unfortunately, most of them are biased in one manner or another. Therefore, be sure to preview any audiovisual materials you plan to present to your students before you use them in the classroom. If you are unable to do so and end up showing a poorly produced film or filmstrip, you might ask your students to critique the material, asking them to (1) point out the ways in which it lacked objectivity, (2) discuss what might have led the producers to introduce bias into their materials, and (c) identify what harmful effects, if any, the material might have on an audience.

The following are among the few audiovisual materials that are relatively objective in their discussions of drinking issues.

Youth Oriented Films

JACKSON JUNIOR HIGH. Four 15-minute films. Grades 5–8.
NCALI, Department OE, Box 2345, Rockville, Md. 20852
Together, the films trace the activities of a class engaged in "Alcohol Education Week" and present well-acted scenarios in the lives of the students and their parents that relate to alcohol use and abuse.

DIAL A-L-C-O-H-O-L. Four 30-minute films. Grades 9–12.
NCALI, Department OE, Box 2345, Rockville, Md. 20852
Together, the films dramatize a number of alcohol issues by following the activities of several high school students and their college advisor who run an Alcohol Hotline.

99 Bottles of Beer. 23 minutes. Available in Spanish. Grades 8–12.
Norm Southerby & Associates. P.O. Box 15403, Long Beach, Calif. 90815
Explores alcohol abuse and alcoholism in youth, pointing out the underlying psychological basis for involvement with alcohol.

Trigger Films for Health (Series Alcohol Education). 1–2 minutes each.
Grades 7–12.
University of Michigan. Television Center, 400 South Fourth St., Ann Arbor, Mich. 48103

Problem Drinking and Alcoholism

And I'm an Alcoholic. 29 minutes. Grades 9–College.
Aspect IV Educational Films. 41 Riverside Avenue, Westport, Conn. 06880
Features interviews with actual recovered alcoholics from various walks of life telling about their stages of alcoholism.

Chalk Talk. 67 minutes. Grades 9–Adult.
Fr. Joseph Martin. 103 Fox Ridge Dr., Havre de Grace, Md. 21078
Compelling lecture on alcoholism.

Living Sober: The Class of '76. 28 minutes. Grades 9–Adult.
Group Three. Human Resource Program. 6135 Mission Gorge Rd., San Diego, Calif. 92120
Presentation of the challenges and rewards of staying sober for recovered alcoholics.

Francesca, Baby. 46 minutes. Grades 6–Adult.
Walt Disney Educational Media. 500 South Buena Vista, Burbank, Calif. 91521
Portrayal of the effects of an alcoholic mother on her children.

The First Step. 27-1/2 minutes. Grades 7–Adult.
Motivision, Ltd. 21 West 46th St., New York, N.Y. 10036
Drama about a family troubled by alcoholism.

Focuses on the effects of the father's alcoholism on the rest of the family.

Soft Is the Heart of a Child. 28 minutes. Grades 6–Adult.
    Operation Cork. P.O. Box 9550, San Diego, Calif. 92109
    Powerful presentation of the effects of an alcoholic father on his children. Requires follow-up discussion.

If You Loved Me. 54 minutes. Grades 6–Adult.
    Operation Cork, P.O. Box 9550, San Diego, Calif. 92109.
    Emphasizes the impact of alcoholism in the family on the nonalcoholic spouse. Requires follow-up discussion.

Drinking and Driving

Point Zero Eight. 30 minutes. Grades 9–Adult.
    CTV Television Network, Ltd. 42 Charles St., Toronto, 5, Canada.
    Tests are performed on eight of Canada's foremost racing drivers after they drink larger and larger quantities of alcohol.

A Snort History. 6-1/2 minutes. Grades 6–Adult.
    AIMS Instructional Media Services, Inc. P.O. Box 1010, Hollywood, Calif. 90028
    Subject is drinking and driving, but the risk-taking aspect can be a basic element in any alcohol education program.

Until I Get Caught. 90 Minutes. Grades 4–College.
    Modern Talking Picture Service. 5000 Park Street North, St. Petersburg, Fla. 33709
    Documentary dealing with community response to drinking and driving in rural New York State, Nashville, Tennessee, and Sweden.

For an annotated list of films and filmstrips which address alcohol use, nonuse, and abuse, see *In Focus: Alcohol and Alcoholism Media.* For a single free copy write to:

National Clearinghouse for Alcohol Information
P.O. Box 2345
Rockville, MD 20852

If the Clearinghouse is out of stock, send $1.50 to the Superintendent of Documents, U.S. Government Printing Office, Washington, D.C. 20402. Request the title above and provide the stock number.

ORGANIZATIONS AND AGENCIES

A list of organizations that can provide additional information or literature regarding alcohol use and abuse follows.

For the Problem Drinker or Alcoholic

Alcoholics Anonymous (AA)
World Services, Inc.
P.O. Box 459
Grand Central Station
New York, New York 10017

For the Families of Problem Drinkers and Alcoholics

Al-Anon Family Group Headquarters, Inc.
P.O. Box 182
Madison Square Garden
New York, New York 10010

Schools and Community

Boys Clubs of America
Alcohol Education Project
771 First Avenue
New York, New York 10017

CASPAR, Inc.
Alcohol Education Program
266 Highland Avenue
Somerville, MA 02143

Comprehensive Health Education Foundation
3002 N. Union Street
Tacoma, Washington 98407

National Congress of Parents and Teachers
Alcohol Education Project
700 North Rush Street
Chicago, Illinois 60611

U.S. Jaycees
Products Division
Box 7
Tulsa, Oklahoma 74102

Community

AFL-CIO Community Service Department
815–16th Street, N.W.
Washington, D.C. 20006

Religious Organizations

North Conway Institute
8 Newbury Street
Boston, Massachusetts 02116

Traffic and Highway Safety

National Highway Traffic Safety Administration
400 7th and D Streets, S.W.
Washington, D.C. 20590

National Safety Council
444 North Michigan Avenue
Chicago, Illinois 60611

General

Addiction Research Foundation (ARF)
33 Russell Street
Toronto, Ontario, Canada M5S 2S1

Alcohol and Drug Problems Association of
North America (ADPA)
1001 15th Street, N.W., Room 204
Washington, D.C. 10005

American Business Men's Research Foundation
Suite 1208
Michigan National Tower
Lansing, Michigan 48933

National Center for Alcohol Information
1601 North Kent Street
Arlington, Virginia 22209

The National Clearinghouse for Alcohol Information (NCALI)
Box 2345
Rockville, Maryland 20852

National Institute on Alcohol Abuse and
Alcoholism
5600 Fishers Lane
Rockville, Maryland 20852

The National Council on Alcoholism
Publications Division
733 Third Avenue
New York, New York 10017

Rutgers Center of Alcohol Studies
Publications Division
Rutgers University
New Brunswick, New Jersey 08903

Women's Christian Temperance Union
1730 Chicago Avenue
Evanston, Illinois 60201

LOCAL SERVICES

State Divisions of Alcoholism
State Departments of Education
State Departments of Mental Health
State Safety Councils
Local AA, Al-Anon, and Alateen groups, listed in most telephone directories
Local chapters of the National Council on Alcoholism
State chapters of the National Council on Alcoholism
State Departments of Motor Vehicles
Governors' Highway Safety Representatives

JOURNALS IN THE ALCOHOL FIELD

Advances in Alcoholism
Alcohol Health and Research World
The Alcohol Newsletter
Alcoholism: Clinical and Experimental Research
The Alcoholism Report
American Journal of Drug and Alcohol Abuse
The Bottom Line
Currents in Alcoholism
DISCUS Newsletter
Health Education
International Journal of the Addictions
The Journal by the Addiction Research Foundation
Journal of Alcohol and Drug Education
Journal of Alcohol Studies
Journal on Alcoholism and Related Addictions
National Council on Alcoholism Friday Letter
News and Views Newsletter of Alcohol and Drug Problems Association of North America
Report on Alcohol
The U.S. Journal of Drugs and Alcohol Dependence

Glossary

Absorption: The process by which alcohol enters the bloodstream primarily from the small intestine but also from the stomach. The rate of absorption is affected by rate of consumption, body weight, presence of food in the stomach, body chemistry, and type of beverage.

Abstinence: Refraining from any use of alcohol-containing beverages.

Addiction: Physiological and/or psychological dependence on a drug. The overpowering physical or emotional urge to do something repeatedly that an individual cannot control, accompanied by a physical tolerance for the drug and *withdrawal* symptoms if use of the drug is stopped. (See also *physiological dependence* and *tolerance*.)

Al-Anon: A world-wide organization of wives and husbands of alcoholics. There are local groups in many towns. Members meet to discuss how to deal with their alcoholic husbands and wives.

Alateen: An organization for teenagers whose mothers or fathers are alcoholics. There are local groups in many towns. Members meet to discuss how to cope more effectively with their common problems.

Alcohol (ethyl): The intoxicating chemical (C_2H_5OH) found in alcoholic beverages and produced by the action of yeast on sugars and starches (fermentation). Often referred to as "beverage alcohol," as opposed to *methyl alcohol* which is poisonous and used primarily for industrial purposes. Alcohol is classified as a central nervous sytem (*CNS*) depressant.

Alcohol education: The process of acquainting people with facts, attitudes, values, and behavior regarding alcohol use, nonuse, and abuse.

Alcoholic: A person whose drinking causes repeated problems. The person usually drinks often, drinks until he or she gets drunk, and cannot control his or her drinking.

Alcoholics Anonymous (AA): A world-wide organization of recovering alcoholics. There are local groups in many towns. Members meet to discuss their problems related to alcohol so they can continue not to drink and help others with drinking problems.

Bender: (slang) A period of continuous drinking in order to get drunk. May last several days or weeks.

Blackout: A period of temporary amnesia that occurs while a person is drinking. During a blackout, the person is conscious and walks, talks, and acts but can't remember any of the events the next day.

Blood Alcohol Content (BAC): The percentage of alcohol in a person's blood. In most states, a driver with a BAC of .10 percent is presumed to be driving while intoxicated (*DWI*).

Breathalyzer: An instrument used to measure the alcohol content of a person's blood through an analysis of the person's breath.

Brewing: The *fermentation* of grains that results in beer or ale.

Cirrhosis: The replacement of liver tissue with scar tissue due either to malnutrition and/or excessive and prolonged alcohol abuse.

Delirium tremens (DTs): Hallucinations, violent shaking, nausea, and other symptoms and alcoholic experiences when he or she suddenly stops drinking for several hours.

Depressant: Any chemical that diminishes the activity of the central nervous system, usually resulting in dulled reflexes, impaired thought processes, and distorted perceptions. Alcohol is a central nervous system depressant.

Detoxification: (1) Also called "drying out." The process of sobering up and withdrawing from the poisonous effects of alcohol. (2) the process carried out by the liver in changing chemicals like alcohol into non-toxic substances.

Distillation: The process of making *hard liquor* by heating wine or beer. The alcohol becomes a gas that, when cooled, becomes liquid alcohol.

Distilled spirits (beverages): Beverages made by the distilling process and usually containing at least 40% alcohol by volume. These include whiskey, gin, rum, brandy, tequila, vodka, and liqueurs.

Drug: Anything that people put on their skin or swallow that can have an effect on how their mind or body works.

Drunk: The way people feel and act when they have had a lot of alcohol. "Drunk" usually means the person has lost all or a great deal of control of his or her actions and thoughts. Same as *intoxicated.*

DWI: Also called *DUIL.* Driving while intoxicated or under the influence of liquor. In most states a driver whose *blood alcohol content (BAC)* is .10 percent or higher is presumed to be *DWI (DUIL).*

Ethyl alcohol: The only kind of alcohol that is safe to drink. It is made from fruit or cereals.

Fermentation: The process of making wine or beer. The yeast acts on the sugar in fruit juices or cereal to produce alcohol.

Hangover: The unpleasant physical sensations (headache, upset stomach, etc.) some people feel several hours after having been drunk or high. People get hangovers *after* all the alcohol has left their body and they are sober again. Only time makes a hangover go away.

Hard liquor: Expression used to refer to *distilled* beverages as opposed to beer and wine.

High: The way people feel when they have had enough alcohol to feel good, but not so much that they have lost significant control over what they say and do.

Impaired driver: A driver whose skill and judgment have been decreased due to alcohol and/or some other drugs or conditions (like fatigue or illness).

Implied consent law: A law that stipulates that by obtaining a driver's license an individual has given his or her tacit consent to submit to a chemical blood-alcohol level (breathalyzer) test upon the request of the police or else lose his or her license for a given period of time.

Intoxication: The physical and emotional effects of excessive drinking. In most states, one is legally presumed intoxicated if one has a blood alcohol level of .10 percent or higher.

Malt beverages: Alcoholic beverages produced from barley, hops, corn, sugar, water, and other ingredients. Includes beer and ale.

Methyl alcohol: A type of alcohol that is poisonous if drunk. It is found in anti-freeze, paint thinner, and fuels. It is made from wood and is sometimes called "wood alcohol."

Minor: A person who is not legally an adult. Every state has its own law saying at what age a person becomes an adult (usually 18) for purposes of voting, signing contracts, and purchasing alcoholic beverages.

Oxidation: The addition of oxygen to another chemical. The liver adds oxygen to alcohol to produce carbon dioxide (which is exhaled), water (which is eliminated as urine), and energy.

Peer: A person of one's own standing and usually age. "Peer pressure" occurs when people with no special authority or power try to get other people like them to do (or not do) something.

Physiological dependence: An uncontrollable physical urge to use a substance. The individual requires an increasing amount of the substance to get the same effect, and symptoms of physical withdrawal develop if the person stops using the substance.

Presumptive level: The level of alcohol concentration in the blood that is legal, although inconclusive, evidence of intoxication (.10 percent in most states). One is presumed, but not proven, to be impaired.

Primary prevention: The forestalling of problems related to the use of alcohol before they occur.

Problem drinker: A person whose drinking causes him or her a problem or causes problems for other people. Problem drinkers have more control over their drinking than alcoholics do. Problem drinking can lead to alcoholism.

Prohibition: The period in American history from 1919 to 1933 when it was illegal nationwide to manufacture, transport, or sell alcoholic beverages.

Proof: A number that is equivalent to double the alcohol content of whiskey (86 proof whiskey contains 43% alcohol). In Colonial America the high alcohol content of a beverage was considered "proven" if, when combined with gunpowder, it was capable of burning with a steady flame. Used only when referring to *whiskey ("hard liquor").*

Psychological tolerance: People's ability over a long period of time to learn what effects drinking has on them and to train themselves to prevent these effects from causing trouble.

Secondary prevention: When alcohol problems have begun in an individual but have not become severe, and intervention is undertaken to prevent the incipient problem from becoming worse.

Skid Row: The part of a town where "bums" live. Most skid row "bums" are *not* alcoholics. Most alcoholics are *not* skid row "bums" either.

Social drinker: A person who drinks occasionally or regularly at social functions, mealtimes, etc., but whose drinking does not create personal or social problems.

Stimulant: Any chemical that increases the activity of the central nervous system, usually resulting in sharpened reflexes and either sharper or distorted perceptions depending on the dose and chemical.

Temperance: Literally, use of alcohol in moderation. Historically, as in the Temperance movement, total abstinence.

Tertiary prevention: Helping people who have recovered from an illness (for example, alcoholism) from suffering relapses.

Tolerance: The body's resistance to alcohol (or to any drug) because of repeated use. As a result of this tolerance, the person must drink more and more alcohol to get the same effects as earlier.

Uniform Alcoholism Act: A law passed in a number of states, recommended by the National Institute on Alcohol Abuse and Alcoholism, that makes it no longer a crime to be *drunk* in public.

Whisky or whiskey: A *distilled* beverage made from *fermented* grain and aged in charred oak barrels. Usually has alcoholic content of 40–60 percent (80–120 proof).

Withdrawal: After developing physical dependence on a drug, this is the result of discontinuing its use. With alcohol this causes various reactions from mild disorientation, hallucinations, shaking, and convulsions to *delirium tremens ("DTs").*

Index